The Complete Green Letters

The Complete Green Letters

Miles T. Stanford

Zondervan Publishing House
Grand Rapids, Michigan

THE COMPLETE GREEN LETTERS
Copyright © 1975, 1976, 1977, 1983 by The Zondervan Corporation
Grand Rapids, Michigan

The Complete Green Letters was formerly published as five small books, *The Green Letters, The Principle of Position, The Ground of Growth, The Reckoning That Counts,* and *Abide Above.*

Library of Congress Cataloging in Publication Data

Stanford, Miles J.
  The complete green letters.
  (Clarion classic)
  "Formerly published as five small books, The green
letters, The principle of position, The ground of
growth, The reckoning that counts, and Abide above."—
Verso t.p.
  Bibliography: p.
  1. Christian life—1960-   . I. Title.
II. Series.
BV4501.2.S7167 1983   248.4   83-21672
ISBN 0-310-33051-3

Designed by Ann Cherryman

Printed in the United States of America

83 84 85 86 87 88 — 10 9 8 7 6 5 4 3 2 1

Contents

Introduction

The complete Green Letters is not a single work, but actually a collection of five works dealing with a common theme—"Not I, but Christ." In these works, Miles J. Stanford of Lakewood, Colorado, presents us with a comprehensive, if somewhat disconnected, treatise on what it means to be a Christian.

Stanford is convinced that the weakness experienced by the church today, whether individually or corporately, as well as throughout its history, is primarily due to its ignorance of the truths pertaining to the deeper life. Most Christians settle for far less than the best after wearying but fruitless struggles with the flesh. Because they rely on their own strength, which is a hopeless thing to do, they never make any significant progress toward true spirituality. Fortunately, there exists the truth of the deeper life, known by some throughout the history of the church, but now explicitly taught by many great writers of our own era, such as F. E. Huegel, Ruth Paxon, Andrew Murray, and Jessee Penn-Lewis, and, above all, by the Keswick Convention.

The five books that make up this manual of spirituality are to be read in order. They are: first, *The Green Letters: Principles of Spiritual Growth;* second, *The Principle of Position: Foundations of Spiritual Growth;* third, *The Ground of Growth: The Christian's Relationship to the Cross and the Risen Christ;* fourth, *The Reckoning That Counts: The Realization of Spiritual Growth;* and fifth, *Abide Above: A Guide to Spiritual Growth.*

Book one, *The Green Letters,* lays the foundation for understanding what spiritual growth is. Stanford bases the numerous principles discussed, such as faith, consecration, discipleship, and the cross, on some essential foundational principles, for example, the futility of the self-life. All that we are, have been, or attempt to be is utterly worthless and totally sinful. Any attempt to operate on this basis is doomed to heartbreaking failure and total defeat. The crux of the matter is "which life is to be consecrated to Him, the old self-life, or the new Christ-life? God can accept absolutely nothing from the old." A second key principle is that of identification. Identification truth teaches us that our old man, or original self, has been crucified with Christ. We are one with Him in death; He is one with us in life. Not I, but Christ. *He* is now my life, and I am dead and gone. Another foundational principle is that of reckoning. We are to live as disciples, reckoning the identification truths to be true. We are dead indeed unto sin. We are to hate ourselves. We must count it so that Christ lives in us. If we do not do this we will be substituting self-will for truth and will certainly fall.

In the second book, *The Principle of Position*, Stanford attempts to work out the implications of dead self, identification, and reckoning by stressing the importance of position. "All spiritual life and growth is based upon the principle of position. It can be summed up in one word: source." By this Stanford means we must allow what we are *in fact* to become what we are *in experience*. The Lord is our source (i.e., our everything) and we are complete in Him. We must let this reality become an experienced reality. "But only the believer who knows, grows. It is faith in the facts of our position that gives us the daily benefits of growth in our condition." Stanford follows this important truth with discussions of such theological concepts as justification, reconciliation, security, sin, conscience, and confession.

The Ground of Growth continues the study of what it means to be in Christ by focusing on our internal conflict and the solution to it. The conflict exists because when we are born again we are given a new nature that immediately wars against the old nature—the flesh—that was not removed when we became Christians. We might wonder why God did not simply destroy the "old man" when we believed, and Stanford gives several speculative reasons as to why He didn't, but the fact remains: the spirit struggles with the flesh because they are contrary to one another. The resolution is to apply identification truth to our lives, reckon that our "old man" is dead, and allow Christ to be our life. When we do this, we find that we are no longer under law but that we walk in liberty, in the Spirit, in Christ. "My liberty from the old is infinite in the Lord Jesus."

In *The Reckoning That Counts,* Stanford isolates the key element in the practical realization of what it means to grow as a Christian. Assuming that all of the identification truths have been understood, the believer who wants to go on to maturity must now "reckon" upon those truths. If we do not do this there will be compounded failure and bondage, because only Spirit-taught and Spirit-ministered identification truth will avail. There are three steps in reckoning: know and reckon; abide and rest; and depend and walk. Stanford follows this with discussions of reckoning truth in Romans 6, Romans 7, Romans 8, Galatians 2:20, Philippians 3:10, and Colossians 3. The basis for certainty in all of this reckoning is the eternal, unconditional security that the believer has in Christ. It is only the believer who realizes that life-union with Christ is forever who will be able to trust Christ for emancipation from sin and maturity for growth.

The final book, *Abide Above,* admonishes us to keep looking down. In contrast to the popular exhortation to "keep looking up" (from ourselves to Christ), we are to "keep looking down" (from our position in Him) upon our circumstances here on earth. This gives us the proper perspective on all things. In this, we are guided by the Holy Spirit, and Stanford shows what that consists of, as well as what he thinks it does not consist of, namely healing and tongue-speaking. "The modern 'gifts' of tongues and healing have a common source. They are not of the Spirit, but of the flesh, and function primarily in the realm of the nervous system."

* * * * *

Stanford ends his series with a four-point summary of

what he is trying to say. In it the whole of the Christian life is comprehended.

Live Positionally
"Cricified, Risen, Seated"
(Gal. 2:20; Eph. 2:6)

Live Positively
"Fully Persuaded"
(Rom. 14:5)

Live Possessively
"All Things Are Yours"
(I Cor. 3:21)

Live Triumphantly
"More Than Conquerors"
(Rom. 8:37)

Walter A. Elwell
Wheaton College
Wheaton, Illinois

Part One
PRINCIPLES OF SPIRITUAL GROWTH

1 Faith

The aim of this book is to carefully bring out some of the more important principles of spiritual growth, to help the reader build on a sound biblical foundation in Christ. He can honor no other.

The Holy Spirit had Paul write to each of us, "Examine yourselves, whether ye be in the faith" (2 Cor. 13:5a), and the recommendation is certainly not out of order at the inception of this series of studies. First of all, we must remind ourselves that "without faith it is impossible to please him" (Heb. 11:6a). Moreover, and this is all-important, true faith must be based solely on scriptural *facts*, for "faith cometh by hearing, and hearing by the word of God" (Rom. 10:17). Unless our faith is established on facts, it is no more than conjecture, superstition, speculation, or presumption.

Hebrews 11:1 leaves no question regarding this: "Faith is the substance of things hoped for, the evidence of things not seen." Faith standing on the *facts* of the Word of God substantiates and gives evidence of things not seen. And everyone knows that evidence must be founded on facts. All of us started on this principle when we were born again—our belief stood directly on the eternal fact of the redeeming death and resurrection of our Lord and Savior Jesus Christ (1 Cor. 15:1-4). This is the faith by which we began, and it is the same faith by which we are to "stand" (1 Cor. 16:13), and "walk" (2 Cor. 5:7), and "live" (Gal. 2:20b). "As ye have therefore received Christ Jesus the Lord, so walk ye in him" (Col. 2:6).

Since true faith is anchored on scriptural facts, we are certainly not to be influenced by *impressions*. George Mueller said, "Impressions have neither one thing nor the other to do with faith. Faith has to do with the Word of God. It is not impressions, strong or weak, which will make the difference. We have to do with the Written Word and not ourselves or our impressions."

Then, too, *probabilities* are the big temptation when it comes to exercising faith. Too often the attitude is, "It doesn't seem probable that he will ever be saved." The way things are going, I wonder if the Lord really loves me." But Mueller wrote: "Many people are willing to believe regarding those things that seem probable to them. Faith has nothing to do with probabilities. The province of faith begins where probabilities cease and sight and sense fail. Appearances are not to be taken into account. The question is—whether God has spoken it in His Word."

Alexander R. Hay adds to this by saying, "Faith must be based upon *certainty*. There must be definite knowledge of God's purpose and will. Without that there can be no true faith. For faith is not a force that we exercise or a striving to believe that something shall be, thinking that if we believe hard enough it will come to pass." That may be positive thinking, but certainly not biblical faith.

Evan Hopkins writes: "Faith needs facts to *rest* upon. Presumption can take fancy instead of fact. God in His Word reveals to us the facts with which faith has to deal." It is on this basis that J. B. Stoney can say, "Real faith is always increased by opposition, while false confidence is damaged and discouraged by it." There can be no steadfastness apart from immovable facts. Peter's burden was, "That the trial of your faith, being much more precious than of gold that perisheth, though it be tried with fire, might be found unto praise and honour and glory at the appearing of Jesus Christ" (1 Peter 1:7).

Once we begin to reckon (count) on facts, our Father begins to build us up in the faith. From his profoundly simple trust in God, Mueller was able to say that "God delights to increase the faith of His children. We ought, instead of wanting no trials before victory, no exercise for patience, to be willing to take them from God's hand as a means. I say—and say it deliberately—trials, obstacles, difficulties, and sometimes defeats, are the very food of faith."

On this same subject, James McConkey wrote: "Faith is *dependence* upon God. And this God-dependence only begins when self-dependence ends. And self-dependence only comes to its end, with some of us, when sorrow, suffering, affliction, broken plans and hopes bring us to that place of self-helplessness and defeat. And only then do we find that we have learned the lesson of faith; to find our tiny craft of life rushing onward to a blessed victory of life and power and service undreamt of in the days of our fleshly strength and self-reliance."

J. B. Stoney agrees by saying, "It is a great thing to *learn* faith: that is, simply dependence upon God. It will comfort you much to be assured that the Lord is teaching you dependence upon Himself, and it is very remarkable that faith is necessary in *everything.* 'The just shall live by faith,' not only in your circumstances, but in everything, I believe the Lord allows many things to happen on purpose to make us feel our need of Him. The more you find Him in your sorrows or wants, the more you will be attached to Him and drawn away from this place where the sorrows are, to Him in the place where He is." "Set your affection on things above" (Col. 3:2a).

Actually, we cannot trust anyone further than we know him. So we must not only learn the facts involved, but must always intimately come to know the One who presents and upholds them! "And this is life eternal, that they might know thee the only true God, and Jesus Christ, whom thou hast sent" (John 17:3). "Grace and peace be multiplied unto you through the knowledge of God, and of Jesus our Lord, According as his divine power hath given unto us all things that pertain unto life and godliness, through the knowledge of him that hath called us to glory and virtue: Whereby are given unto us exceeding great and precious promises: that by these ye might be partakers of the divine nature" (2 Peter 1:2-4).

2 Time

It seems that most believers have difficulty in realizing and facing up to the inexorable fact that God does not hurry in His development of our Christian life. He is working from and for eternity! So many feel they are not making progress unless they are swiftly and constantly forging ahead. Now it is true that the new convert often begins and continues for some time at a fast rate. But this will not continue if there is to be healthy growth and ultimate maturity. God Himself will modify the pace. This is important to see, since in most instances when seeming declension begins to set in, it is not, as so many think, a matter of backsliding.

John Darby makes it plain that "it is God's way to set people aside after their first start, that self-confidence may die down. Thus Moses was forty years. On his first start he had to run away. Paul was three years also, after his first testimony. Not that God did not approve the first earnest testimony. We must get to know ourselves and that we have no strength. Thus we must learn, and then leaning on the Lord we can with more maturity, and more experientially, deal with souls."

Since the Christian life matures and becomes fruitful by the principle of growth (2 Peter 3:18), rather than by struggle and "experiences," much time is involved. Unless we see and acquiesce to this there is bound to be constant frustration, to say nothing of resistance to our Father's development processes for us.

A. H. Strong illustrates it for us: "A student asked the President of his school whether he could not take a shorter course than the one prescribed. 'Oh yes,' replied the President, 'but then it depends upon what you want to be. When God wants to make an oak, He takes an hundred years, but when He wants to make a squash, He takes six months.' " Strong also wisely points out to us that "growth is not a uniform thing in the tree or in the Christian. In some single months there is more growth than in all the year besides. During the rest of the year, however, there is solidification, without which the green timber would be useless. The period of rapid growth, when woody fiber is actually deposited between the bark and the trunk, occupies but four to six weeks in May, June and July."

Let's settle it once and for all—there are no shortcuts to reality! A meteor is on a shortcut as it proceeds to burn out, but not a star, with its steady light so often depended on by navigators. Unless the time factor is acknowledged from the heart, there is always danger of turning to the false enticement of a shortcut via the means of "experiences," and "blessings," where one becomes pathetically enmeshed in the vortex of ever-changing "feelings," adrift from the moorings of scriptural facts.

Concerning this subject George Goodman writes: "Some have been betrayed into professing perfection or full deliverance, because at the time they speak they are happy and confident in the Lord. They forget that it is not a present experience that ensures fruit unto maturity, but a patient continuance in well doing. To taste of the grace of God is one thing; to be established in it and manifest it in character, habit, and regular life, is another. Experiences and blessings, though real gracious visitations from the Lord, are not sufficient to rest upon, nor should they lead us to glory in ourselves, as if we had a store of grace for time to come, or were yet at the end of the conflict. No. Fruit ripens slowly; days of sunshine and days of storm each add their share. Blessing will succeed blessing, and storm follow storm before the fruit is full grown or comes to maturity."

In that the Husbandman's method for true spiritual growth involves pain as well as joy, suffering as well as happiness, failure as well as success, inactivity as well as service, death as well as life, the temptation to shortcut is especially strong unless we see the value of and submit to the necessity of the time element; in simple trust resting in His hands, "Being confident of this very thing, that he which hath begun a good work in you will perform it until the day of Jesus Christ" (Phil. 1:6). And, dear friends, it will take that long! But since God is working for eternity, why should we be concerned about the time involved?

Graham Scroggie affirmed: "Spiritual renewal is a gradual process. All growth is progressive, and the finer the organism, the longer the process. It is from measure to measure: thirtyfold, sixtyfold, an hundredfold. It is from stage to stage: 'first the blade, then the ear, and after that, the full corn in the ear.' And it is from day to day. How varied these are! There are great days, days of decisive battles, days of crisis in spiritual history, days of triumph in Christian service, days of the right hand of God upon us. But there are also idle days, days apparently useless, when even prayer and holy service seem a burden. Are we, in any sense, renewed in these days? Yes, for any experience which makes us more aware of our need of God must contribute to spiritual progress, unless we deny the Lord who bought us."

We might consider some familiar names of believers whom God obviously brought to maturity and used for His glory names such as Pierson, Chapman, Tauler, Moody, Goforth, Mueller, Taylor, Watt, Trumbull, Meyer, Murray, Havergal, Guyon, Mabie, Gordon, Hyde, Mantle, McCheyne, McConkey, Deck, Paxson, Stoney, Saphir, Carmichael, and Hopkins. The average for these was fifteen years after they entered their life work before they began to know the Lord Jesus as their Life, and ceased trying to work for Him and began allowing Him to be their All in all and do His work through them. This is not to discourage us in any way, but to help us to settle down with our sights on eternity, by faith "apprehend[ing] that for which also I am apprehended of Christ Jesus. . . . press[ing] toward the mark for the prize of the high calling of God in Christ Jesus" (Phil. 3:12b, 14).

Certainly this is not to discount a Spirit-fostered experience, blessing, or even a crisis; but it is to be remembered that these simply contribute to the overall, and all-important process. It takes time to get to know oneself; it takes time and eternity to get to know the infinite Lord Jesus Christ. Today is the day to put the hand to the plow, and irrevocably set the heart on His goal for us—that we "may know him, and the power of his resurrection, and the fellowship of his sufferings, being made conformable unto his death" (Phil. 3:10).

"So often in the battle," says Austin-Sparks, "we go to the Lord, and pray, and plead, and appeal for victory, for ascendancy, for mastery over the forces of evil and death, and our thought is that in some way the Lord is going to come in with a mighty exercise of power and put us into a place of victory and spiritual ascendancy as in an act. We must have this mentality corrected. What the Lord does is to enlarge us to possess. He puts us through some exercise, through some experience, takes us by some way that means our spiritual expansion, and exercise of spirituality so we occupy the larger place spontaneously. 'I will not drive them out from before thee in one year; lest the land become desolate, and the beast of the field multiply against thee. By little and little I will drive them out before thee, until thou be increased' (Exod. 23:29, 30).

"One day in the House of Commons, British Prime Minister *Disraeli* made a brilliant speech on the spur of the moment. That night a friend said to him, 'I must tell you how much I enjoyed your extemporaneous talk. It's been on my mind all day.' 'Madam,' confessed Disraeli, 'that extemporaneous talk has been on my mind for twenty years!' "

3 Acceptance

There are two questions that every believer must settle as soon as possible. The one is, Does God fully accept me? and, if so, on what basis does He do so? This is crucial. What devastation often permeates the life of one, young or old, rich or poor, saved or unsaved, who is not sure of being accepted, even on the human level.

Yet so many believers, whether "strugglers" or "vegetators," move through life without this precious fact to rest and build on: "Having predestined us unto the adoption of children by Jesus Christ to himself, according to the good pleasure of his will, to the praise of the glory of his grace, wherein he hath made us accepted in the beloved" (Eph. 1:5, 6).

Every believer is accepted by the Father, in Christ. "Being justified by faith, we have peace with God through our Lord Jesus Christ" (Rom. 5:1). The peace is God's toward us, through His beloved Son—on this, our peace is to be based. God is able to be at peace with us through our Lord Jesus Christ, "having made peace through the blood of his cross" (Col. 1:20). And we must never forget that His peace is founded solely on the work of the cross, totally apart from anything whatsoever in or from us, since "God commendeth his love toward us, in that, while we were yet sinners, Christ died for us" (Rom. 5:8).

Our faith becomes a fixed attitude, once it begins to rest in this wonderful fact. This is the steadying influence most believers are in need of today. A century ago, J. B. Stoney wrote: "The blessed God never alters nor diverges from the acceptance in which He has received us because of the death and resurrection of Jesus Christ. Alas! we diverge from the state in which God can ever be toward us as recorded in Romans 5:1-11. Many suppose that because they're conscious of sins, that hence they must renew their acceptance with God.

"The truth is that God has not altered. His eye rests on the work accomplished by Christ for the believer. When you are not walking in the Spirit you are in the flesh; you have turned to the old man which was crucified on the cross (Rom. 6:6). You have to be restored to fellowship, and when you are, you find your acceptance with God unchanged and unchangeable. When sins are introduced there is a fear that God has changed. He has not changed, but you have. You are not walking in the Spirit but in the flesh. You have to judge yourself in order to be restored. 'For this is my blood of the new testament which is shed for many for the remission of sins' (Matt. 26:28). But if your sins are not met there, where can they be met? 'Now where remission of sin is, there is no more offering for sin' (Heb. 10:18). God has effected the reconciliation; He always remains true to it. Alas! we diverge from it; and the tendency is to suppose that the blessed God has altered toward us. He certainly will judge the flesh if we do not, but He never departs from the love which He has expressed to the prodigal, and we find that when the cloud, which walking in the flesh produced, has passed away, His love, blessed be His Name, had never changed."

God's basis must be our basis for acceptance. There is none other. We are "accepted in the Beloved." Our Father is fully satisfied with His Beloved Son on our behalf, and there is no reason for us not to be. Our satisfaction can only spring from and rest in His satisfaction. It is from God to us, not from us to God. J. N. Darby was very clear on this: "When the Holy Spirit reasons with man, He does not reason from what man is for God, but from what God is to man. Souls reason from what they are in themselves as to whether God can accept them. He cannot accept you thus; you are looking for righteousness in yourself as a ground of acceptance with Him. You cannot get peace whilst reasoning in that way.

"The Holy Spirit always reasons down from what God is, and this produces a total change in my soul. It is not that I abhor my sins; indeed I may have been walking very well; but it is 'I abhor myself.' This is how the Holy Spirit reasons; He shows us what we are, and that is one reason why He often seems to be very hard and does not give peace to the soul, as we are not relieved until we experientially, from our hearts, acknowledge what we are.

"Until the soul comes to that point He does not give it peace— He could not; it would be healing the wound slightly. The soul has to go on until it finds there is nothing to rest on but the abstract goodness of God; and then, 'If God be for us, who can be against us?' (Rom. 8:31b)."

Sad today, most believers actually reason just the opposite—from themselves to God. When all is going well, and God seems to be blessing, then it is that they feel He loves and accepts them. But when they are stumbling, and everything seems dry and hard, then they feel He does not love and accept them. How can this be? There is nothing about us to commend us to God, our acceptance being in Christ, plus the fact that most of our true spiritual development comes through the dry and hard times. Thank God, He has accepted us in His Son, and upon this *fact* we must rest our faith. As in justification, our acceptance is by *grace* alone. In his classic, *Romans, Verse by Verse,* Wm. R. Newell presents some penetrating thoughts regarding this grace:

"There being no cause in the creature why grace should be shown, the creature must be brought off from trying to give cause to God for His care." "He has been accepted in Christ, who is his standing!" "He is not on probation." "As to his life past, it does not exist before God: he died at the cross, and Christ is his Life." "Grace, once bestowed, is not withdrawn: for God knew all the human exigencies beforehand; His action was independent of them, not dependent upon them."

"To believe, and to consent to be loved while unworthy, is the great secret."

"To refuse to make 'resolutions' and 'vows'; for that is to trust in the flesh."

"To expect to be blessed, though realizing more and more lack of worth."

"To rely on God's chastening (child training) hand as a mark of His kindness."

"To 'hope to be better' (hence acceptable) is to fail to see yourself in Christ only."

"To be disappointed with yourself is to have believed in yourself."

"To be discouraged is unbelief—as to God's purpose and plan of blessing for you."

"To be proud, is to be blind! For we have no standing before God, in ourselves."

"The lack of Divine blessing, therefore, comes from unbelief, and not from failure of devotion."

"To preach devotion first, and blessing second, is to reverse God's order, and preach law, not grace. The Law made man's blessing depend on devotion; Grace confers undeserved, unconditional blessing: our devotion may follow, but does not always do so—in proper measure."

Have we been afraid to really believe God? Have some even been afraid to allow others to really believe Him? We must never forget that "God's ways are not always man's ways. To some men constant peril is the only spur to action, and many religions and psychologies are dependent on fear to keep their disciples in line. Fear, too, has a place in Christianity, but God has higher and more effective motivations than fear, and one of these is love. Often fear after a while produces only numbness, but love thrives on love. To promise a man the certainty of his destiny may seem, on the human level, like playing with fire; but this leaves God out of the picture. Those who have the deepest appreciation of grace do not continue in sin. Moreover, fear produces the obedience of slaves; love engenders the obedience of sons."—J. W. Sanderson, Jr.

"For if the trumpet give an uncertain sound, who shall prepare himself to the battle?" (1 Cor. 14:8). Until the Christian is absolutely and scripturally sure of his standing, he is not going to do much standing. "Stand therefore" (Eph. 6:14a).

"Now our Lord Jesus Christ himself, and God, even our Father, which hath loved us, and hath given us everlasting consolation and good hope through grace, comfort your hearts, and stablish you in every good word and work" (2 Thess. 2:16, 17).

4 *Purpose*

How wonderful and encouraging it is to know that our heavenly Father has made it crystal clear in His Word exactly what His purpose is for each one of us. Now is the time, in these next few moments, to make sure, on the authority of His eternal Word, as to His purpose for your personal life.

"And God said, Let us make man in our image" (Gen. 1:26). The first Adam, the head of the human race, was made in God's image in the realm of personality, intellect, emotions, will, etc., so that there could be communion, fellowship, and cooperation between them; with God Sovereign, and man subject—subject to His will, which is perfect freedom. But we know that Adam was beguiled into choosing his own way in preference to God's way, relying on himself only, loving just himself. As a result, he immediately became self-centered instead of God-centered; dead to God who is the Source of all Life, dead in trespasses and sins. In this condition Adam "begat a son in his own likeness, after his [fallen] image" (Gen. 5:3). Thus he brought forth a sinful, ungodly, self-centered race, born "dead in trespasses and sins" (Eph. 2:1).

"God . . . hath in these last days spoken unto us by his Son . . . who being the brightness of his glory, and the express image of his person" (Heb. 1:1-3). Here is the image of God back on earth, this time in the person of our Lord Jesus Christ, God's Last Adam (1 Cor. 15:45, 47). Our natural birth made us members of the fallen, sinful first-Adam race. Our transition from the old sinful race to the new godly race is known as the "new birth." When we were "born again," through "repentance toward God, and faith toward our Lord Jesus Christ" (Acts 20:21), we were born into Him—He became our

Life (Col. 3:3, 4). "Thou wert cut out of the olive tree which is wild by nature, and wert grafted contrary to nature into a good olive tree" (Rom. 11:24). "For as by one man's disobedience [Adam's] many were made sinners, so by the obedience of one [Christ] shall many be made righteous" (Rom. 5:19).

Our heavenly Father is still carrying out His purpose of making man in His image. Although His original purpose is the same, He is not using the original man to bring it about. *All* is now centered in the Last Adam, our Lord Jesus. Being born into Him through faith we became "partakers of the divine nature" (2 Peter 1:4). And as the Lord Jesus is allowed to express Himself through our personality this poor sin-sick world will see "*Christ in you,* the hope of glory" (Col. 1:27). In 1 Corinthians 15:49, Paul gives us the heartening promise: "As we have borne the image of the earthly [Adam], we shall also bear the image of the heavenly [Christ]."

"And we know that all things work together for good to them that love God, to them who are the called according to his purpose. For whom he did foreknow, he also did predestinate to be conformed to the image of His Son" (Rom. 8:28, 29). Here is the "good" for which God is working all things together—His original purpose of making us in His image, which is centered and expressed in His Son, Christ who is our life. Paul's determination for each of his converts was, "My little children, of whom I travail in birth again until Christ be formed in you" (Gal. 4:19).

The open secret of healthy spiritual growth is to know and settle down on this fact as set forth in Romans 8:28 and 29. When we see that all things are working together to make us more and more like the Lord Jesus we will not be frustrated and upset when some of these "things" are hard, difficult to understand, and often contain an element of death. We will be able to rest in our Lord Jesus and say to our Father, "Thy will be done." And our constant attitude of faith will be, "Though he slay me, yet will I trust in him" (Job 13:15). This is our matriculation to spiritual maturity!

"But we all, with open face beholding as in a glass the glory of the Lord, are changed into the same image from glory to glory, even as by the Spirit of the Lord" (2 Cor. 3:18). It is one thing to know what God's purpose is for our lives, and it is another to know something of the "how" as to entering into it all right here and now. One of God's most effective means in the process is failure. So many believers are simply frantic over the fact of failure in their lives, and they will go to all lengths to try to hide it, ignore it, or rationalize about it. And all the time they are resisting the main instrument in the Father's hand for conforming us to the likeness of His Son!

Failure where self is concerned in our Christian life and service, is allowed and often engineered by God in order to turn us completely from ourselves to His Source for our life— Christ Jesus, who never fails. Rejoice, dear friend, in your need and hunger of heart, for God says, "Blessed are they which do hunger and thrist after righteousness: for they shall be filled" (Matt. 5:6). As we, in our abject need, consistently and lovingly look on our Lord Jesus revealed to us in the Word, the Holy Spirit will quietly and effortlessly change the center and source of our lives from self to Christ—hence for each of us it will be, "Not I, but Christ."

God has a natural law in force to the effect that we are conformed to that on which we center our interest and love. Hawthorne brought out this fact in "The Great Stone Face." Then too, think of Germany some years ago, full of little Hitlers all because of fanatical devotion to a second-rate paper-hanger! Here in our country comic books, radio, T.V. and movies have all contributed in giving us a rising generation of young policemen, cowboys, gangsters, etc. And what of the believer? If we are attracted to this present evil world, we become increasingly worldly; if we pamper and live for self, we become more and more self-centered; but when we look to Jesus Christ, we become more and more like Him.

Norman Douty writes, "If I am to be like Him, then God in His grace must do it, and the sooner I come to recognize it the sooner I will be delivered from another form of bondage. Throw down every endeavor and say, I cannot do it, the more I try the farther I get from His likeness. What shall I do? Ah, the Holy Spirit says, You cannot do it; just withdraw; come out of it. You have been in the arena, you have been endeavoring, you are a failure, come out and sit down, and as you sit there behold Him, look at Him. Don't try to be like Him, just look at Him. Just be occupied with Him. Forget about trying to be like Him. Instead of letting that fill your mind and heart, let Him fill it. Just behold Him, look upon Him through the Word. Come to the Word for one purpose and that is to meet the Lord. Not to get your mind crammed full of things about the sacred Word, but come to it to meet the Lord. Make it to be a medium, not of Biblical scholarship, but of fellowship with Christ. Behold the Lord."

Thou sayest, Fit me, fashion me for Thee.
　Stretch forth thine empty hands, and be thou still:
O restless soul, thou dost but hinder Me
　By valiant purpose and by steadfast will.
Behold the summer flowers beneath the sun,
　In stillness his great glory they behold;
And sweetly thus his mighty word is done.
　And resting in his gladness they unfold.
So are the sweetness and the joy Divine
　Thine, O beloved, and the work is Mine.

　　　　　　　　　　　　　　　—Ter Steegen

"For it is God which worketh in you both to will and to do of his good pleasure" (Phil. 2:13). And what is His "good pleasure" He is "performing" in us? He is working everything together for this one purpose: "That the life also of Jesus might be made manifest in our mortal flesh" (2 Cor. 4:11). This is life: "For to me to live is Christ" (Phil. 1:21). This is service: "And there were certain Greeks . . . saying . . . Sir, we would see Jesus" (John 12:20, 21).

5 Preparation

Once we know His eternal plan and purpose for us, plus His method of preparation and process to that end, there is rest and confidence. Now it so happens that God's basic ingredient for growth is need. Without personal needs, we would get nowhere in our Christian life. The reason our Father creates and allows needs in our lives is to turn us from all that is outside of Christ, centering us in Him alone. "Not I, but Christ."

For both our growth and service it is all-essential that we see and understand this principle, which J. B. Stoney sets forth in a sentence: "The soul never imbibes the truth in living power but as it requires it." As for our growth, needs cause us to reach out and appropriate by faith, from our Lord Jesus, what we require. And in the matter of service, in witnessing and helping others, we must watch and wait for the hungry, the needy heart, if there is to be abiding fruit. Again Stoney says, "The true value of anything is known only when it is wanted." J. N. Darby makes this doubly clear by writing, "Wisdom and philosophy never found out God; He makes Himself known to us through our needs; necessity finds Him out. I doubt much if we have ever learned anything solidly except we have learnt it thus."

In this light, our needs are invaluable! We must face up to the fact that without spiritual hunger, we cannot feed on the Lord Jesus Christ. From our personal experience, Matthew 5:6 should mean much to every one of us—"Blessed are they which do hunger and thirst after righteousness: for they shall be filled." All too often believers are exhorted and even pressured to grow before there is an acute awareness of need, before there is true spiritual hunger. And, sad to say, in most instances when there is real heart-hunger, very little spiritual food is offered. One of the main reasons for so much evangelistic effort and personal work coming to little or nothing is that truths are forced on the "victim" to be saved before he is aware that he is lost. The work will soon come to naught unless an overpowering conviction of sin causes the lost to reach out with the grip of personal faith, and find their need fully ment in the Savior.

Watchman Nee puts first things first in saying, "The Lord does not set us here first of all to preach, or to do any work for Him. The first thing for which He sets us here is to create hunger in others. No true work will ever begin without a sense of need being created. We cannot inject that into others; we cannot drive people to be hungry. That hunger is to be created, and that hunger can be created only through those who carry the impressions of God."

In preparation, there is a tearing down before there can be a building up. "Come, and let us return unto the LORD: for he hath torn, and he will heal us; he hath smitten, and he will bind us up" (Hos. 6:1). This applies to both growth and service.

J. C. Metcalfe faithfully writes: "It is more than comforting to realize that it is those who have plumbed the depths of failure to whom God invariably gives the call to shepherd others. This is not a call given to the gifted, the highly trained, or the polished as such.

"Without a bitter experience of their own inadequacy and poverty they are quite unfitted to bear the burden of spiritual ministry. It takes a man who has discovered something of the measures of his own weakness to be patient with the foibles of others. Such a man also has a first-hand knowledge of the loving care of the Chief Shepherd, and his ability to heal one who has come humbly to trust in Him and Him alone. Therefore he does not easily despair of others, but looks beyond sinfulness, willfulness, and stupidity, to the might of unchanging love. The Lord Jesus does not give the charge, 'Be a shepherd to My lambs . . . to My sheep,' on hearing Peter's self-confident affirmation of undying loyalty, but He gives it after he has utterly failed to keep his vows and has wept bitterly in the streets of Jerusalem."

Yes, there must be deep, thorough, and long preparation if there is to be reality—if our life is to be Christ-centered, our work controlled by the Holy Spirit, and our service glorifying to God. Sooner or later the Holy Spirit begins to make us aware of our basic problem as believers—the infinite difference between self and Christ. "There are other laborers besides those who are seeking for pardon—for justification. There are laborers for sanctification—after personal holiness—after riddance of the power of the old Adam; and to such, as well as to those who are seeking after salvation, Christ promises, with this great 'I will' (Matt. 11:28-30). It is highly possible for a man, after having found justifying rest in Christ, to enter upon a state of deep need as regards sanctifying rest. We think we shall not go far wrong if we say that this has been the experience of almost every believer who has ever lived" (P. B. Power).

Much of His preparation in our lives consists of setting up this struggle—our seeing self for what it is, and then attempting to get free from its evil power and influence. For there is no hope of consistent abiding in the Lord Jesus as long as we are under the dominion of the self-life, in which "dwelleth no good thing" (Rom. 7:18a). "Not in babyhood are we able to continually abide in His presence, regardless of our surroundings and that which we are doing. Not when we serve Him with intermittent zeal does our own soul grow and thrive; not when we are indifferent are we watered from the presence of the Lord. It is after we have been subdued, refined, and chastened; when love of self and the world is gone, that we learn to abide in touch with Him at all times, and in all places or surroundings."

The value of both the struggle to free ourselves from the old Adam-life, and the equally fruitless efforts to experience the new Adam-life, the Christ-life, is to finally realize that it is utterly futile. Our personal, heart-breaking failure in every phase of our Christian life is our Father's preparation for His success on our behalf. This negative processing of His finally brings us into His positive promise of Philippians 1:6, "Being confident of this very thing, that he which hath begun a good work in you will perform it until the day of Jesus Christ." His "good work" in us is begun through failure, and this includes our strongest points, which continues on into His success, by His performance, and not ours. "For it is God which worketh in you both to will and to do of his good pleasure" (Phil. 2:13). There is no question but that we all began in sheer grace, and we must continue and arrive on the very same basis: "Stand fast therefore in the liberty wherewith Christ hath made us free" (Gal. 5:1).

Charles Trumbull said, "The effortless life is not the will-less life. We use our will to believe, to receive, but not to exert effort in trying to accomplish what only God can do. Our hope for victory over sin is not 'Christ plus my efforts,' but 'Christ plus my receiving.' To receive victory from Him is to believe His Word that solely by His grace He is, this moment, freeing us from the dominion of sin. And to believe on Him in this way is to recognize that He is doing for us what we cannot do for ourselves." We learned this principle at the time of our spiritual birth, and it seems that most of us have to learn it all over again for our spiritual growth and service. Fear not, dear friend; just hold firm to the fact of His purpose for you in Christ, and He will faithfully take you step by step into all the necessary preparation—He will do it. Once you are sure of the purpose you can be equally positive of the preparation. Simply remember that Romans 8:28 and 29 go together, and thank Him for Philippians 1:6.

"The Lord is glorified in a people whose heart is set at any cost, by any road, upon the goal which is God himself. A man who is thus minded says, 'By any road!' Here is a very difficult road; a road beset by enemies, but the passionate desire for the goal will hold him steadfast in the way. It is the man who lacks the yearning to know Him that will easily be turned aside. Along that road the Man Christ Jesus has already gone before, and at every point has overcome for us. We have not to climb up; we are to be brought through in the train of His triumph. Every enemy has been met; every foe has been overcome; there remains nothing that has not been put potentially beneath His feet, and there remains nothing in this universe that is able to overcome the least child of God who has taken the hand of the Lord and said: 'Lord, bring me through to the place where Thou art, in virtue of the blood which Thou hast already taken through in victory.' There is great glory of the Lord in a quiet, confident walk in a day of adversity, a day of dread, when things about us are shaking and trembling" (G. P.).

6 *Complete in Him*

We continue to deal with foundational facts, since the life can be no better than its roots, its source. Youth and immaturity tend to act first and think later, if at all. Maturity has learned to take time to assess the facts. Our patient Husbandman is willing for us to take time and learn the eternal facts, without which we cannot be brought to maturity.

Our Lord Jesus so often uses natural facts to teach us the deepest spiritual truths. He first teaches us about our natural, Adamic life before we can understand and appreciate our new spiritual, Christ-life. This involves the vital source principle—"after his kind." Every believer first learns that he is complete in Adam—he sprang from him: he is like him. "For as by one man's disobedience many were made sinners" (Rom. 5:19a). "For I know that in me (that is, in my flesh), dwelleth no good thing" (Rom. 7:18a). When, through our failures and struggles, He has taught us about the natural, we will be ready to learn of our spiritual Source. "By the obedience of one shall many be made righteous" (Rom. 5:19). "For in him dwelleth all the fullness of the Godhead bodily. And ye are complete in him" (Col. 2:9, 10a).

There are two main aspects to this source principle. First, the Lord Jesus is the Source of our Christian life—we were born into Him; God has made us complete in Him. This truth we are to hold by faith; it is true of each of us. "If any man be in Christ, he is a new creature . . ." (2 Cor. 5:17a). Second, as we hold to this fact by faith, we are brought into the practical reality of it day by day in our experience. Little by little we receive what is already ours. The important thing to know and be sure of is that all is ours, we are complete in Him, *now.* This fact enables us to hold still while He patiently works into our character that life of ours which is hid with Christ in God.

"Progress is only advancing in the knowledge, the spiritual knowledge, of what we really possess at the outset. It is like ascending a ladder. The ladder is grace. The first step is, we believe, that the Lord Jesus was sent of God; second, that in the fullness of His work we are justified; third, we make His acquaintance; fourth, we come to see Him in heaven; we know our association with Him there, and His power here; fifth, we learn the mystery, the great things we are entitled to because of being His body; sixth, that we are seated in heavenly places in Christ; seventh, lost in wonder and in praise in the knowledge of Himself" (J. B. Stoney).

Since we are complete in our Lord Jesus, it will not do to try and add to that finished work. It is now a matter of walking by faith and receiving, appropriating, from the ever-abundant Source within. Walter Marshall is concise here: "Christ's resurrection was our resurrection to a life of holiness, as Adam's fall was our fall into spiritual death. And we are not ourselves the first makers and formers of our new holy nature, any more than of our original corruption, but both are formed ready for us to partake of them. And by union with Christ, we partake of that spiritual life that He took possession of for us at His resurrection, and thereby we are enabled to bring forth the fruits of it; as the Scripture showeth by the similitude of a marriage union. Romans 7:4: 'Married to another, even to him who is raised from the dead, that we should bring forth fruit unto God.' "

Our part is not production, but reception of our life in Christ. This entails Bible-based fact-finding; explicit faith in Him and His purpose for us in Christ; and patient trust while He takes us through the necessary processing involved. No believer ever fell into maturity, even though he is complete in Christ. Spiritual growth necessitates heart-hunger for the Lord Jesus; determination, based on assurance, to have that which is ours in Him, plus meditation and thought. We will never come into the knowledge of our spiritual possessions through a superficial understanding of the Word. How can we ever expect to have intimate fellowship with One of whom we know little?

The following truth may be a good opportunity to exercise and develop some of that meditation and thought. "What is needed is a mediation, in which God concentrates His own peculiar Spirit and Life as a principle in a human individual to be personally appropriated. In a revelation, which is really to translate the divine into man's individual personal life, in truth, to form men of God, the divine as such—that is, as a personal life—must first be embodied in a personal center in humanity. For this reason, as soon as something strictly new is concerned, something that in its peculiarity has not yet existed, every new type of life, before it can multiply itself to a number of specimens, must first have its full contents combined in perfect unity, in an adequate new principle. And so, for the making personal of the divine among men, the first thing needed is one in whom the principle of the divine life has become personal.

"Christianity concentrates the whole fullness of revelation in the one human personality of Jesus Christ as Mediator—that is, as the mediating central principle of the new Divine organism, in its fullness of Spirit and Life, in and for the human personal life. With the entrance of Christ into the human individual, the Divine life becomes immanent in us, not in its universal world-relation, but as a personal principle, so that man is not only a being made of God, but a being begotten of God. And with the growing transformation of the individual into the life-type of Christ there is perfected the development of the personal life out of God, in God, and to God—the development not only of a moral or theocratic communion, but a communion of nature" (J. T. Beck).

A seed embodies in full the reproduction of the life from which it came. That much is complete, and can never be added to. "Being born again, not of corruptible seed, but of incorruptible" (1 Peter 1:23a). "Thou shalt not sow thy field with mingled seed" (Lev. 19:19). It is to be "not I, but Christ." The Seed has been implanted—now the entire question is one of growth and maturity. This alone will bring forth fruit that abides. "The development of the divine life in the Christian is like the natural growth in the vegetable world. We do not need to make any special effort, only place ourselves under the conditions favorable to such growth."

Only those who have sought to grow by effort and failed are in the position to appreciate the fact that God is the aggressor in the realm of development. "All the powers of Deity which have already wrought together in the accomplishment of the first part of the eternal purpose, the revealing of the Father's perfect likeness in the Man Christ Jesus, are equally engaged to accomplish the second part, and work that likeness in each of God's children" William Law agrees: "A root set in the finest soil, in the best climate, and blessed with all that sun and air and rain can do for it, is not so sure a way of its growth to perfection, as every man may be whose spirit aspires after all that which God is ready and infinitely desirous to give him. For the sun meets not the springing bud that stretches toward him with half that certainty as God, the Source of all good, communicates Himself to the soul that longs to partake of Him."

Not only is our life complete in Him, but likewise the essential victory in all the many exigencies of that life. "When you fight to get victory, then you have lost the battle at the very outset. Suppose the Enemy assaults you in your home or in your business. He creates a situation with which you cannot possibly deal. What do you do? Your first instinct is to prepare yourself for a big battle and then pray to God to give you the victory in it. But if you do so defeat is sure, for you have given up the ground that is yours in Christ. By the attitude you have taken you have relinquished it to the Enemy. What then should you do when he attacks? You should simply look up and praise the Lord. 'Lord, I am faced with a situation that I cannot possibly meet. Thine enemy the Devil has brought it about to compass my downfall, but I praise Thee that Thy victory is an all-inclusive victory. It covers this situation, too. I praise Thee that I have already full victory in this matter.' "

P.S. Don't rush—He won't. "The Japanese artist, Hokusai, said, 'From the age of six I had a mania for drawing the forms of things. By the time I was fifty I had published an infinity of designs; but nothing I produced before seventy is worth considering.' He died at eighty-nine, declaring that if he could have only another five years he would have become a great artist."

7 Appropriation

Here is an important subject that has to do with faith, and the practical reception of that for which we are able to trust Him. Appropriation does not necessarily mean to gain something new, but to set aside for our practical possession something that already belongs to us.

To appropriate something for our daily walk in Christ, we face two essentials: to see what is already ours in Christ; and to be aware of our need for it. On these two factors rests the ability to appropriate, to reach out in steadfast faith and receive what belongs to us in our Lord Jesus Christ.

Regarding the first essential, to *see* what is already ours, William R. Newell wrote: "Paul does not ask a thing of the saints in the first three chapters of Ephesians but just to listen while he proclaims that wondrous series of great and eternal *facts* concerning them; and not until he has completed this catalogue of realities about them does he ask them to do anything at all!

"And when he does open his plea for their high walk as saints, everything is based on the revelation before given—the facts of their high character and destiny as saints: 'I therefore . . . beseech you that ye walk worthy of the vocation wherewith ye are called (Eph. 4:1). Let us cease laying down to the saints long lists of 'conditions' of entering into the blessed life in Christ; and instead, as the primal preparation for leading them into the experience of this life, show them what their position, possessions, and privileges in Christ already are. Thus shall we truly work with the Holy Spirit, and thus shall we have more, and much more abiding fruit of our labors among the people of God."

Once we see what is ours in Christ Jesus, practical need will cause us to appropriate, to receive the answer to that need. "There was a 'supply of the Spirit of Jesus Christ' for Paul, and that made it possible for Christ to be magnified in him. It was a supply which was always available, but only appreciated and appropriated as and when the Apostle came to know his need. Life is meant to bring a succession of discoveries of our need of Christ, and with every such discovery the way is opened for a new inflow of the supply. This is the explanation of so much that we cannot otherwise understand—this plunging of us into new tests where only a fresh supply of the Spirit of Jesus Christ will meet our need. And as our need is met, as we prove the sufficiency of Christ to meet our inward need, so there can be a new showing forth of His glory through us" (H. F.).

These two realities of seeing and needing bring us from childish meandering into a responsible, specific walk of faith. They take us from the "help me" attitude to that of giving thanks; from begging to appropriation. Notice what L. L. Letgers, co-founder of Wycliffe Bible Translators, has to say about this: "Blessed be the God and Father of our Lord Jesus Christ, who hath blessed us with every spiritual blessing in the heavenly places in Christ Jesus' (Eph. 1:3, A.S.V.). If you run over in your mind and find one single blessing with which God might bless us today, with which He has not already blessed us, then what He told Paul was not true at all, because He said, 'God hath.' It is all done. 'It is finished.' God hath blessed us with every spiritual blessing in the heavenlies! The great pity of it all is that we are saying, 'O God bless us, bless us in this, bless us in that!' and it is all done. He has blessed us with every spiritual blessing in the heavenlies." As C. A. Coates said, "It is appropriation that tests us. How often we stop at admiration."

From time to time the Holy Spirit will bring to our attention a certain aspect of the Word in a striking manner, and we will rejoice to see and believe that it is ours in Christ. It may be, for instance, the truths of Matthew 11:28, "Come unto me, all ye that labour and are heavy laden, and I will give you rest." Besides the usual personal situations, the uncertainty, strife, and tensions of world conditions provide just what is needed for the believer to abide, to rest in the Lord Jesus. The need exists, and when he sees the rest in Him, all there remains to do is appropriate!

So far so good. The believer sees what he possesses in Christ, and the need enables him to reach out and confidently appropriate and accept the required rest. This appropriation must be a case of clear, scriptural, specific trust. We are not to "ask amiss." And now comes the critical phase, the key to it all. In most instances of appropriation, there is a waiting period between the acceptance and the receiving—often of years. Our responsibility is to patiently wait on Him during the time necessary for Him to work into our character, our life, that which we have appropriated in Christ—in this instance, His rest, steadiness, assurance, security. "A God . . . who acts in behalf of the one who waits for him" (Isa. 64:4b, NASB).

T. Austin-Sparks gives us two valuable thoughts regarding this all-important gap—usually a matter of years—between the actual appropriation, and the practical experience. "Every bit of truth we receive, if we receive it lovingly, will take us into conflict and will be established through conflict. It will be worthless until there has been a battle over it. Take any position the Lord calls you to take, and, if you are taking it with Him, you are going through things in it, and there will be an element added by reason of the battle. You have taken a position—yes, but you have not really got it yet, the real value of it has not been proved. You have not come into the real significance of it until there has been some sore conflict in relation to it.

"As the result of the work of His cross, and as the grand issue of His resurrection, eternal life is received already by those who believe. But while that life is itself victorious, incorruptible, indestructible, the believer has to come by faith to prove it, to live by it, to learn its laws, to be conformed to it. There is a deposit in the believer, which in itself needs no addition, so far as its quality is concerned. So far as its victory, its power, its glory, its potentialities are concerned nothing can be added to it. But the course of spiritual experience, of spiritual life, is to discover, to appropriate, and to live by all that the life represents and means."

Now we have seen a third element involved in our appropriation. After we have seen our possessions in Christ, and become aware of our need, then we must give Him the necessary time to work the appropriation into our everyday walk. If we are looking for our needs to be met in the next interview, the next devotional book, the next series of special meetings, the next hoped-for "revival," then reality will never come.

In this matter of Christian development, there is no short-cut, no quick and easy way. The Husbandman builds into the believer that which He intends to minister through him to others. To minister Life to others, what one does and says must flow from what he is. "For it pleased the Father that in him [Christ Jesus] should all fullness dwell"; "For we are made partakers of Christ"; "That ye might be filled with all the fullness of God"; For your life is hid with Christ in God"; "That the life also of Jesus might be made manifest in our mortal flesh" (Col. 1:19; Heb. 3:14; Eph. 3:19; Col. 3:3; 2 Cor. 4:11b).

How often we simply admire and talk about truths the Holy Spirit reveals to us in the Word, whereas His primary purpose in giving them to us is that we might stand on them in faith, waiting confidently for Him to make them an integral part of our life. "A prophet is one who has a history, one who has been dealt with by God, one who has experienced the formative work of the Spirit. We are sometimes asked by would-be preachers how many days should be spent in preparation of a sermon. The answer is: At least ten years, and probably nearer twenty! For the preacher matters to God at least as much as the thing preached. God chooses as His prophets those in whom He has already worked what He intends to use as His message for today."

8 Identification

As our thinking moves along from the Substitutionary (birth) truths, on to the Identification (growth) truths, it might be good to consider briefly what leaders, honored of God through the years, have to say about identification, as centered in Romans 6.

Evan H. Hopkins: "The trouble of the believer who knows Christ as his justification is not sin as to its guilt, but sin as to its ruling power. In other words, it is not from sin as a load, or an offense, that he seeks to be freed—for he sees that God has completely acquitted him from the charge and penalty of sin—but it is from sin as a master. To know God's way of deliverance from sin as a master he must apprehend the truth contained in the sixth chapter of Romans. There we see what God has done, not with our sins—that question the Apostle dealt with in the preceding chapters—but with ourselves, the agents and slaves of sin. He has put our old man— our original self—where He put our sins, namely, on the cross with Christ. 'Knowing this, that our old man was crucified with him' (Rom. 6:6). The believer there sees not only that Christ died for him—substitution—but that he died with Christ—identification" (*Thoughts on Life and Godliness,* p. 50).

Andrew Murray: "Like Christ, the believer too has died to sin; he is one with Christ, in the likeness of His death (Rom. 6:5). And as the knowledge that Christ died for sin as our atonement is indispensable to our justification; so the knowledge that Christ and we with Him in the likeness of His death, are dead to sin, is indispensable to our sanctification" (*Like Christ,* p. 176).

J. Hudson Taylor: "Since Christ has thus dwelt in my heart by faith, how happy I have been! I am dead and buried with Christ—ay, and risen too! And now Christ lives in me, and 'the life which I now live in the flesh I live by the faith of the Son of God, who loved me, and gave himself for me.' Nor should we look upon this experience, these truths, as for the few. They are the birthright of every child of God, and no one can dispense with them without dishonoring our Lord" (*Spiritual Secret*, p. 116).

William R. Newell: "To those who refuse or neglect to reckon themselves dead to sin as God commands, we press the question, How are you able to believe that Christ really bare the guilt of your sins and that you will not meet them at the judgment day? It is only God's Word that tells you that Christ bare your sins in His own body on the tree. And it is that same Word that tells you that you as connected with Adam, died with Christ, that your old man was crucified, that since you are in Christ you shared His death unto sin, and are thus to reckon your present relation to sin in Christ—as one who is dead to it, and alive unto God" (*Romans, Verse by Verse*, p. 227).

Lewis Sperry Chafer: "The theme under consideration is concerned with the death of Christ as that death is related to the divine judgments of the sin nature in the child of God. The necessity for such judgments and the sublime revelation that these judgments are now fully accomplished for us is unfolded in Romans 6:1-10. This passage is the foundation as well as the key to the possibility of a 'walk in the Spirit' " (*He That Is Spiritual*, p. 154).

R. Paxson: "The old 'I' in you and me was judicially crucified with Christ. 'Ye died' and your death dates from the death of Christ. 'The old man,' the old 'self' in God's reckoning was taken to the cross with Christ and crucified and taken into the tomb with Christ and buried. Assurance of deliverance from the sphere of the 'flesh' and of the dethronement of 'the old man' rests upon the apprehension and acceptance of this fact of co-crucifixion" (*Life on the Highest Plane*, Vol. II, pp. 78, 79).

Watchman Nee: "Our sins were dealt with by the blood, we

ourselves are dealt with by the cross. The blood procures our pardon, the cross procures deliverance from what we are in Adam. The blood can wash away my sins, but it cannot wash away my old man: I need the cross to crucify me—the sinner" (*The Normal Christian Life*, p. 25).

L. E. Maxwell: "Believers in Christ were joined to Him at the cross, united to Him in death and resurrection. We died with Christ. He died for us, and we died with Him. This is a great fact, true of all believers" (*Christian Victory*, p. 11).

Norman B. Harrison: "This is the distinctive mark of the Christian—the experience of the cross. Not merely that Christ died for us, but that we died with Him. 'Knowing this, that our old man is crucified with him' (Rom. 6:6)" (*His Side Versus Our Side*, p. 40).

F. J. Huegel: "If the great Luther, with his stirring message of justification by faith, had with Paul moved on from Romans 5 to Romans 6 with its amazing declarations concerning the now justified sinner's position of identification with his crucified Lord, would not a stifled Protestantism be on higher ground today? Might it not be free from its ulcerous fleshiness?" (*The Cross of Christ*, p. 84).

Alexander R. Hay: "The believer has been united with Christ in His death. In this union with Christ, the flesh, 'the body of sin—the entire fallen, sin-ruined being with its intelligence, will and desires—is judged and crucified. By faith, the believer reckons (counts) himself 'dead unto sin' (Rom. 6:3-14)" (N.T. *Order for Church & Missionary*, p. 310).

T. Austin-Sparks: "The first phase of our spiritual experience may be a great and overflowing joy, with a marvelous sense of emancipation. In this phase extravagant things are often said as to total deliverance and final victory. Then there may, and often does, come a phase of which inward conflict is the chief feature. It may be very much of a Romans 7 experience. This will lead, under the Lord's hand, to the fuller knowledge of the meaning of identification with Christ, as in Romans 6. Happy the man who has been instructed in this from the beginning" (*What Is Man?* p. 61).

J. Penn-Lewis: "If the difference between 'Christ dying for us,' and 'our dying with Him,' has not been recognized, acknowledged, and applied, it may safely be affirmed that the self is still the dominating factor in the life" (*Memoir*, p. 26).

William Culbertson: "Who died on the cross? Of course, our blessed Lord died on the cross; but who else died there? 'Knowing this, that our old man is crucified with him, that the body of sin might be destroyed, that henceforth we should not serve sin. Now if we be dead with Christ, we believe that we shall also live with him' (Rom. 6:6-8)" (*God's Provision for Holy Living*, p. 46).

Reginald Wallis: "God says in effect, 'My child, as you reckoned on the substitutionary work of the Lord Jesus Christ for your salvation, now go a step farther and reckon on His representative work for your victory day by day.' You believe the Lord Jesus died for your sins because God said so. Now take the next step. Accept by faith the further fact that you died with Him, i.e., that your 'old man was crucified with Him' " (*The New Life*, p. 51).

James R. McConkey: "Because He died 'death hath no more dominion over Him,' and because of our union with Him 'sin shall not have dominion over you,' even though it is present in you. Our 'reckoning' ourselves dead to sin in Jesus Christ does not make it a fact—it is already a fact through our union with Him. Our reckoning it to be true only makes us begin to realize the fact in experience" (*The Way of Victory*, p. 16).

9 Consecration

It might be good to stress several points just here. (1) Never was a believer brought into healthy spiritual maturity by means of pressure meetings, and constant exhortation, nor before he was prepared by the Spirit. (2) Healthy progress is based on the apprehension, understanding, and appropriation of the truths in Christ that make for real growth. (3) The experiential aspect of all truth, and especially these so-called deeper truths, is closed to all but the needy heart. Until one is aware of his need to progress spiritually, he will never be brought beyond the birth truths—a mere babe in Christ. "Therefore let us go on and get past the elementary stage in the teachings *and* doctrine of Christ, the Messiah, advancing steadily toward the completeness *and* perfection that belongs to spiritual maturity. Let us not again be laying the foundation of repentance *and* abandonment of dead works [dead formalism], and of the faith [by which you turned] to God" (Heb. 6:1, Amplified).

This subject of consecration seems to be badly misunderstood by so many believers. Many, especially those young in the Lord, have been victimized time and time again in this matter of surrender, or commitment. The bludgeon most commonly used is: "The Lord Jesus gave His all for you, now the least you can do is give your all for Him!" The believer is exhorted and pressured to consecrate, surrender, commit his life to Christ on the basis of his love and gratitude for what has been done on his behalf at Calvary.

How often the average congregation is put through this routine. How often the individual believer is maneuvered down front to consecrate and reconsecrate, surrender and re-surrender, commit and recommit himself to Christ! Why is it that after awhile the believer comes to dread such meetings and messages? Well, there are a number of reasons for all this frustration, floundering, and failure; and, praise the Lord, there are scriptural answers available to all who need and want them.

First, it is utterly futile to expect a believer, by means of consecration, surrender, or commitment, to step from his ground of substitution (Rom. 3-5), onto that of the deeper truths in Romans 8 and 12:1.

There is the all-important area of identification truth in Romans 6 and 7 that cannot be skipped over. Every hungry-hearted Christian yearns to be fully consecrated and conditioned for effective life and service. And from the outset, until hard experience teaches him otherwise, the well-meaning believer thinks that since he has the will to obey God and to be what He intends for him, he should attempt to carry it out through personal consecrated effort with His help. He seeks to struggle forward via the love motive, i.e., He did for me, so I must do for Him.

The following two thoughts by Andrew Murray will help here. "A superficial acquaintance with God's plan leads to the view that while justification is God's work, by faith in Christ, sanctification (growth) is our work, to be performed under the influence of the gratitude we feel for the deliverance we have experienced, and by the aid of the Holy Spirit. But the earnest Christian soon finds how little gratitude can supply the power. When he thinks that more prayer will supply it, he finds that, indespensable as prayer is, it is not enough. Often the believer struggles hopelessly for years, until he listens to the teaching of the Spirit, as He glorifies Christ again, and reveals Christ, our Sanctification, to be appropriated by faith alone.

"God works to will, and He is ready to work to do (Phil. 2:13), but, alas! many Christians misunderstand this. They think because they have the will it is enough, and that now they are able to do. This is not so. The new will is a permanent gift, an attribute of the new nature. The power to do is not a permanent gift, but must be each moment received from the

Holy Spirit. It is the man who is conscious of his own impotence as a believer who will learn that by the Holy Spirit he can lead a holy life." Now and then one is called on to speak out against something that is good, in order to present His best. The love motive from which to live the Christian life and serve the Lord is good, it is high, but it is not adequate—especially because it is not the motivation underwritten by Him.

As growing Christians, it is time for us to see the necessity of going beyond the love motive to the life motive. "For to me to live is Christ" (Phil. 1:21a). Our consecration, surrender, or commitment will never hold up if it is our responding to Him from any other motivation than the response of His life in us. Yielding to Him on any different basis will simply amount to our trying to live for Him in the self-life. And even if that were possible He could never accept it, since in that realm there dwells no good thing (Rom. 7:18); plus the fact that He has already taken the old life to the cross and crucified it (Rom. 6:6; Gal. 2:20; 2 Tim. 2:11; 1 Peter 2:24).

J. C. Metcalfe sees both the problem and the answer: "The modern teaching of consecration, which is tantamount to the consecration of the 'old man,' seeks to bypass the death sentence and, therefore, only leads to frustration and failure. When, however, you and I are prepared, in simple humility, to make the *fact* of our death with Christ our daily basis of life and service, there is nothing that can prevent the uprising and outflow of new life, and meet the need of thirsty souls around us."

Here is the crux of the matter. The question is, Which life is to be consecrated to Him, the old self-life, or the new Christ-life? God can accept absolutely nothing from the old—He sees and acknowledges only that which is centered in His Son, who is our Life. Hence God has but one stipulation for consecration: "Yield yourselves unto God, as those that are alive from the dead" (Rom. 6:13). This is our only ground, and from this platform we are to count ourselves dead unto sin, self, the law, the world, and alive unto God in Christ risen—to walk in "newness of life," "risen life" (Rom. 6:11, 4b).

" 'Present yourselves unto God as those alive from the dead'

(Rom. 6:13, **NASB**). This is the true place of consecration. For believers to 'consecrate themselves to God' ere they have learnt their union with Christ in death and resurrection (identification) is only to present to God the members of the natural man, which He cannot accept. Only those 'alive from the dead'—that is, having appropriated fully their likeness with Him in death—are bidden to present their members as instruments unto God."

"God asks us to present our bodies as living sacrifices to Him (Rom. 12:1). Until we have done this, there is nothing else we can do. Notice this exhortatation comes after Romans 6. There is a reason for this order—crucifixion comes before consecration. Uncrucified self refuses to be consecrated. This is why so many people with all sincerity walk down the aisles again and again, consecrating uncrucified self to God" (H. Duncan). This is why the identification truths must be carefully and throughly presented, ultimately understood, and their reality entered into. We cannot even get as far as consecration without them! Many feel that identification is an "emphasis," an interesting subject ministered at a few Deeper Life Conferences, and Keswick Conventions. But these truths are not peripheral; they are foundational. "The sixth of Romans is not an aspect of the truth, but the foundation truth upon which every believer must stand to know anything about victory."

"All the (identification) truths we have learned about the cross, of our death with Christ, our death to sin with Him, of our conformity to death like the grain of wheat falling into the ground to die, are preparatory to the overcoming life. They are the foundation of, and fundamental to it."

"A careful study of all the Epistles of Paul will show that they are written on the basis of the cross set forth in Romans 6—the fact that God consigns the old fallen Adam-life to the cross, and has nothing to say to it. God deals with all believers on the ground—'In Christ you died.' But the Church of Christ, as a whole, ignores this fact. It treats the fallen creation (self-life) as capable of improvement, and the meaning of the cross bringing to death the old Adam race as fallen beyond repair, is thus nullified."

10 Self

One of the most important factors in Christian growth is the Holy Spirit's revelation of the self-life to the believer. Self is the fleshly, carnal life of nature, the life of the first Adam— "dead in trespasses and sins" (Eph. 2:1); thoroughly corrupt before God (Gal. 5:19-21); the life in which there is no good thing in the sight of God (Rom. 7:18). Nowhere do spiritual principles mean more than here. Plato, with his "Know thyself," was more right than he knew, but still only half right. Paul, with God's "Not I, but Christ," was all right!

For one to get beyond just knowing about the Lord Jesus, and enter into a consistent and growing personal knowledge of and fellowship with Him, one must *first* come to know oneself. Introspection is not involved here—the Holy Spirit uses experiential revelation. First, the believer learns "Not I," then, "but Christ." First, "Except a corn of wheat fall into the ground and die, it abideth alone," then "but if it die, it bringeth forth much fruit" (John 12:24). First, "alway delivered unto death," then, "that the life also of Jesus might be made manifest" (2 Cor. 4:11). In service: first, "death worketh in us," then, "but life in you" (2 Cor. 4:12). All resurrection life springs out of death, else it would not be resurrection life— His risen life (Rom 6:5, 6). We are to yield ourselves to God as those who are alive from the dead (Rom. 6:13).

For some years now the evangelistic scene has been dominated by a conversion known as "commitment," which often, sad to say, amounts to little more than a spiritual miscarriage. When there is a bit of life it usually blossoms overnight into full bloom, and soon becomes heavy with the fruit of "dynamic," "radiant," personality coupled with busy, rushing service. The tragedy of this sort of thing is that self is at home and thrives in the glow of it all, and is rarely found out for what it really is. All is indiscriminate "hearts and flowers."

The healthy new birth, based on deep conviction of sin, and repentance toward God, starts out clear and strong with love and devotion to the Savior. But, before long, there comes the sickening realization of an element within that pulls one back to self-centeredness, to the world, to the rule of the law, to sin. This learning by heartbreaking experience of the utter sinfulness and reigning power of self in the everyday Christian life, is the means whereby we come to know the Lord Jesus beyond the birth phase—as our Savior; on to the growth-phase—as our Lord and Life. "To me to live is Christ." No believer will truly come to know the Lord Jesus as his Life until he knows by experience the deadly self-life deep within for what it is.

At a Spiritual Life Conference many years ago, Dr. C. I. Scofield said, "Not everyone, by any means, has had the experience of the seventh of Romans, that agony of conflict, of desire to do what we cannot do, of longing to do the right we find we cannot do. It is a great blessing when a person gets into the seventh of Romans and begins to realize the awful conflict of its struggle and defeat; because the first step toward getting out of the struggle of the seventh chapter and into the victory of the eighth, is to get into the seventh. Of all the needy classes of people, the neediest of this earth are not those who are having a heartbreaking, agonizing struggle for victory, but those who are having no struggle at all, and no victory, and who do not know it, and who are satisifed and jogging along in a pitiable absence of almost all the possessions that belong to them in Christ."

J. C. Metcalfe gives this same fact an added witness: "Many a young Christian, who has not been warned of this necessary voyage of discovery upon which the Holy Spirit will certainly embark him (Rom. 7), has been plunged into almost incurable despair at the sight of the sinfulness which is his by nature. He has in the first place rejoiced greatly in the forgiveness of his sins, and his acceptance by God; but sooner or later he begins to realize that all is not well, and that he has failed and fallen from the high standard which he set himself to reach in the first flush of his conversion.

"He begins to know something of the experience which Paul

40

so graphically describes: "What I would, that do I not; but what I hate, that do I' (Rom. 7:15), and, in consequence, he feels that the bottom has fallen out of his Christian life; and then perhaps the Devil whispers to him that it is just no good his going on, because he will never be able to make the grade. Little does he know how healthy his condition is, and that this shattering discovery is but the prelude to a magnificent series of further discoveries of things which God has expressly designed for his eternal enrichment. All through life God has to show us our utter sinfulness and need, before He is able to lead us on into realms of grace, in which we shall glimpse His glory."

Self-revelation precedes divine revelation—that is a principle for both spiritual birth and spiritual growth. The believer who is going through struggle and failure is the Christian who is being carefully and lovingly handled by his Lord in a veıy personal way. He is being taken through the experience (years in extent) of self-revelation and into death, the only basis upon which to "know him, and the power of his resurrection, and the fellowship of his sufferings, being made conformable unto his death" (Phil. 3:10).

God works by paradox. Success comes via failure; life springs out of death, etc. The only element in the believer's life that crumbles is that which has to go anyway—the new life can never be harmed or affected. This disintegration is something the believer cannot enter into nor engineer on his own—self will never cast out self. He has to be led into it by the mercy of the Holy Spirit—into failure; abject and total. "For we which live are alway delivered unto death for Jesus' sake, that the life also of Jesus might be made manifest in our mortal flesh" (2 Cor. 4:11). So often the means utilized by the Spirit is an unsaved mate, or even a saved one! Or poor health, yes, and good health, too! A thousand and one things are used by Him—in fact, everything (Rom. 8:28, 29), to bring out the worst in us, ultimately enabling us to see that the Christian life has to be "not I, but Christ." People, circumstances, etc., are never the cause of failure. Self's reaction to them is the cause, and the one problem to be dealt with. "It's me, it's me, O Lord."

"Many of us have probably known what it was to rejoice in the grace of God without having apprehended very much the true character of the flesh. It has often been noticed that where there is the greatest exuberance of joy in young converts, there is often a levity which fails to take into account that the flesh is unchanged. In such cases the grace of God is taken up in a self-confident way; there is a very little self-distrust, or sense of weakness and dependence. And the inevitable consequence is a fall, or a succession of falls, that gradually bring home to the consciences of believers their utter weakness and incapacity as in the flesh" (C. A. Coates).

Evan Hopkins shares some important light on our subject: "How infinite are the forms in which self appears. Some are occupied with good self. They pride themselves on their excellencies. Others are just as much occupied with bad self. They are forever groaning over their imperfections, and struggling with the flesh as if they hoped in time to improve it. When shall we be convinced it is so utterly bad that it is beyond all recovery? Our experience, upward, in the power of God, is just in proportion to our experience, downward, in ceasing from self.

"Is it, Reckon yourself to be weak in reference to sin? No, it is lower than that. Is it, Reckon yourself to be dying? No, lower still. 'Reckon yourself to be dead—(Rom. 6:11)—indeed unto sin.' Some believe they are very weak. But what does that imply? That they have some strength. But when a man is dead he has no strength. We must act on the fact that we are dead in reference to sin. We shall not then speak of difficulty as to resisting temptation in reference to ourselves. We shall take the lowest place, and say it is impossible. But we shall know that what is impossible with self is possible with God. We shall take our place on the resurrection side of the cross, and in so doing we leave behind the old self-life for the new Christ-life. To live in Him who is our Life, is to be in the power of God." Someone has rightly said that "there are many 'separated from the world' Christians who are not 'separated from themselves' Christians."

11 Self-Denial

When a believer begins to discover something of the awful tyranny of the self-life, or has been endlessly struggling against that tyranny, he becomes intensely concerned about the denial of self with the resultant freedom to rest and grow in Christ. Man has many ways of seeking to escape the thralldom of self; God has but one way. First then, some of these man-centered methods.

Mortification   Denying oneself certain things for a time, or even for all time, is not even close to the answer since the old nature will adjust and thrive under any conditions—anything short of death to self. "There have been those who have thought that to get themselves out of the way it was necessary to withdraw from society; so they denied all natural human relationships and went into the desert or the mountain or the hermit's cell to fast and labor and struggle to mortify the flesh. While their motive was good it is impossible to commend their method. For it is not scriptural to believe that the old Adam nature can be conquered in that manner. It yields to nothing less than the death of the cross. It is altogether too tough to be killed by abusing the body or starving the affections" (A. W. Tozer).

Conquest   Probably the most drawn out and exhausting effort of all is the believer's struggle to conquer and control this rebel self. More meetings, more Bible study, more prayer are all resorted to, but neither are these God's answer to this problem.

Training   Here is a favorite that has been tried and found wanting down through the ages. Good Christian training and culture in the right homes, churches, and schools have been relied on to subdue the old nature and bring it into line.

Revivalism   Another failure has been the practice of holding special meetings once or twice a year. This involves outside leadership (a stranger to the individual problems), and the devastating revival routine (confession, new resolutions, etc.), in the hope that something will change—but it rarely does, and then not for long.

Growth   So many dear Christians just keep plodding (or racing) through the deadening routine of their multitudinous church activities and duties, expecting that in time self will change for the better as they grow. But self never changes into anything but more of the same! "That which is born of the flesh is flesh" (John 3:6a). "Sometimes this self is entirely bad, as when it is angry, spiteful, unkind, unjust, untruthful, unloving, catty. In other cases a good exterior conceals an evil heart, as when we are proud of our humility, conceited about our Christian service, boastful of our orthodoxy. And an overforwardness and obvious conceit at the sound of one's own voice spoils many a prayer meeting."

Cleansing   Up-to-the-moment confession and consequent cleansing have also constituted a popular method. However, 1 John 1:9 has to do with sins already committed, and not with the source (self) from which they emanate. "Our sins are dealt with by the blood, we ourselves are dealt with by the cross. The blood procures our pardon, the cross procures deliverance from what we are in Adam. The blood can wash away my sins, but it cannot wash away my old man: I need the cross to crucify me—the sinner."

Experiences   Today one of the prevalent attempts for something better is to go in for "the baptism of the Spirit," speaking in tongues, etc. This is by far the most dangerous and pathetic trap of all, as it is simply self, neurotically and religiously rampant. "Calvary precedes Pentecost. Death with Christ precedes the fullness of the Spirit. Power! Yes, God's children need power, but God does not give power to the old creation, nor to the uncrucified soul. Satan will give power to the 'old Adam,' but not God."

Which of us does not know something of the failure of our ways, well-intentioned as they may be? What most do not know is what this very failure is the path to learning, and entering into, God's way. "For my thoughts are not your thoughts, neither are your ways my ways, saith the LORD. For as the heavens are higher than the earth, so are my ways higher than your ways, and my thoughts than your thoughts" (Isa. 55:8, 9). Now just what is God's way of self-denial? He has but one way, and it is on the basis of all His other ways: the principle of the finished work. His way for us in everything is the way He has already traveled, conquered, and completed in Christ.

The Cross
God's Way

It was on the Cross of Calvary that God, in Christ, dealt fully and finally with self, the nature from which all our sins flow. "We know that our old (unrenewed) self was nailed to the cross with Him in order that [our] body, [which is the instrument] of sin, might be made ineffective and inactive for evil, that we might no longer be the slaves of sin" (Rom. 6:6, Amplified). The reason there is no other way for self to be denied is that God has done the work in this way: our identification with Christ Jesus in His death and resurrection! It is done; now ours to believe.

"The 'flesh' will only yield to the cross; not to all the resolutions you may make at a conference, not to any self-effort, not to any attempted self-crucifixion; only to co-crucifixion, crucified together with Christ (Gal. 2:20). It is not by putting yourself to death, but by taking, through faith and surrender, your place of union with Christ in His death. That is the blessed barrier of safety between you and all the attractions of the flesh, and that makes the way open to do the will of God" (G. Watt).

The Cross of Calvary resulted in the death of the Lord Jesus, both for sin, and to sin. In that He died to sin, He died out of the realm of sin, and He arose into the realm of "newness of life," eternal life. And our identification with Him on Calvary took us into death; down into the tomb; up into "newness of life" (Rom. 6:4). First, Romans 6:3—"baptized into [his] death"; then, Romans 6:4—"buried with him"; then, Romans 6:5—"For if we have been planted together in the likeness of his death, we shall be also in the likeness of his resurrection"; also, Colossians 3:3—"For ye are dead, and your life is hid with Christ in God"; therefore, Romans 6:11—"reckon ye also yourselves to be dead indeed unto sin, but alive unto God through Jesus Christ our Lord."

Praise the Lord! it all happened at Calvary: our sins were paid for, our sinfulness was dealt with, and both by the ultimate—*death*. And we receive the benefits of the work of the Cross simply by reckoning on, believing in, the finished work of the Cross. First, through the Word, we find out what God did about our problem. Then, as we become thoroughly convinced of the fact and begin to understand it clearly, we are able to agree to "reckon" it true. And as we exercise faith in God's fact, we begin to receive the benefits of that finished work in experience. Was it not true in the matter of our justification? Yes, and we will likewise find it to be true in the matter of our emancipation from the slavery of the self-life.

"The powerful effect of the cross was God, in heaven, in the blotting out of guilt, and our renewed union with God, is inseparable from the other effect—the breaking down of the authority of sin over man, by the crucifixion of self. Therefore Scripture teaches us that the cross not only works out a disposition or desire to make such a sacrifice, but it really bestows the power to do so, and completes the work. This appears with wonderful clarity in Galatians. In one place the cross is spoken of as the reconciliation for guilt (3:13). But there are three more places where the cross is even more plainly spoken of as the victory over the power of sin; as the power to hold in the place of death the 'I' of the self-life; of the flesh (the outworking of self); and of the world (2:20; 5:24; 6:14). In these passages our union (identification) with Christ, the crucified One, and the conformity to Him resulting from the union, are represented as the result of the power exercised within us and upon us by the cross" (Andrew Murray).

As we learn to stand on the finished work of Calvary, the Holy Spirit will begin to faithfully and effectively apply that finished work of the Cross to the self-life, thereby holding it in the place of death—inactive—resulting in the "not I, but Christ" life.

12 The Cross

Studying these truths is hard work, is it not? Although spiritual hunger and need are prime requisites for light and understanding, the Holy Spirit does not release the treasures of the Word quickly nor easily. "Deep calleth unto deep." We have to be prepared, and even then there is much time, digging, praying, meditation, yearning, and experiencing involved. True spiritual reality comes in no other way, but, praise the Lord, it does come in this way!

Understanding and appropriating the facts of the Cross proves to be one of the most difficult and trying of all phases for the growing believer. Our Lord holds his most vital and best things in store for those who mean business, for those who hunger and thirst for His very best as it is in our Lord Jesus Christ. The believer's understanding of the two aspects of Calvary gives the key to both spiritual growth, and life-giving service.

"Calvary is the secret of it all. It is what He did there that counts, and what He did becomes a force in the life of a Christian when it is appropriated by faith. This is the starting point from which all Godly living must take its rise. We shall never know the experience of Christ's victory in our lives until we are prepared to count (reckon) upon His victory at the cross as the secret of our personal victory today. There is no victory for us which was not first His. What we are to experience He purchased, and what He purchased for us we ought to experience. The beginning of the life of holiness is a faith in the crucified Savior which sees more than His substitutionary work. It is a faith which sees myself identified with Christ in His death and resurrection."

Actually, our Father has trained every one of us for clear-cut, explicit faith in this second aspect of Calvary: our individual identification with the Lord Jesus in His death to sin and rising to resurrection ground. This training taught us thoroughly in the first realm: believing and appropriating the finished work of His dying for our sins—justification. Now we are asked just as definitely to believe and appropriate the further aspect: "Knowing this, that our old man is crucified with him" (Rom. 6:6a); "Likewise reckon ye also yourselves to be dead indeed unto sin, but alive unto God" (Rom. 6:11).

Our intelligent faith standing on the facts of Calvary gives the Holy Spirit freedom to bring that finished work into our daily lives. We stood on the fact of His dying *for* our sins, and this act of faith allowed the Holy Spirit to give us our freedom from the penalty of sin—justification. Now, once we come to see this further fact, we are urged in the Word to stand on the liberating truth of our dying with Christ in His death to sin, which allows the Holy Spirit to bring into our lives freedom from the power, the enslavement, of sin—progressive sanctification. And of course when we stand with Him in Glory, we will be forever free from the presence of sin—entirely sanctified and glorified.

"As our Substitute He went to the cross alone, without us, to pay the penalty of our sins; as our Representative, He took us with Him to the cross, and there, in the sight of God, we all died together with Christ. We may be forgiven because He died in our stead; we may be delivered because we died with Him. God's way of deliverance for us, a race of hopeless incurables, is to put us away in the cross of His Son, and then to make a new beginning by re-creating us in union with Him, the Risen, Living One (2 Cor. 5:17). It is the Holy Spirit who will make these great facts real and true in our experience as we cooperate with Him; and so the plague of our hearts will be stayed, and we shall be transformed into the likeness of Christ.

"Through the crucifixion of the old man with Christ the believer has been made dead unto sin, he has been completely freed from sin's power, he has been taken beyond sin's grip, the claim of sin upon him has been nullified. This is the flawless provision of God's grace but this accomplished fact can only become an actual reality in the believer's experience as faith lays hold upon it and enables him moment by moment, day by day, though temptation assail him, 'to reckon' it true. As he reckons, the Holy Spirit makes real; as he continues to reckon, the Holy Spirit continues to make real. Sin need have no more power over the believer than he grants it through unbelief. If he is alive unto sin it will be due largely to the fact that he has failed to reckon himself dead unto sin" (R. Paxson).

The Reformation brought into focus once again the emphasis on spiritual birth, without which there can be no beginning. What is lacking among believers to this day is the proper emphasis on *growth*—not just to be saved, and heaven by and by. What sort of salvation would we have if our Father simply saved us from the penalty of sins, and then left us on our own to deal with the power of sin in our Christian life and walk? But most believers feel this is about as far as He went, and are struggling to get on the best they can, with His help. And this is the Galatian error, so prominent even now throughout born-again circles. We must be brought back to the basics: freed from the penalty of sin by His finished work; freed from the power of sin by His finished work. ". . . justified by faith . . ." (Gal. 3:24); ". . . we walk by faith . . ." (2 Cor. 5:7); "As ye have therefore received Christ Jesus the Lord, so walk ye in him" (Col. 2:6).

"We are not left to deal with the old life ourselves; it has been dealt with by Christ on the cross. This is the fact which must be known, and upon that fact is built the New Testament principle and doctrine of holiness. In other words, Calvary is as much the foundation of sanctification as of justification. Both gifts spring from the same work and are two aspects of the same salvation."

Now, as long as the believer does not know this dual aspect of his salvation, the best he can do is seek to handle his sins via confession (1 John 1:9)—that is, after the damage has been done! This takes care of the penalty of the product, but not the source. Is it not time we allowed the Holy Spirit to get at the source, and cut off this stream of sins before they are committed? Is this not infinitely better than the wreckage caused by sin, even though confessed? When believers get sick and tired of spinning year after year in a spiritual squirrel cage—sinning, confessing, but then sinning again—they will be ready for God's answer to the source of sin, which is death to self, brought forth from the completed work of the Cross.

"When God's light first shines into our heart our one cry is for forgiveness, for we realize that we have committed sins before Him; but once we have known forgivenss of sins, we make a new discovery—the discovery of sin, and we realize that we have the nature of a sinner. There is an inward inclination to sin. There is a power within that draws us to sin, and when that power breaks out we commit sins. We may seek and receive forgiveness, but then we sin again; and life goes on in a vicious circle—sinning and being forgiven, but then sinning again. We appreciate God's forgiveness, but we want something more than that, we want deliverance. We need forgiveness for what we have done, but we need deliverance from what we are."

Our reckoning on the finished work of our death to sin, in Christ at Calvary, is God's *one* way of deliverance—there is no other way because that is the way He did it. We learned not to add a finished work in the matter of justification, and now we must learn not to add to the finished work of emancipation. We will be freed when we enter His prepared freedom—there is no other. "The believer can never overcome the old man even by the power of the new apart from the death of Christ, and therefore the death of Christ unto sin is indispensable, and unless the cross is made the basis upon which he overcomes the old man, he only drops into another form of morality; in other words, he is seeking by self-effort to overcome self, and the struggle is a hopeless one" (C. Usher).

Marcus Rainford refused to stop short of God's ultimate for freedom: "It is not to be a mere passing impression of the mind when we are undisturbed by active temptation; no mere happy frame of spirit when under temporary refreshing from the presence of the Lord; no self-flattering consciousness of a heart exercised in good works; from none of these is the believer to infer his practical mastery over sin, but on the ground that Christ died unto sin, and liveth unto God through Jesus Christ our Lord."

"I must recognize that the enemy within the camp—the flesh, the old nature, self, I, the old Adam—is a usurper. By faith I must reckon him to be in the place that God put him—crucified with Christ. I must realize that now my life is hid with Christ in God; that He is my life" (Ian Thomas).

13 Discipleship

A disciple is one who first maintains the fellowship of the Cross, which results in fellowship with his Lord: discipleship. "The atonement of the cross and the fellowship of the cross must be equally preached as the condition of true discipleship." "Christ is the answer, but the cross is needed to clear the way for Him."

In spiritual progress, our Lord never pushes. He is our "file leader" (Heb. 12:2), and He leads us step by step. We struggle and fail (self-effort), which sets up a yearning for the answer to this depressing failure. In time, we see the scriptural facts of deliverance in the Cross (identification), and that in turn produces the required hunger to enter into that freedom, freedom for fellowship with the answer—our risen Lord Jesus.

"Nothing can set us apart for God, nothing can make us holy, except as the cross is working in us, because the cross alone can keep the hindrances to holiness in the place of death" (G. Watt.) "Back of all successful work for the lost is an inward spiritual impulse; and back of the impulse is the Holy Spirit who reproduces Christ in us; and the brand mark of it all is the cross, the living experience of which must both enter and control the life before we are fit for service" (J. E. Conant).

Nowhere was our Lord Jesus more explicit and firm than when He mentioned discipleship. "And he said to them all, If any man will come after me, let him deny himself, and take up his cross daily, and follow me . . . And whosoever doth not bear his cross, and come after me, cannot be my disciple" (Luke 9:23; 14:27). His reason for this is simple: self cannot and will not follow Him, but taking one's Cross results in death to self, and newness of life in Christ Jesus.

A disciple is one who is free from the old, and free for the new. In other, scriptural words: "dead . . . unto sin, but alive unto God" (Rom. 6:11). And for this the Lord Jesus states that each must take up his Cross. Here is the ultimatum, so now to the how.

But first, how not to take up one's Cross. "Christians need to understand that bearing the cross does not in the first place refer to the trials which we call crosses, but to the daily giving up of life, of dying to self, which must mark us as much as it did the Lord Jesus, which we need in times of prosperity almost more than adversity, and without which the fullness of the blessing of the cross cannot be disclosed to us" (Andrew Murray).

"May we cease to confuse the words 'a cross' with 'the cross.' Sometimes believers in self-pity bemoan themselves, and say, 'I have taken, or must take up my cross, and follow Jesus.' Would that we would lose sight of our 'cross' in His cross, then His cross becomes our cross; His death, our death; His grave, our grave; His resurrection, our resurrection; His risen life, our newness of life." No, taking up our Cross does not mean the stoical bearing of some heavy burden, hardship, illness, distasteful situation or relationship. Enduring anything of this nature is not bearing one's Cross. Taking up the Cross may or may not involve such things, but things do not constitute our Cross.

The believer's Cross is the Cross of Calvary, the Cross on which he was crucified with Christ (Gal. 2:20). There the eternal emancipation proclamation was signed with the blood of the Lamb, and sealed by the Spirit of God. Every believer is thereby freed from all bondage, but every believer is not aware of this liberating truth.

Sad to say, the only believers who are interested in freedom are those who have come to the place of hating instead of hugging their chains. "It is true that the intellect is stumbled by the cross; yet the antagonism to the cross is mainly moral, both in the sinner and in the saint, for its message is only welcomed by those who desire freedom from the bondage of their sins, and who hunger and thirst after the experiential righteousness of God." Yes, the need must be intense, as Norman Douty says: "The Divine way (via the cross) for spiritual emancipation is just as offensive to the child of God as the Divine way for salvation is to the lost."

When the believer begins really to see the Cross for what it is—a place of death—he is inclined to hesitate about choosing such fellowship. Our Lord Jesus understands this well, but there is no other way, since that is the manner in which He finished the work on our behalf. So He simply allows our needs to continue their relentless pressure until we finally bend.

We will be ready to take up our Cross when self becomes intolerable to us, when we begin to hate our life—"and hate not . . . his own life . . . cannot be my disciple" (Luke 14:26). The deep burden of self and hunger to be like Him cause the function of the Cross—crucifixion—to become attractive. The long devastating years of abject bondage make freedom in the Lord Jesus priceless—the cost becomes as nothing to us! Think of it, we begin to share the attitude of our Lord Jesus, and of Paul. "For the joy that was set before Him," the Lord Jesus "patiently endured the cross" (Heb. 12:2, Weymouth). The attitude of the apostle Paul became: "But God forbid that I should glory, save in the cross of our Lord Jesus Christ" (Gal. 6:14). "Let this mind [attitude] be in you, which was also in Christ Jesus" (Phil. 2:5).

Yes we begin to glory in the Cross, our very own freedom from all that enslaves, from all that would keep us from fellowship with our risen lord. So we begin to take up our Cross, our liberation, our personal finished work held in trust for us so long and patiently by the Holy Spirit. Talk about your trust funds!

And here is how we take up and bear our Cross: finally prepared by our needs, aware that our bondage was broken in Christ on Calvary, we definitely begin to rely on that finished work—we appropriate. Our attitude becomes: I gladly and willingly take, by faith in the facts, my finished work of emancipation that was established at Calvary; I consider myself to be dead to sin, and alive to God in Christ. This is taking up one's Cross. As we learn to do this, we begin to find these facts true in experience. The Holy Spirit brings that finished work of death and applies it to all of the old nature, which is thus held in the place of death—the death of Calvary. If and when we turn from the facts and begin to rely on anything or anyone else, including ourselves, self is released from the Cross—active and enslaving as ever. Through this process we are patiently taught to walk by faith, to maintain our attitude of reliance on the finished work of the Cross.

Adolph Saphir wrote, "The narrow path, commencing with the cross—'Ye have died with Christ'—ending with the glory of the Lord Jesus, is the path on which the Lord draws near and walks with His disciples.

" 'Christ liveth in me.' The Lord within lives as the sole source of life. The old 'I' has no contribution he can make to Christian life and service; he can never be harnessed to the purposes of God. Death is his decreed portion. There cannot be two masters in our lives. If the old 'I' is an active possession of us then Christ cannot be. But if we gladly take hold of the great fact of redemption—'I have been crucified with Christ'— then Christ by His Spirit takes up the exercise of the function of life within us, and leads us as His bond-slaves (disciples), in the train of His triumph."

14 Process of Discipleship

In the Parable of the Sower, the seed sown "on the good ground are they, which in an honest and good heart, having heard the word, keep it, and bring forth fruit with patience" (Luke 8:15). The principle of growth is always, "first the blade, then the ear, after that the full corn in the ear" (Mark 4:28). Therefore, "the husbandman waiteth for the precious fruit of the earth, and hath long patience for it" (James 5:7). As this clearly exemplifies, "he that believeth shall not make haste" (Isa. 28:16).

For most of us it has been a long season of growth from the tiny green blade up to the "full corn in the ear." So many seek to settle for this stage; saved, with heaven assured—plus a pacifying measure of Christian respectability, at least in church circles. Here we have the believer as a normal kernel of wheat containing life inside a more or less shiny golden covering, in fellowship high up on the stalk with similar kernels of wheat. This is but a stage, not the goal. And, like middle age, this can be a dangerous stage: one of seeking a "much deserved" rest; of basking aimlessly in the fellowship of meetings, classes, etc.; of ignoring or forgetting the struggles and growing pains of the tiny green blades down at one's feet, and expecting and exhorting them to shape up and mature without delay.

This is all very cozy, but costly; snug, but sterile. "The seed corn may be beautiful, but it is hard. The germ of life is locked up within its shell and cannot get out. Therefore it produces nothing. Here is the reason why so many Christians, even preachers, are so unfruitful. Only one here and there is a soul winner. When the grain of corn is buried it dies, and that hard exterior surface softens and decays, in order to give nutriment to the young sprout, which would otherwise die and thus cause a crop failure. One must reckon himself dead to the hard, cold, selfish 'I' before the softening influence of the Holy Spirit can operate, qualifying the believer in the service of God. Many want to do God's work but are unable, because of the 'flesh' in their lives."

Our Father understands all this, and He it is who takes the initiative in the matter. He drops the seed of dissatisfaction into our hearts; He begins to show us that there is far more to this Christian life than just being saved and active for Him. And it is necessary for Him to engineer our exchange from carnal kernel Christians to fruitful fellowshiping disciples. From an infinite number of ways, He chooses the most effective for each individual's transition. And in the hand of the Husbandman, there is no fear, but freedom.

"We often come across Christians who are bright and clever, and strong and righteous; in fact, a little too bright, and a little too clever—there seems so much of self in their strength, and their righteousness is severe and critical. They have everything to make them saints, except . . . crucifixion, which would mold them into a supernatural tenderness and limitless charity for others. But if they are of the real elect, God has a winepress prepared for them, through which they will some day pass, which will turn the metallic hardness of their nature into gentle love, which Christ always brings forth at the last of the feast."

"Another parable put he forth unto them saying, The kingdom of heaven is likened unto a man which sowed good seed in his field: He that soweth the good seed is the Son of Man; the field is in the world; the good seed are the children of the kingdom" (Matt. 13:24, 37, 38a). The Lord of the harvest plants, buries Christians as seeds in a field, which is the world.

Through the Husbandman's patient and loving cultivation the grain of wheat high on the stalk begins to fear being garnered alone, and hungers to bring forth "much fruit." Here is God's motivation for discipleship: that filial heart-hunger for fruit bearing. He finally pleads to be made fruitful at any cost, and then it is that he hears the Lord say, "Verily, verily, I say unto you, Except a corn of wheat fall into the ground and die, it abideth alone: but if it die, it bringeth forth much fruit" (John 12:24). "Whosoever shall lose his life for my sake and the gospel's, the same shall save it" (Mark 8:35). In loving response to this hunger the Holy Spirit silently and gently begins to loosen the grain from its comfortable bindings and supports in the kernel. "When the fruit is brought forth, immediately he putteth in the sickle, because the harvest is come" (Mark 4:29). As a result, sooner or later the grain of wheat finds itself, not high up on the stalk, but dropped to the earth, into the cold and strange darkness. And still worse, the earth smears and injures that nice shiny golden coat. Worst of all, the coat begins to disintegrate and fall to pieces. All that is not Christ, no matter how nice in appearance and profession, is revealed for what it is—just self.

There is a further stripping, right down to the germ of life, right on down until there is nothing left but Christ, who is our life. Down, down into death. Patience, grain of wheat: "Though he slay me, yet will I trust in him" (Job 13:15).

"Except it fall into the ground and die" . . .
　　Can "much fruit" come alone at such a cost?
Must the seed corn be buried in the earth,
　　All summer joy and glory seemingly lost?
He buries still His seed corns here and there,
　　And calls to deeper fellowship with Him
Those who will dare to share the bitter cup,
　　And yet while sharing, sing the triumph hymn.

"Except it fall into the ground and die" . . . ?
　　But what a harvest in the days to come;
When fields stand thick with golden sheaves of corn
　　And you are sharing in the Harvest Home.
To you who "lose your life," and let it "die,"
　　Yet in the losing "find" your life anew,
Christ evermore unveils His lovely face,
　　And thus His mirrored glory rests on you.

—Selected

When the believer takes up his cross for discipleship, the process of death begins to set in. The disciple finds himself a seed sown by the Son, planted in a home, office, hospital, church, manse, or mission station. Whatever or wherever it is, there will be the death from which resurrection life follows. "For we which live are alway delivered unto death for Jesus' sake, that the life also of Jesus might be made manifest in our mortal flesh. So then death worketh in us, but life in you" (2 Cor. 4:11, 12). "We need to enter deeply into the truth that Christ the Beloved Son of the Father could not enter to the glory of heaven until He had first given Himself over to death. And this great truth, as it opens to us, will help us to understand how in our life, and in our fellowship with Christ, it is impossible for us to share His life until we have first in every deed surrendered ourselves every day to die to sin and self and the law and the world, and so to abide in the unbroken fellowship of discipleship with our crucified and Risen Lord."

P.S. "All the truths we have learned about the cross, of our death with Christ, our death unto sin with Him, of our conformity to death like the corn of wheat falling into ground to die, are preparatory to the overcoming life. They are the foundation of, and fundamental to it."

15 Rest

"There remaineth therefore a rest to the people of God. For he that is entered into his rest, he also hath ceased from his own works, as God did from his. Let us labour therefore to enter into the rest" (Heb. 4:9-11a). So many of the life-giving truths in the Word consist of two intertwining halves that are inseparable. "Let us labour therefore to enter into the rest." As for labor, it is true that there is a great deal of struggling and searching, pleading and agonizing, in the process of discovering and understanding truths fitted to our needs. And much of the same pathway is trod (or crawled) in an effort to appropriate and enter in. All this is not in vain; it is necessary. But it is not the key that opens the door to reality. Rest is the key to entering into rest!

In the important but exhausting labor process we come to see the needed truth; we become sure of our facts; we begin to realize something of what is ours in the Lord Jesus Christ. The appropriation of, the resting in the reality must be on the basis of faith, not struggle and labor. We are told to reckon, to count on what we now know to be true of us in Him as set forth in the Word. "In quietness and in confidence shall be your strength" (Isa. 30:15). We are to quietly and steadily look to our Father in confident trust, and thankfully receive that which He has given to us in His Son. "These wait all upon thee; that thou mayest give them their meat in due season. That thou givest them they gather: thou openest thine hand, they are filled with good" (Ps. 104:27, 28).

Norman Grubb shares a good word on the principle of labor and rest: "Take as an example the learning of a foreign language. You are faced with a series of hieroglyphics in a book, you hear a medley of sounds around, which mean absolutely nothing. Yet you know that it is a language that can be learned. More than that, you have gone there to learn it. Now that is the first rung in the ladder of faith. However weak or waveringly, in your heart you do believe that you can and will get it. Otherwise, obviously you wouldn't try to learn it. So you plod on. Many a time faith and courage fail, the mind is weary and the heart is heavy, and you almost give up. But not quite. To give up is faith's unforgivable sin. On you go at it. Months pass. It seems largely to go in one ear and out the other. Then—the length of time depends on the difficulty of the language and the ability and industry of the pupil of course—a miracle seems to happen. The day or period comes when, without your hardly realizing it, what you are seeking has found you; what you are trying to grasp has grasped you! You just begin automatically to speak the language, to think it, to hear it. What was an incomprehensible jumble of sounds without, has become an ordered language within the mind.

"So, in the spiritual labor of faith, the moment or period comes when we know. Every vestige of strain and labor is gone. Indeed, faith, as such, is not felt or recognized any more. The channel is lost sight of in the abundance of the supply. As we came to know that we were children of God by an inner certainty, a witness of the Spirit in our spirits; so now we come to know that the old 'I' is crucified with Christ, the new 'I' has Christ as its permanent life, spirit with Spirit have been fused into one; the branch grafted into the vine; the member joined to the body, the problem of abiding becomes as natural as breathing."

Thank God for the needs that just will not allow the hungry heart to stop short of finding them met in Him. "It is necessary to remember a fundamental principle in the spiritual life: that God only reveals spiritual truths to meet spiritual needs." "How many rest on the initial stage of the new birth: "Begotten again . . . of incorruptible seed through the Word of God' (1 Peter 1:23), and fail to press on to know 'Begotten . . . by the resurrection of Jesus Christ . . . unto an inheritance' (1 Peter 1:3)."

Through the years the hungry-hearted believer finds he has

been brought a long way, and each step of the way has been personally experienced: reality that springs from faith founded on the facts of the Word. "The more clearly we enter by faith into objective truth, or what is true of us in Christ, the deeper, more experiential, and practical, will be the subjective work in us, and the more complete will be the manifestation of the moral effect in our life and character" (C.H.M.).

Yes, brought a long way, walking a step at a time, by faith: The rest of faith concerning our justification; the rest of faith concerning our acceptance; the rest of faith concerning our position in Christ Jesus; the rest of faith concerning our identification with Christ in death, resurrection, and ascension. Each step established in the rest of faith brings us to the next one. Each must be settled before the next can be rested on.

It cannot be too strongly stated that unless the believer is firmly established in the steps of Romans 1-5, he cannot truly enter and rest on the truths of Romans 6-8, no matter how many special meetings and conferences he attends or so-called revivals he becomes involved in. "Dr. James of Albany, who was used to bring hundreds into the deeper truths, declared that he usually found that 'failure in the higher stages of the Christian life was due to imperfect understanding and acceptance of the gospel of salvation in its fundamental principles.' It is a rare thing to be able to sit down and teach, because in most settings today one is limited to dealing with 'the first principles of the oracles of God'; and can go little further than the basic facts of the new birth. You cannot deepen spiritual life that is not there! You will only build askew if the foundations are not properly laid! A lack of appreciation of the wonder of a full salvation in Christ, opens the door to every kind of overbalance, and spells continual frustration and failure."

Believers often manage to trust God for truths they need, only to slip from grace into the legal realm in seeking to produce the particular truth in their life or service. Once in possession of a truth, we are to rest—He will produce. "In actual experience, when we have apprehended our deliverance through death with Christ, the self-life often appears more alive than ever! Just here God would have us stand firm (rest) upon His written Word. The increasing revelation proves the surrender to the cross to be real, because the Holy Spirit takes us at our word, and reveals all that He has seen lying underneath—reveals it that it may be dealt with at the cross. Our part is to yield our wills, and take God's side against ourselves, whilst the Holy Spirit applies the death of the cross to all that is contrary to Him, that it may be really true that we who are of Christ have crucified the flesh with the affections and lusts (Gal. 5:24).

"The faith that receives from the hand of the Father is in two stages, and we are not to give up just because the struggle-and-labor phase does not produce the prize. 'According to your faith be it unto you.' And, do not let us forget, faith begins by being a labor (Heb. 4:11) or fight (1 Tim. 6:12), although it is consummated in a rest (Heb. 4:3). That is to say, the first stage of faith is always the battle of taking hold by the will, heart, and intelligence of some truth or promise which is not real to us in experience, and declaring it to be ours in spite of appearances. We do not appear to be dead unto sin and alive unto God. We are told to believe it, and so we dare to do so and declare so. A thousand times, maybe, faith will be assaulted and fall: unbelief will say 'nonsense,' and we shall belie our declaration of faith; but the labor of faith means that we deliberately return to the assault. Once again we believe and declare it. This we persist in doing. As we thus follow in the steps of those who 'by faith and patience inherit the promises,' a new divine thing will happen within us. The Spirit will cooperate with our faith (as He is invisibly doing all the time), and to faith will be added assurance. Labor will be replaced by rest. The consummation of faith has been reached."

"True activity is that which springs out of, and is ever accompanied by, rest. It is only as we know what it is to be 'still,' that we are ready to 'go forward.' 'We rest on Thee, and in Thy Name we go' " (E.H.).

"Let us take care lest we get out of soul-rest in seeking further blessing. God cannot work whilst we are anxious, even about our spiritual experience. Let us take Him at His Word, and leave the fulfillment of it to Him."

16 Help

For most of us, it is time to stop asking God for help. He didn't help us to be saved, and He doesn't intend to help us live the Christian life.

Immaturity considers the Lord Jesus a Helper. Maturity knows Him to be Life itself. J. E. Conant wrote, "Christian living is not our living with Christ's help, it is Christ living His life in us. Therefore that portion of our lives that is not His living is not Christian living; and that portion of our service that is not His doing is not Christian service; for all such life and service have but a human and natural source, and Christian life and service have a supernatural and spiritual source." Paul insisted, "For to me to live is Christ"; and, "I can do all things through Christ" (Phil. 1:21; 4:13a).

William R. Newell said, "Satan's great device is to drive earnest souls back to beseeching God for what God says has already been done"! Each of us had to go beyond the "help" stage for our new birth, and thank Him for what He has already done on our behalf. God could never answer a prayer for help in the matter of justification. The same principle holds true for the Christian life. Our Lord Jesus waits to be wanted, and to be all in us and do all through us. "For in him dwelleth all the fullness of the Godhead bodily. And ye are complete in him" (Col. 2:9, 10).

God is not trusted, not honored, in our continually asking Him for help. In the face of "my God shall supply all your need according to his riches in glory by Christ Jesus" (Phil. 4:19), how can we beg for help? Our responsibility is to see in the Word all that is ours in Christ, and then thank and trust Him for that which we need.

Sooner or later we must face up to what F. J. Huegel declares: "When a Christian's prayer life springs from a right position (a thorough adjustment to Christ in His death and resurrection), a vast change in procedure follows. Much of the mere begging type (though of course asking is always in order for the Lord says, 'Ask and ye shall receive') gives way to a positive and unspeakably joyous appropriation. Much of our begging fails to register in heaven because it fails to spring from right relations with the Father in union with Christ in death and resurrection: in which position one simply appropriates what is already his. 'All things,' says the Apostle Paul, 'are yours . . . and ye are Christ's; and Christ is God's' (1 Cor. 3:21, 23)."

Since ". . . without faith it is impossible to please him" (Heb. 11:6a), we might consider several more strong but true statements to further clarify the attitude of faith that does please His heart.

"In our private prayers and in our public services," A. W. Tozer writes, "we are forever asking God to do things that He either has already done or cannot do because of our unbelief. We plead for Him to speak when He has already spoken and is at that very moment speaking. We ask Him to come when He is already present and waiting for us to recognize Him. We beg the Holy Spirit to fill us while all the time we are preventing Him by our doubts."

S. D. Gordon admonished: "When you are in the thick of the fight, when you are the object of attack, plead less and claim more, of the ground of the blood of the Lord Jesus. I do not mean, ask God to give you victory, but claim His victory, to overshadow you."

Watchman Nee startles many by saying, "God's way of deliverance is altogether different from man's way. Man's way is to try to suppress sin by seeking to overcome it; God's way is to remove the sinner. Many Christians mourn over their weakness, thinking that if only they were stronger all would be well. The idea that, because failure to lead a holy life is due to our impotence, something more is therefore demanded of us, leads naturally to this false conception of the way of deliverance. If we are preoccupied with the power of sin and with our inability to meet it, then we naturally conclude that to gain the victory over sin we must have more power.

" 'If only I were stronger,' we say, 'I could overcome my violent outbursts of temper,' and so we plead with the Lord to strengthen us that we may exercise more self-control. But this is altogether wrong; this is not Christianity. God's means of delivering us from sin is not by making us stronger and stronger, but by making us weaker and weaker. This is surely a peculiar way of victory, you say; but it is the divine way. God sets us free from the dominion of sin, not by strengthening our old man but by crucifying him; not by helping him to do anything but by removing him from the scene of action."

The believer does not have to beg for help. He does have to thankfully appropriate that which is already his in Christ; for, ". . . the just shall live by faith . . ." (Heb. 10:38a). And dear old Andrew Murray encourages us with, "Even though it is slow, and with many a stumble, the faith that always thanks Him—not for experiences, but for the promises on which it can rely—goes on from strength to strength, still increasing in the blessed assurance that God himself will perfect His work in us (Phil. 1:6)."

17 *Cultivation*

There can be little question concerning the importance of balance, so vital in the mechanical, physical, esthetic, and spiritual realms. Faulty balance often results in disintegration; and possible devastation to the surrounding area.

Our self-life is out of balance—it is all one-sided. Like the universal Tea Party:

> I had a little tea party,
>   One afternoon at three;
>
> 'Twas very small, three guests in all,
>   Just I, myself and me.
>
> Myself ate up the sandwiches,
>   While I drank up the tea,
>
> 'Twas also I who ate the pie
>   And passed the cake to me.

Because He is the great Husbandman, the beginning of God's cultivation of the hungry-hearted believer is downward. Patiently, persistently, and painfully our Father digs down into the recesses of self, more and more fully revealing to us just what we are, and are not, in ourselves. His reason for this preparation is twofold: that the Lord Jesus might be free to manifest Himself in us; and through us for the sake of others—growing and sharing. "The LORD shall guide thee continually, and satisfy thy soul in drought, and make fat thy bones: and thou shalt be like a watered garden, and like a spring of water, whose waters fail not" (Isa. 58:11).

Each of us must be thoroughly cultivated before He can effectively cultivate others through us. It is not that there will be no service for us until we are spiritually mature, but that most of our service on the way to maturity is for our own development, and not so much that of others. At first the growing believer thinks, and would have others feel, that all his service is effective; but in time he comes to realize that the Lord is not doing so much *through* him as He is *in* him. Our Lord always concentrates on the greater need.

"Since the work of God is essentially spiritual, it demands spiritual people for its doing; and the measure of their spirituality will determine the measure of their value to the Lord. Because this is so, in God's mind the servant is more than the work. If we are going to come truly into the hands of God for His purpose, then we shall be dealt with by Him in such a way as to continually increase our spiritual measure. Not our interest in Christian work; our energies, enthusiasm, ambitions, or abilities; not our academic qualification, or anything that we are in ourselves, but simply our spiritual life is the basis of the beginning and growth of our service to God. Even the work, when we are in it, is used by Him to increase our spiritual measure.

"It is a mistake to measure spiritual maturity merely by the presence of gifts. By themselves they are an inadequate basis for a man's lasting influence to God. They may be present and they may be valuable, but the Spirit's object is something far greater—to form Christ in us through the working of the cross. His goal is to see Christ inwrought in believers. So it is not merely that a man does certain things or speaks certain words, but that he is a certain kind of man. He himself is what he preaches. Too many want to preach without being the thing themselves, but in the long run it is what we are, and not simply what we do or say, that matters with God, and the difference lies in the formation of Christ within."

We are not saved to serve; we are matured to serve. Only to the extent that cultivation reveals self for what it is are we in position to assist others in their cultivation. We find out everyone else by first finding ourselves out. "As in water face answereth to face, so the heart of man to man" (Prov. 27:19). To counterbalance knowledge of self our Father enables us to "grow in grace, and in the knowledge of our Lord and Saviour Jesus Christ" (2 Peter 3:18).

This is not only true concerning general service, but also in the matter of our ministry of intercession. More than anything else the service of prayer for others necessitates a triune understanding: that of our Father, of ourselves, and of others. "Praying for others can only flow from a heart at rest about itself, and knowing the value of the desires which it expresses for another. I could not be true or happy in praying otherwise" (Stoney). Paul wrote that he would "pray with the spirit—by the Holy Spirit that is within me; but I will also pray intelligently—with my mind and understanding" (1 Cor. 14:15, Amplified).

So many of us, after having entered into some of the deeper realities of our Lord, seek to immediately pull or push others into this wonderful advancement; and then we wonder why they are so slow to learn, and seemingly apathetic in their understanding and concern. We so easily forget the many years it took, and what wandering wilderness ways our Lord had to traverse with us to bring us over Jordan and into Canaan. "Moses had all the wisdom of the Egyptians, yet his idea of delivering Israel was to slay an Egyptian! He had to be trained in God's ways, having forty years in Midian, and when he was sent back to Egypt God said for him not to trouble about Israel—go direct to Pharoah—the cause of their chains! God didn't train Israel at the first, but a leader to lead Israel. God seeks to get leaders trained in the knowledge of His ways."

To the extent that we learn how our Father has had to handle us through the years will we understand how He would have us share with others. We must be cultivated to be cultivators. "It is injurious for one believer to be forcing another into 'blessing' which that soul may not be ready for. Forced advance really gives the enemy his opportunity to mislead, for those who try to rush on at the push of others cannot stand alone, nor bear the tests of their assumed positions."

Then too, in all our service, there is the proper motive to be fully considered. "Work should be regarded less with reference to its immediate results, or as to how it may affect this or that person; the great question is, will it, when sifted in

His presence, be acceptable to Him? and this acceptability to Him is my reward: Wherefore we labor that, whether present or absent, we may be acceptable to him" (2 Cor. 5:9). Many seem to droop because there are no grapes and are not happy unless they are doing. Doing is right enough in itself, but the order ought to be from happiness to work, and not work to be happy. It is from the inner circle, the hive, the heart where Christ reigns, the only green spot, the fond enclosure—the sanctuary, that one should come forth to work. The quality of one's work depends on the nature of one's rest—and the rest should be like His own, known and enjoyed with Him. We have but small ideas of how our outward bears the color of our inward, and if our inward is not restful, there cannot be a rest-imparting service, however it may be attempted" (J. B. Stoney).

P.S. "The greatest proof of our love for Christ is that we care for those who belong to Him; '. . . if you love me, feed my sheep.' "

18 Continuance

When we first start out hungry and zealous for Him it is often imagined that extensive progress has been made, when as yet we have barely begun. As our Lord takes us along through the years it slowly dawns on us that there are vast, almost infinite, areas of development through which He must still lead us.

Many of these development areas are just plain desert—no spiritual activity, no service, little or no fellowship with Him, or others. What prayer there is has to be forced and is sometimes dropped altogether for months at a time. Bible study finally grinds to a halt; everything seems to add up to nothing. It is during these necessary times that the believer often feels that God has ceased to carry out His part, and there is little or no use in seeking to continue on. And yet there is a hunger deep within that will not allow him to quit. "The foundation of God standeth sure, having this seal, The Lord knoweth them that are his" (2 Tim. 2:19a).

Are we to love and trust and respond to Him only when He seems to be "blessing" us? What sort of love is that? Self-love? Our Father strips everything away from time to time to give us the opportunity of loving and trusting and responding to Him just because He is our Father. He knows what the cross is going to mean in our lives; He knows the death march that lies ahead of us in order that there may be resurrection life; He knows the barren, bleeding hearts beyond to whom He must minister through us—hence He is going to bring us to the place where we don't care what happens: He is all that matters!

"Sonship is something more than being born again. It represents growth into fullness. It is quite a good thing to be a babe while babyhood lasts, but it is a bad thing to be a babe when that period is past. This is the condition of many Christians. While sonship is inherent in birth, in the New Testament sense sonship is the realization of the possibilities of birth. It is growth to maturity. So the New Testament has a lot to say about growing up, leaving childhood and attaining unto full stature. With this growth comes the greater fullness of Christ and the abundant wealth unto which we are saved. It is a matter not so much of that from which we are saved, as of that unto which we are saved. The grand climax of the new creation is 'the revealing of the sons of God' (Rom. 8:19, ASV)" (T.A.S.).

In the beginning we are mainly taken up with the externals of our Christian life, and the Lord allows this for a time. Then, to get us and our externals out of the way so that the Lord Jesus Christ can be our *All*, our Father begins to take away much of what we thought we had. Here begins the long cross-centered transition from "do" to "be."

All this paradoxical progress—the way up being down—has a strong tendency to make us feel that the Lord is not taking us on. This is simply a weapon of the enemy, easily parried by letting God be God in the scriptural knowledge that He is our Father.

"It is true that God does take up those who are not worthy and permit them to speak His words years before they fully understand their import; but He does not wish any of us to stop there. We may go on in that way for awhile, but it is not true that, from the time when He begins in us His work of formation through discipline and chastening, it growingly dawns on us how little in fact we knew of the true meaning of what we had been saying and doing? He intends that we should reach the place where we can speak, with or without manifest gifts, because we are the thing we say. For in Christian experience the spiritual things of God are less and less outward, that is, of gift, and more and more inward, of life. In the long run it is the depth and inwardness of a work that counts. As the Lord Himself becomes more and more to us, other things—yes, and this must include even His gifts—

matter less and less. Then, though we teach the same doctrine, speak the same words, the impact on others is very different, manifesting itself in an increasing depth of the Spirit's work within them also" (Watchman Nee).

His relentless processing will discourage and baffle us if we simply want heaven when we die. But if we want what He wants, all that we are taken through, including the desert, will encourage us. Thus we will continue because we know that He ever continues to work in and through us that which He began and finished on our behalf in our Lord Jesus Christ.

"If our hearts are really true to Him we may be assured He will lead us on in the knowledge of Himself just as fast as we are able to advance. He knows how much we can take in, and He does not fail to minister to us the very food that is suitable to our present need. We may sometimes feel inclined to be impatient with ourselves because we do not make more rapid progress, but we have to learn to trust the Lord without spiritual education. If our eyes are upon Him, and we follow with simple hearts as He leads us, we shall find that He leads us by a right way and brings us through all the exercises we need to form our souls in the appreciation of Himself, and of all those blessed things which are brought to pass in Him. We have to trust His love all through, and to learn increasingly to distrust ourselves" (C. A. Coates).

Paul writes to us, as he did to Timothy: "Thou therefore, my son, be strong in the grace that is in Christ Jesus. And the things that thou hast heard of me among many witnesses, the same commit thou to faithful men, who shall be able to teach others also. Thou therefore endure hardness, as a good soldier of Jesus Christ" (2 Tim. 2:1-3). We rejoice with you as you continue in Him. "The Lord is faithful, who shall stablish you" (2 Thess. 3:3a).

Part Two
FOUNDATIONS OF SPIRITUAL GROWTH

19 *Position Defined and Illustrated*

The Principle of Position   All spiritual life and growth is based upon the principle of position. It can be summed up in one word: source.

Through physical birth we entered our human family position, from which source we derive certain characteristics. We are the product of our position. Just so in our spiritual birth. When we are born again, the risen Lord Jesus is the source of our Christian life; in Him we are positioned before our Father, in whom "we live, and move, and have our being" (Acts 17:28), "for we are his workmanship, created [born anew] in Christ Jesus" (Eph. 2:10). Our Father, in redeeming and recreating us, "raised us up with Him, and seated us with Him in the heavenly *places,* in Christ Jesus" (Eph. 2:6, NASB).

Our position, the source of our Christian life, is perfect. It is eternally established in the Father's presence. When we received the Lord Jesus as our personal Savior, the Holy Spirit caused us to be born into Him. He created us in the position that was established through His work at Calvary. "Therefore if any man be in Christ, he is a new creature [creation]" (2 Cor. 5:17). This is the eternal position in which every believer has been placed, whether he is aware of it or not. The Christian who comes to see his position in the Lord Jesus begins to experience the benefit of all that he is in Him. His daily state is developed from the source of his eternal standing.

Our condition is what we are in our Christian walk, in which we develop from infancy to maturity. Although our position remains immutable, our condition is variable. Through the exercise of faith, our eternal position (source) affects our daily condition, but in no way does our condition affect that heavenly position. "If [since] ye then be risen with Christ, seek those things which are above, where Christ sitteth on the right hand of God" (Col. 3:1). "Be strong *in the Lord*—be empowered through your union with Him; draw your strength from Him" (Eph. 6:10, Amplified).

When we concentrate on our condition, we are not living by faith but by feelings and appearances. The inevitable result is that we become increasingly self-conscious and self-centered. Our prime responsibility is to pay attention to the Lord Jesus, to rest (abide) in Him as our position. There will then be growth, and He will be more and more manifested in our condition. "But we all, with open face beholding as in a glass the glory of the Lord, are changed into the same image from glory to glory, even as by the spirit of the Lord" (2 Cor. 3:18).

If the believer does not know of his position in the Lord Jesus, and how to abide in Him as his very life, there will be but one result. He will struggle in his un-Christlike condition rather than rest in his Christ-centered position.

In most cases, a believer is more aware of his condition than of his position. This is the reason for so much failure and stagnation. If we are to grow and become fruitful, our faith must be anchored in the finished work of our position— in Christ. There is no basis for faith in our changeable, unfinished condition. ". . . Your faith should not stand in the wisdom of men, but in the power of God" (1 Cor. 2:5).

Scriptural, fact-centered faith in the Lord Jesus as our position before the Father is the one means of experiencing that finished work in the growth of our daily condition. Spiritual birth placed us in our accepted position, from which our spiritual condition is being completed, by faith. ". . . created in Christ Jesus unto good works, which God hath before ordained that we should walk in them" (Eph. 2:10).

Every Christian has been positioned forever in the risen Lord by spiritual birth. But only the believer who knows, grows. It is faith in the facts of our position that gives us the daily benefits of growth in our condition. If the believer is not clearly aware of the specific truths of the Word, he cannot exercise the necessary faith for growth and service. He can only seek his resources in the realm of self. Some of the wonderful positional truths are set forth for our faith in the scriptural illustrations of the grain of wheat, and the vine and the branch.

The Grain of Wheat   In John 12:24 the Lord Jesus said, "Except a corn (grain) of wheat fall into the ground and die, it abideth alone: but if it die, it bringeth forth much fruit." This principle of life out of death was then established at Calvary's cross, where He, as *the* Grain of Wheat, died and rose again. In His resurrection He brought forth the "much fruit" out of His death.

Everyone who would ever place his trust in Christ as Savior, every grain of wheat, was resident in (identified with) *the* Grain of Wheat, the Head of the new spiritual harvest. Every believer is included in the "much fruit" of His death and resurrection. "For if we have been planted together in the likeness of his death, we shall be also in the likeness of his resurrection" (Rom. 6:5).

The Principle of Reproduction   There is another wonderful principle involved here: *like produces like.* "And God said, Let the earth bring forth grass, the herb yielding seed, and the fruit tree yielding fruit *after his kind*" (Gen. 1:11, italics mine). Our Lord Jesus, as the Grain of Wheat having fallen into the ground in death, and having risen again to life eternal, is still bringing forth the "much fruit," "after his kind." "For whom he [God] did foreknow, he also did predestinate to be conformed to the image of his Son, that he might be the *firstborn among many brethren*" (Rom. 8:29, italics mine). The Lord Jesus is our life; therefore, as we grow spiritually, the family likeness is manifested. We are gradually conformed to His image, who Himself is the "express image of his [God's] person" (Heb. 1:3). And, "when he shall appear, we shall be [completely] like him; for we shall see him as he is" (1 John 3:2).

In the natural realm, the first grain of wheat contained, complete and perfect, the life of every subsequent grain of wheat to this day. It did not abide alone, retaining all, but fell into the ground and died, finding resurrection in the "much fruit" of life out of death. This same principle applies in the spiritual realm. The position, the source of life, of every believer as a grain of wheat, is God's firstborn Grain of Wheat, our Lord Jesus Christ. Each of us is "after his kind"; we have His life. Thus, when we speak of our position, we refer to our place in the risen Lord—our "life is hid with Christ in God" (Col. 3:3).

The principle of position, therefore, both natural and spiritual, is that life in its fullness and completeness is resident in the source, and is transmitted through birth and growth. Resurrection life is explicitly after its kind; it is "conformed to the image" of its positional source. The Lord Jesus Christ as the Father's Grain of Wheat took our place at Calvary, and His death and resurrection brought forth the "much fruit" of similar grains of wheat, believers predestined to be conformed to the image of God's Son.

There is a stillness in the Christian's life:
    The grain of wheat must fall into the ground
And die; then, if it die, out of that death
    Life, fullest life, will blessedly abound.
It is a mystery no words can tell,
    But known to those who in this stillness rest;
Something divinely incomprehensible:
    That for my nothingness, I get God's best!

                    —Selected

The Vine and the Branch Consistent with *the principle of position* and *the principle of reproduction,* our risen Lord Jesus is the Vine. As such, He brings forth fruit "after his kind." "I am the vine, ye are the branches; He that abideth in me, and I in him, the same bringeth forth much fruit: for without me ye can do nothing" (John 15:5).

In the natural realm, the life that is already complete in the vine is increasingly supplied to the growing branches. The healthy condition of the branches is contingent on their abiding in their position in the vine. The branch is not only a product and a living part of the vine, but that which is produced in the branch is also the fruit of the vine. Actually, the branch produces nothing, either for the vine, for others, or for itself. The vine, the positional source, has everything to do with the development and fruitfulness of all its branches. The chief responsibility of the branch is to rest just where it was born, to abide in its living position in its living source.

As the believer rests in his position, the life of the Vine (the "fruit of the Spirit") is manifested in his condition—"love, joy, peace, patience, kindness, goodness, faithfulness, gentleness, self-control" (Gal. 5:22, 23 NASB). The life of the Vine is the life of the branch. The True Vine is established at the right hand of our Father in glory and is the source from which our Christian life flows. The indwelling Spirit of Christ is the living link between Him in heaven and our spirit here on earth. ". . . he that is joined unto the Lord is one spirit" (1 Cor. 6:17).

Taking Our Position   We take our position, not by attempting to get into it, but simply by seeing that we are already positioned in the Lord Jesus. We abide in Him by resting in the fact. We have been in this risen position ever since our new birth. As we come to realize this truth and to "stand in our standing" in Him, we begin to experience the daily benefits of our life that is hid with Christ in God. Our attitude becomes, "I see my position in the Lord Jesus, and I abide there; I rest in Him, not only as my Savior, but as my life." Faith in our position will bring growth in our condition.

Paul prayed for believers, "That the God of our Lord Jesus Christ, the Father of glory, may give unto you the spirit of wisdom and revelation in the knowledge of him: the eyes of your understanding being enlightened; that ye may know what is the hope of his calling, and what the riches of the glory of his inheritance in the saints" (Eph. 1:17, 18). He also said, "Blessed be . . . God . . . who has blessed us with every spiritual blessing in the heavenly *places* in Christ" (Eph. 1:3, NASB).

Our Father intends us to know and understand that He has already provided, in Christ our life, everything required for our Christian life both in time and eternity. He is patiently teaching us to have no faith in the old man (self), and to exercise all of our faith in the new Man (Christ). We are told to do in faith what our Father has already done in fact. At the cross He freed us from the reign of sin and self; in the Resurrection He united us to the risen Lord Jesus. By faith in the work of the cross, the old man is put off; by faith in our heavenly position in Christ, the new man is put on. Hence we are free to dwell within the very Source of every spiritual blessing with which our Father has blessed us.

By considering the old man to have been crucified at Calvary, he is "put off" daily (Rom. 6:11a). By considering ourselves as newly created in the risen Lord Jesus, we "put on" the new man (Rom. 6:11b). As we escape self's reign of death, we enter into Christ's reign of life.

1. Put Off the Old

a. *Fact*

"Knowing this, that our old self was crucified with Him" (Rom. 6:6, NASB). ". . . seeing that ye have put off the old man" (Col. 3:9). Positionally, we were separated from the old Adamic nature in our identification with Christ on the cross.

b. *Faith*

"That ye put off concerning the former conversation (manner of life) the old man" (Eph. 4:22). By faith in our new, sanctified position, we turn from, we consider as crucified, the principle of sin and self within. We count ourselves to be new creations in Christ, having died to sin and self. That is our part in putting off the old man that God put off from us at the cross.

2. Put On the New

a. *Fact*

"For as many of you as have been baptized [spiritually] into Christ have put on Christ" (Gal. 3:27). "And have put on the new man, which is renewed in knowledge after the image of him that created him" (Col. 3:10). At our new birth we were recreated in Christ, and our Christian life is now hid with Him in God (Col. 3:3, 4).

b. *Faith*

"Put ye on the Lord Jesus Christ" (Rom. 13:14). ". . . put on the new man, which after God is created in righteousness and true holiness" (Eph. 4:24). By faith in the positional fact that our Father has placed us in His Son, we abide in Him, we acknowledge our place in Him. By faith, we stand in the position He has already given us. "Stand therefore, having your loins grit about with truth" (Eph. 6:14).

20 *Justification and Assurance*

It may help us to see the importance of the principle of position in our Christian life if we consider the fact that God began training us in positional truth before we were born again!

Justification   According to His faithful ministry, the Holy Spirit brought about an initial conviction of sin by revealing our needy condition. Through varied pressures and circumstances, we came to realize our sinful state before God.

Then the Holy Spirit may have used a faithful witness to make clear to us from the Word that we were lost sinners, *positionally.* We were in the wrong family—we had been born into the fallen, sinful, condemned Adamic line. ". . . as in Adam all die" (1 Cor. 15:22). In our natural birth, we were born "dead in trespasses and sins" (Eph. 2:1). ". . . by one man's [Adam's] offence death reigned . . ." (Rom. 5:17).

In His perfect love and holiness, God made it possible for us to be removed from our position of death in Adam, and to be eternally born anew into His family through our position in the Lord Jesus Christ. By His grace we were brought to turn from our natural, fallen condition and position, and to believe on His Son as our own personal Savior, our new position before God.

Much of this wonderful transaction and transition, no doubt, was not understood at the time. However, it is all-important that the truths of our new birth and justification become crystal clear if we are to experience the *benefits* of our position in Christ. Superficiality in this foundational step inevitably makes for shallowness and immaturity throughout our subsequent walk.

The meaning of justification is to pronounce righteous, not to make righteous; what is imputed is not, in fact, imparted. To be justified means that the believer is viewed in Christ as righteous, and is treated as such by God. The righteousness of our position in the Lord Jesus is increasingly manifested in our condition, as we "grow in grace, and in the knowledge of our Lord and Saviour Jesus Christ" (2 Peter 3:18). "But of him are ye in Christ Jesus who of God is made unto us . . . righteousness, and . . . redemption" (1 Cor. 1:30).

Until we clearly see the positional perfection of our justification in Christ, our conception of, and faith in, all the other aspects of our position will be out of focus. In the Old Testament type, God explained to Israel that "the life of the flesh is in the blood: and I have given it to you upon the altar to make an atonement for your souls: for it is the blood that maketh an atonement for the soul" (Lev. 17:11). Now, the value of the life sacrificed is the measure of the worth of the blood shed. In that these type-sacrifices were animals, innocent and spotless though they were, still "it is not possible that the blood of bulls and of goats should take away sins" (Heb. 10:4). All this was a cancellation in anticipation of God's perfect sacrifice of "the Lamb of God, which taketh away the sin of the world" (John 1:29).

God the Son became also the perfect Son of Man in order that He might go to the Father's altar, the cross of Calvary, and there willingly shed His precious blood in full atonement for our sins. Complete payment made, He was free to rise again in resurrected, ascended, and glorified eternal life. "In whom we have redemption through his blood, the forgiveness of sins, according to the riches of his grace" (Eph. 1:7). There are two important factors in this verse: (1) "In whom we have redemption." Here we have our position of justification. When we received Him as our Savior, He received us and we were born into Him in "newness of life"—His life. (2) Because of the perfection of His atonement, it was all "according to the riches of his grace." Complete and eternal justification is a gracious *gift*, utterly impossible to be earned in any way whatsoever. ". . . to him that worketh not, but believeth on him that justifieth the ungodly, his faith is counted for righteousness" (Rom. 4:5).

A further fact to be remembered is that all of our sins were future at the time they were paid for, since the work of the Cross was accomplished when we were yet unborn. Our Father took everything into consideration before He made a single move on our behalf. Hence we can be fully assured that all our sins, past, present, and future, have been forever forgiven. ". . . through this man is preached unto you the forgiveness of sins: and by him all that believe are justified from *all things*" . . . (Acts 13:38, 39, italics mine.)

Since justification is in Christ and not in ourselves, it is a truth of position, not condition. We receive justification in the Lord Jesus by faith in the Word; it is a fact believed, not an experience received. It has nothing to do with our condition, but everything to do with our position. However, as we rest in our justified position, our spiritual condition is affected. We experience something of the new-found peace and joy of the Lord, and His love for us.

Assurance   The blessed assurance of salvation, and of justification in particular, is based squarely on our position in the Lord Jesus as our righteousness. Being non-experiential, justification can never be founded on our condition. Assurance of justification results when we realize what our Father has done and said; it is never based on feelings. Someone has said, "Because God has spoken, I am *sure*; because I am sure, I *feel* at rest." "Set your mind on the things above, not on the things that are on earth" (Col. 3:2, NASB).

It is here that the first major mistake in our Christian life is often made. In taking the position of justification by faith in the Lord Jesus, this new standing of life began to make a marked difference in our state. Because of this, we shifted the basis of our assurance from eternal position to temporal condition. We looked, and felt, and sounded saved, hence we were assured of our salvation.

But then, one morning came the dawn! We didn't look very saved, we didn't feel at all saved, and so we didn't sound saved either. All day long everything and everybody went wrong, and by nightfall we found ourselves at the end of our assurance. Thoroughly shaken, we determined to rectify matters the next day. On that day we strove to look saved, to feel saved, and to sound saved. But, because we were centered in our condition, all was wretched failure. We even began to question our salvation. ". . . If the LORD be with us, why then is all this befallen us?" (Judg. 6:13).

In the Lord's time, the Comforter refocused our faith on our position by means of the Word, and our assurance of salvation was again anchored on the Rock, Christ Jesus. With this assurance reestablished, our condition began to improve as a result of the position in which we stood by faith. We had learned our first important lesson: the necessity of knowing and abiding in our position. Apart from this abiding, there is nothing but frustration and failure. "And the work of righteousness shall be peace; and the effect of righteousness quietness and assurance forever" (Isa. 32:17).

| The Witness of | "The Spirit Himself [thus] testifies together |
| the Spirit | with our own spirit, [assuring us] that we |

are children of God" (Rom. 8:16), Amplified). It is a temptation from many to yearn after something more tangible than the positional testimony of the Word, in order to be more sure of their assurance. But it is at this point that the faithful Spirit would teach us total reliance on the Word, *nothing* added. ". . . receive with meekness the engrafted word . . ." (James 1:21).

There may be other ground for assurance of our salvation, such as, "We know that we have passed from death unto life, because we love the brethren" (1 John 3:14), but this is secondary, not foundational. Besides, there will be times when our love for some brethren may falter, and then what of our assurance?

The witness of the Spirit is His witness to the Word wherein lies God's revelation of our eternal position. And in that Word He testifies concerning the Lord Jesus, who is our position before God. Although the Holy Spirit abides within and witnesses to our spirit, we must remember that the human spirit lies beyond the range of consciousness. Therefore, assurance of salvation is not gained through the senses. As we rest in our position by faith in the scriptural facts, the Spirit of truth gives us a deep, inexplicable assurance that cannot be altered. We not only believe, we *know;* our knowledge is established in the eternal, Spirit-ministered Scriptures. ". . . for I know whom I have believed, and am persuaded that he is able to keep that which I have committed unto him against that day" (2 Tim. 1:12).

All seems so simple and solved during the infant stage of our Christian life. But the Lord must take us on from milk to meat, to become responsible, spiritually intelligent, adult believers. We must not only become firmly and clearly established in the deeper truths ourselves, but we must be qualified to share them effectively with others. Once we are sure and sound, the Lord can establish others through us. But, "if the trumpet give an uncertain sound, who shall prepare himself to the battle?" (1 Cor. 14:8).

Until we are soldily founded on the first principles of spiritual birth, we cannot be taken on to the principles of growth and maturity. "For every one that useth milk is unskillful in the word of righteousness: for he is a babe. But strong meat belongeth to them that are of full age, even those who by reason of use have their senses exercised to discern both good and evil. Therefore leaving the principles of the doctrine of Christ, let us go on unto perfection [maturity]" (Heb. 5:13, 14; 6:1).

As the electronic eye of the space capsule locks onto its designated star for guidance and maintenance on its heavenly course, so are we to fix our eye of faith on our heavenly position—the Bright and Morning Star. Thus, in our "fixing our eyes on Jesus, the author and perfecter of faith," we shall find experientially that "the path of the righteous is like the light of dawn, that shines brighter and brighter until the full day" (Heb. 12:2; Prov. 4:18, NASB).

21 Reconciliation and Acceptance

The settled assurance of our justification is not simply to make us sure of getting to heaven, but to prepare us for further spiritual progress. Assurance of our justified position in Christ gives us sureness in each subsequent step of our spiritual development. By grace we were born anew: "Being justified freely by his grace . . ." (Rom. 3:24); and by grace we will grow: "But grow in grace . . ." (2 Peter 3:18). We must stand in the first principles before we can go on from them to maturity. Until we rest assured in our position of justification, we are not spiritually prepared for the positional truths of our reconciliation to, and acceptance by, God.

Reconciliation   The ground of our reconciliation to God is justification from the penalty of sin. In the Lord Jesus we were justified from the death penalty of sin, thereby enabling God to reconcile us to Himself. Justification frees us *from death;* reconciliation brings us *into life.* "For if while we were enemies we were reconciled to God through the death of His Son, it is much more [certain], now that we are reconciled, that we shall be saved [daily delivered from sin's dominion] through His [resurrection] life" (Rom. 5:10, Amplified).

To be reconciled is to be brought into right relationship, into harmony. Being dead in our sins, we were completely cut off from any relationship with the God of life; spiritually, we were the children of the devil (John 8:44). Instead of seeking to bring to life and reconcile the fallen Adamic nature—an impossibility, because that life is enmity toward God and cannot be subject to the law of God (Rom 8:7)—our Father recreated us in the life of the Lord Jesus. He placed us in a totally new position, out of Adam, into Christ. "Even when we were dead . . . He made us alive together in fellowship and in union with Christ. He gave us the very life of Christ Himself, the same new life with which He quickened Him" (Eph. 2:5, Amplified).

Self cannot be reconciled to God. Since we were born sinners and therefore were enmity against God, our reconciliation to Him was no simple matter. It took the cross of Calvary to solve the problem. There, as lost and alienated sinners, we were identified with the Lord Jesus in His death unto sin and resurrection unto God; we were raised from the dead as new creatures (creations) in Christ (2 Cor. 5:17). Being made "partakers of the divine nature" (2 Peter 1:4), we were completely and eternally reconciled to the Father. "Having made peace through the blood of his cross, by him to reconcile all things unto himself. . . . And you, that were sometime alienated and enemies in your mind by wicked works, yet now hath he reconciled in the body of his flesh *through death,* to present you holy and unblameable and unreproveable in his sight" (Col. 1:20-22, italics mine).

Our present condition is infinitely inferior to our eternal position, but our Father accepts us—not in ourselves, but in His Son. Our Lord Jesus so completely justified us in His death and resurrection that our Father is absolutely just in eternally reconciling us. His love and life are free to flow. "For he hath made him to be sin for us, who knew no sin; that we might be made the righteousness of God in him" (2 Cor. 5:21). ". . . All things are from God, Who through *Jesus* Christ reconciled us to Himself (received us into favor, brought us into harmony with Himself)" (2 Cor. 5:18, Amplified). Due to His work of justification and reconciliation, there is full acceptance for us.

Acceptance   Here we have one of the most vital positional subjects, and yet it is relatively unknown among believers today. All too few are enjoying the benefits of acceptance in their daily walk. The believer who is not aware of his position of acceptance *in Christ* is caught in

the struggle to improve his condition in order to feel acceptable to God. But the believer who abides in the Lord Jesus as
his righteousness and acceptance is freed from futile self-effort.
Standing in his position, he trusts Christ to manifest Himself
increasingly in his life. He is free from the burden of himself
and has become burdened on behalf of others. God "hath
given to us the ministry of reconciliation" (2 Cor. 5:18).

Condition   First of all, we must consider the area in
                  which we are not accepted by God, nor ever
can be. It is only natural for us to feel that our spiritual walk
and service make us acceptable to our Father. We imagine
that it is our responsibility (with His help) to live and serve
so faithfully and fruitfully that He will approve of us, and
therefore continually and abundantly bless us. We are making
the natural mistake of depending on condition, instead of
position, for our acceptance.

Important as it is, service is often a condition-centered detriment in the lives of many zealous believers. When service is
given predominance over fellowship with and growth in the
Lord Jesus, *doing,* instead of *being,* takes over in the life.
Fellowship and growth must ever take precedence over service
and activity, otherwise spiritual declension sets in.

In this reversal of God's order for us, the heart seeks satisfaction and a sense of acceptance through production (law),
instead of reception (grace). Bible study and prayer, as well
as one's outlook, become almost exclusively service-centered.
Instead of life bringing forth service, service becomes the life.
Thus, as long as the service goes well, the servant is happy
and feels accepted. But once the service wanes, or fails to
produce results, all else falls with it. We are to be sons, not
servants. "Wherefore thou art no more a servant, but a son
. . ." (Gal. 4:7).

In time, we begin to realize that there is something very
wrong with this entire concept. We become aware that our
walk and service are less and less acceptable, even to ourselves. In seeking to *do* rather than to *be,* in attempting to
give out more than we take in, our condition becomes barren
and carnal. We have been depending on self to do what only

Christ our life can do; the farther we move on this tangent, the more active and malignant the self-life appears to be.

What the condition-centered believer does not realize is that God Himself is causing this shattering revelation of self. He takes us into situations and relationships that finally cause us to face up to the fact of our failure as Christians—our nothingness, our total unacceptability in ourselves. Not until we understand that in our flesh there "dwelleth no good thing" (Rom. 7:18), can we rest in our position of complete acceptance in the Lord Jesus, just as we are. To abide in Christ, and to consent to be loved while unworthy, is the believer's positional privilege and responsibility. Love functions according to its nature, not according to the quality of its object.

The believer who is not abiding by faith in the acceptable One, but who is relying on his personal condition for acceptance, is hopelessly handicapped in the matter of fellowship, growth, and service. He is entangled in the self-effort of working to improve his condition, and is inevitably cast down in utter defeat. How can a defeated, depressed, self-centered Christian enjoy fellowship with the Father, or be at peace with Him? Yet, devastating as this Romans 7 trek is, it is our Father's preparation of us in order that we may shift our reliance and faith from our condition in ourselves, to our position in Christ. ". . . not I, but Christ . . ." (Gal. 2:20).

Position   "Having predestinated us unto the adoption of children by Jesus Christ to himself, according to the good pleasure of his will, to the praise of the glory of his grace, wherein he hath made us *accepted in the beloved.* In whom we have redemption through his blood, the forgiveness of sins, according to the riches of his grace" (Eph. 1:5-7, italics mine). In learning to take our position in the Lord Jesus and thereby to abide in Him as our acceptance, we grow to expect less and less from ourselves, and more and more from Him. "My soul, wait thou only upon God; for my expectation is from him" (Ps. 62:5).

As we become more fully established in our position, we are increasingly willing to reject self, to leave all that sinful source on the cross for daily crucifixion. This progressive freedom from the dominion of self gives us a deepening rest in the Lord Jesus; we become rooted and grounded in the Source of life, where we grow effortlessly and fruit is born to His glory. Self-effort produces the works of the flesh (Gal. 5:19-21), while positional rest fosters the fruit of the Spirit (Gal. 5:22, 23).

"Abide in me [your position], and I in you. As the branch cannot bear fruit of itself, except it abide in the vine; no more can ye, except ye abide in me. I am the vine, ye are the branches: He that abideth in me, and I in him, the same bringeth forth much fruit: for without me ye can do nothing" (John 15:4, 5). Although we abide in the Lord Jesus as our position, we are ever aware of our condition in ourselves. We are concerned about the sinfulness of self, but no longer do we depend on improvement in that realm for our acceptance. We are resting in a position, in a Person who is fully and forever accepted by God, One in whom there is no improvement necessary or possible. We have exchanged unimproveable self for the perfect One.

Established in our position, we become increasingly aware of our acceptance in Him and are more free to fellowship with our Father. In this blessed communion we grow, becoming more manifestly conformed to His image. ". . . we all, with open face beholding as in a glass the glory of the Lord, are changed into the same image from glory to glory, even as by the Spirit of the Lord" (2 Cor. 3:18). We are basically Christ-centered, instead of self-centered. Through our position in Him we have peace, joy, and fellowship which abide all along our Cross-centered path as our spiritual condition is developed.

One of the foremost benefits of resting in our position of acceptance is the deep and undying assurance that God is *for* us. "For I know the thoughts that I think toward you, saith the LORD, thoughts of peace, and not of evil, to give you an expected end" (Jer. 29:11). ". . . having made peace through the blood of his cross . . ." (Col. 1:20). "There is therefore now no condemnation to them which are in Christ Jesus. . . . If God be for us, who can be against us?" (Rom. 8:1, 31).

As the Holy Spirit applies the finished work of the cross to the sinful source within, this inner crucifixion may lead us to think God is against us. But it is just the opposite; everything He takes us through is for our spiritual growth. ". . . *all* things work together for good to them that love God, to them who are the called according to his purpose. For whom he did foreknow, he also did predestinate to be conformed to the image of his Son . . ." (Rom. 8:28, 29). Therefore, "in every thing give thanks: for this is the will of God in Christ Jesus concerning you" (1 Thess. 5:18). "He that spared not his own Son, but delivered him up for us all, how shall he not with him also freely give us all things?" (Rom. 8:32). "For all things are for your sakes, that the abundant grace might through the thanksgiving of many redound to the glory of God" (2 Cor. 4:15).

What a safe and impregnable position is ours in Christ! "The LORD is my rock, and my fortress, and my deliverer; my God, my strength, in whom I will trust; my buckler, and the horn of my salvation, and my high tower" (Ps. 18:2). When the "accuser of the brethren" points his maligning finger at the self-life within, at our condition in ourselves, seeking to get us to question our acceptance, we are able to rest in our position and point to Christ. We are well aware of self's unacceptability, but we are much more aware of our acceptance in the Beloved. The enemy can never touch Him, and our "life is hid with Christ in God" (Col. 3:3). Satan may be the counsel for the prosecution, but we have two Counsels for defense— an Advocate at the throne, and an Advocate within—to say nothing of the fact that the righteous Judge is our Father!

"Wherefore in all things it behooved him to be made like unto his brethren, that he might be a merciful and faithful high priest in things pertaining to God, to make reconciliation for the sins of the people" (Heb. 2:17). Our Father has reconciled us to Himself in a way that enables Him to be consistent with Himself, being both "just, and the justifier of him which believeth in Jesus" (Rom. 3:26).

22 Completeness and Security

Each step of faith we take concerning the facts of our position prepares us for the following one, since every succeeding step is established on all that precedes. Our faith grows by feeding on properly related scriptural truth. "For precept must be upon precept . . . line upon line . . ." (Isa. 28:10). "The steps of a good man are ordered by the LORD . . ." (Ps. 37:23).

Many hungry-hearted believers are struggling to get into the experience of Romans 8 when they are not yet resting in the facts of Romans 3. They feel guilty because they fall far short of the heights of Ephesians and Colossians, when in fact they do not adequately know peace with God in Romans 5, to say nothing of identification with Christ in Romans 6. The experience of Romans 7 is well known, however. It is absolutely necessary to allow the Holy Spirit to take us along in God's sequence of Scripture, as each plane of truth is foundational for the next. Skip over one, and firm footing for the next is lost. "Hold up my goings in thy paths, that my footsteps slip not" (Ps. 17:5).

Complete in Him   Once we are scripturally assured of our justification, reconciliation, and acceptance in the Lord Jesus, we are to feed on the truth of our completeness in Him. "As ye have therefore received Christ Jesus the Lord [by faith], so walk ye in him: rooted and built up in him, and stablished in the faith, as ye have been taught, abounding therein with thanksgiving. . . . For in him dwelleth all the fullness of the Godhead bodily. And ye are complete in him . . ." (Col. 2:6, 7, 9, 10).

All we will ever need for our Christian life, now and forever, is ready and waiting in the Lord Jesus, complete and accessible. Our condition is absolutely dependent on our completed Source. Faith rests on our Father's scriptural testimony as to what He has already done for and with us in Christ, never on what He is doing for and with us in our present condition. Faith in the Vine brings forth fruit in the branches.

Resting in our position in the Lord Jesus has a direct effect on our condition. When we know that our Father has already made us complete in Christ, we are able to trust Him in the midst of His development of that completeness in our spiritual condition. Without the knowledge of this finished work in the Lord Jesus, our faith lacks the necessary confidence that He will make sure progress in our daily growth.

Think for a moment of the positional truth of 2 Corinthians 5:17, ". . . if any man be in Christ, he is a new creature [creation]: old things are passed away; behold, all things are become new." In the Lord Jesus we are altogether new creations, born anew and complete in Him. He is the eternal Source from which our condition is to develop. "For we are God's [own] handiwork (His workmanship), recreated in Christ Jesus, [born anew] that we may do those good works which God predestined (planned beforehand) for us, (taking paths which He prepared ahead of time) that we should walk in them—living the good life which He prearranged and made ready for us to live" (Eph. 2:10, Amplified).

Even though the work is complete in Christ, there is nothing automatic about our experience of it. Ours is the responsibility of faith. We were not only born anew by faith, but we are to live, walk, and grow by faith. To enter intelligently and cooperatively into that which our Father has established for us in Christ, by faith we are to "put on the new man, which after God is created in righteousness and true holiness" (Eph. 4:24). This simply means that we are to rest in our position in the Lord Jesus as our life. We are to abide there because we have already been established (born) there. "And have put on the new man, which is renewed in knowledge after the image of him that created him" (Col. 3:10). "For as many of you as have been baptized [spiritually, by the Holy Spirit] into Christ have put on Christ" (Gal. 3:27).

"But put ye on the Lord Jesus Christ, and make not provision for the flesh, to fulfill the lusts thereof" (Rom. 13:14). The Lord Jesus is "put on" as we abide *in* Him by faith. Our risen Lord is full provision for our Christian life and service; and the cross is the only provision we have for the self-life. As we confidently rest in the Lord Jesus, the Holy Spirit gives us the things of Christ by means of growth. As a result, our condition begins to reflect what we already are in position. By faith, we abide and live in Him; by faith, His life is developed and manifested in us. "My little children, of whom I travail in birth again until Christ be formed in you" (Gal. 4:19).

Secure in Christ   Based on the preceding facts, the eternal security of the believer becomes a foregone conclusion; once the Holy Spirit establishes the Christian in the previous steps, there can be no question about this one. But without the required scriptural preparation, there is bound to be a nagging question mark hovering in the background: am I unconditionally and forever saved, or am I on probation?

The secure believer may now and then be accosted by those who strongly oppose any thought of unconditional, eternal security. They refer to it as "that damnable doctrine," and insist that such a belief results in lawlessness. What these dear people fail to grasp is that the believer who truly stands in the grace of positional security is the one who most fully fears God and hates sin. And he hates sin for what it is, not just for its consequences. Moreover, his is not a slavish fear; it is not a fear of losing God's love, but of offending and grieving it.

"But there is forgiveness with thee, that thou mayest be feared" (Ps. 130:4). The fear of the secure believer is a reverential trust, coupled with hatred of evil. "The fear of the LORD is to hate evil . . ." (Prov. 8:13). "For the grace of God that bringeth salvation hath appeared to all men, teaching us that, denying ungodliness and worldly lusts, we should live soberly, righteously, and godly, in this present world" (Titus 2:11, 12). Grace banishes all guesswork, and gives one assurance; the law keeps one guessing.

The truth of security holds the Christian firm in the midst of the process of growth. It is the insecure believer who is naturally unstable and flounders from one "experience" to another, never learning and therefore never arriving at the truth. Resting in our eternal position frees us from the futile and sinful self-effort of trying to make our condition the basis of our security. Abiding in our eternal security in Christ gives the steadiness of faith necessary for the Holy Spirit to carry on His gracious ministry within—that of dealing with self in crucifixion, and thereby causing us to "grow in *grace*, and in the knowledge of our Lord and Saviour Jesus Christ" (2 Peter 3:18).

The spiritual explanation for opposition to true eternal security is not the claim that it produces lawlessness. It is rather that those who oppose do not exercise faith in the Word, which would enable them to see and accept their position in the risen Lord for assurance, acceptance, and security. They are condition-centered, hence self-centered and earthbound.

On the other hand, the believer who knows he has died to sin and has been recreated in the risen Lord Jesus, understands that he has no other position before God than the very life of Christ. "For ye are all the children of God by faith in Christ Jesus" (Gal. 3:26). "And if children, then heirs; heirs of God, and joint-heirs with Christ . . ." (Rom. 8:17). "Beloved, now are we the sons of God, and it doth not yet appear what we shall be: but we know that, when he shall appear, we shall be like him . . ." (1 John 3:2).

It certainly is not yet manifest in our condition what we already are in our position, or what we shall be when He appears. But the resting believer does not rely on appearances, neither is he affected one way or another by his condition. He knows he is accepted and secure on a different basis altogether, that of his position in Christ, the Man of God's choosing. This is not carelessness, but confidence in Him. In quietness and assurance we are to continue, "waiting for the coming of our Lord Jesus Christ: who shall also confirm you unto the end, that ye may be blameless in the day of our Lord Jesus Christ" (1 Cor. 1:7, 8).

The believer who rests in the *Son of God* knows he is eternally secure. "For you have died and your life is hidden with Christ in God. When Christ, who is our life, is revealed, then you also will be revealed with Him in glory" (Col. 3:3, 4 NASB). "And not only so, but we also joy in God through our Lord Jesus Christ, by whom we have now received the atonement" (Rom. 5:11).

The believer who rests in the *sovereignty of God* knows he is eternally secure. "For whom he did foreknow, he also did predesitnate to be conformed to the image of his Son, that he might be the firstborn among many brethren. Moreover whom he did predestinate, them he also called: and whom he called, them he also justified: and whom he justified, them he also glorified" (Rom. 8:29, 30). "Now unto him that is able to keep you from falling, and to present you faultless before the presence of his glory with exceeding joy . . ." (Jude 24).

The believer who rests in the *justice of God* knows he is eternally secure. "To declare . . . his righteousness: that he might be just, and the justified of him which believeth in Jesus" (Rom. 3:26). "For Christ also hath once suffered for sins, the just for the unjust, that he might bring us to God . . ." (1 Peter 3:18). "There is therefore now no condemnation for those who are in Christ Jesus. For the law of the Spirit of life in Christ Jesus has set you free from the law of sin and of death" (Rom. 8:1, 2 NASB).

The believer who rests in the *will of God* knows that he is eternally secure. "Ye have not chosen me, but I have chosen you, and ordained you, that ye should go and bring forth fruit, and that your fruit should remain . . ." (John 15:16). "But of him are ye in Christ Jesus, who of God is made unto us . . . redemption" (1 Cor. 1:30).

The believer who rests in the *love of God* knows he is eternally secure. ". . . I have loved thee with an everlasting love: therefore with lovingkindness have I drawn thee" (Jer. 31:3). "Who shall separate us from the love of Christ? shall tribulation, or distress, or persecution . . . ? . . . For I am persuaded, that neither death, nor life, nor angels, nor principalities, nor powers, nor things present, nor things to come, nor height, nor depth, nor any other creature, shall be able to separate us from the love of God, which is in Christ Jesus our Lord" (Rom. 8:35, 38, 39).

23 Sanctification and Consecration

There need be no difficulty with the subject of sanctification once the meaning of the term is understood. In both the Hebrew and the Greek, sanctification is synonymous with separation. To be sanctified means to be "set apart" for God's possession and use.

It is important to realize that the term has nothing whatsoever to do with the thought of cleansing or purification, as so many seem to think. For example, it is recorded that, prior to the advent of sin into the world, "God blessed the seventh day, and sanctified it" (Gen. 2:3). He set apart the Sabbath as a special day. Further, the sinless Lord Jesus said, "I sanctify myself" (John 17:19). He willingly set Himself apart, He separated Himself, He completely devoted Himself to the work the Father gave Him to do.

Position   It is all-important to keep in mind the clear scriptural distinction between our fully-sanctified position and our being-sanctified condition. Positionally, our Father has already done the work on our behalf, just as He has already justified, reconciled, accepted, and secured us—in the Lord Jesus. Note the difference between the Corinthians' position, and their condition: (1) "Unto the church of God which is at Corinth, to them that are sanctified in Christ Jesus, called to be saints, will all that in every place call upon the name of Jesus Christ our Lord . . ." (1 Cor. 1:2); (2) "For it hath been declared unto me of you, my brethren . . . that there are contentions among you" (1 Cor. 1:11).

In the first place, it is heartening to realize that our sanctification is both *the will, and the work, of God.* "For this is the will of God, even your sanctification . . ." (1 Thess. 4:3). "And the very God of peace sanctify you wholly. . . . Faithful is he that calleth you, who also will do it" (1 Thess. 5:23, 24). He has sanctified us positionally because we looked to Him for salvation; He will sanctify us experientially as we look to Him for growth.

Every believer, whether babe or veteran, is already separated to God in Christ Jesus. What makes the difference in the believer's condition is that he becomes clearly aware of his sanctified position in the risen Lord. Jude wrote his epistle "to them that are sanctified by God the Father, and preserved in Jesus Christ, and called" (v. 1). Our Father has eternally set us apart and preserved us in His Son, and called us to His Service. All of the growing believer's life is considered service, whether it be formal or otherwise.

Our sanctification is not only the will and the work of the Father, but it is *in and through the Son.* "But of him are ye in Christ Jesus, who of God is made unto us . . . sanctification . . ." (1 Cor. 1:30). Here we can see that our positional sanctification is a gift, just as is our righteousness. When through faith we were born into the Lord Jesus, *He* became our righteousness and our sanctification, not partially, but completely. "For in him dwelleth all the fullness of the Godhead bodily. And ye are complete in him . . ." (Col. 2:9, 10).

It is a great relief and joy for the struggling believer to realize that when he received Christ as his righteousness by faith, he also received Him as his sanctification. Many people struggle and work for a righteousness of their own, until they finally receive His righteousness by faith. Then, as believers, they set about to labor through the whole futile process again, struggling to produce a sanctification of their own instead of resting in His sanctification as a gift. The Lord Jesus sent Paul unto the Gentiles "to open their eyes . . . that they may receive forgiveness of sins and an inheritance among those who have been sanctified by faith in Me" (Acts 26:18, NASB).

As is everything else in our position in Christ, our sanctification is perfect, once for all, complete, eternal. It could not be otherwise, since the Lord Jesus Himself is our sanctification. Hebrews 10:10 and 14 leave no question about this wonderful fact: "By the which will we are sanctified through the offering of the body of Jesus Christ once for all. . . . For by one offering he hath perfected forever them that are sanctified." Through the cross of the Lord Jesus Christ, and in His life, our Father has created us anew and given us a completely separated position before Himself—separated from all that would hinder that blessed relationship. "Therefore if any man be in Christ, he is a new creature [creation]: old things are passed away; behold, all things are become new" (2 Cor. 5:17). "I know that, whatsoever God doeth, it shall be forever: nothing can be put to it, nor any thing taken from it: and God doeth it . . ." (Eccl. 3:14).

Condition   As we abide in our position of sanctification, there is growth in our condition of sanctification. Although the Holy Spirit participated in establishing our positional sanctification—"But you were washed, but you were sanctified . . . in the name of the Lord Jesus Christ, and in the Spirit of our God" (1 Cor. 6:11, NASB)—He is mainly concerned with our condition of sanctification. He it is who brings us into experiential separation to our Father. Peter wrote his first epistle to the "elect according to the foreknowledge of God the Father, through sanctification of the Spirit" (1 Peter 1:2).

Truth is the basis on which the Holy Spirit carries out His ministry. He is the Spirit of truth, the truth of the Scriptures (John 16:13). ". . . God hath from the beginning chosen you to salvation through sanctification of the Spirit and belief of the truth" (2 Thess. 2:13). The Lord Jesus prayed to the Father, "Sanctify them through thy truth: thy word is truth" (John 17:17).

It is by means of the Spirit-ministered Word that we see and understand the facts concerning our position of sanctification in the Lord Jesus. Without the spiritual facts, there would be nothing on which we could base our faith. But as we see that the Holy Spirit has already sanctified us in Christ, we are able to trust Him to separate us to God in our condition. The Spirit carries out His *subjective work* in our lives from the basis, the source, the standing, the position, the *objective truth,* of our eternal completeness in our risen Lord Jesus Christ.

In this matter of faith in the Word, it is essential to distinguish between God's *promises* and His *facts.* Promises are to be anticipated; facts are to be accepted. We wait on our Father to fulfill His promises in His own time, according to His will and His integrity. On the other hand, facts are to be appropriated and enjoyed now; we are to accept them with thanksgiving.

By faith we know that we are justified (Rom. 5:1), that we are reconciled (Col. 1:20-22), that we are accepted (Eph. 1:5-7), and that we are sanctified (Acts 26:18). Since the Holy Spirit ministers to us through the channel of faith, He gives us in our condition what we appropriate from our position. For instance, in the matter of peace, from our position of justification we receive peace concerning the penalty of our sins; for our reconciliation, peace with God; from our acceptance, the peace of God; and from our sanctification, peace and assurance that He will conform us to the image of our Lord Jesus.

Consecration   Without a clear understanding of our position of sanctification, there can be no valid consecration. To dedicate, to separate, to consecrate ourselves to God is simply our response of faith to the separation, the sanctification in which God has already placed us. It is acknowledging our position of sanctification. Consecration does not call on us to do anything, but to rest in what God has already done. Unless we know that we have been sanctified in the Lord Jesus, we cannot respond in consecration to Him.

Pseudo   Why does so much sincere consecration
Consecration   amount to nothing? The main reason is that most well-meaning Christians seek to consecrate to God that which He has totally and forever rejected. Not yet understanding their position of sanctification as new creations in Christ, they consecrate *self* to God in the hope

that the "old man" will become spiritual and thus usable in His service.

The believer must learn by two means the fact that the self-life is unimprovable. (1) Specific Scripture: God never intends to improve the old man, because "the natural man receiveth not the things of the Spirit of God . . .neither can he know them, because they are spiritually discerned" (1 Cor. 2:14). Further, "the flesh lusteth against the Spirit, and the Spirit against the flesh: and these are contrary the one to the other" (Gal. 5:17). Everything of the first Adam is unalterably opposed to everything of the Last Adam. Self is implacable in its attitude toward God, having the very essence of the enemy. "Because the carnal mind is enmity against God: for it is not subject to the law of God, neither indeed can be" (Rom. 8:7). (2) Personal experience: One's daily life proves beyond a doubt that the sinful Adamic source within never changes. The awakened and honest believer must admit that self is as capable of sin after fifty years of the Christian life as it was before he was saved—sometimes, it seems, even more so!

No, our Father can accept nothing of the Adamic life, no matter how "good" or "religious" it may seem in the natural realm. And when the believer sees that God has taken all the old life to the cross and crucified it with Christ, he will likewise count (reckon) it crucified, and take his place of consecration as alive to God in Christ Jesus.

Scriptural True, acceptable, abiding consecration is
Consecration expressed most clearly in Romans 6:13, "Neither yield to your members as instruments of unrighteousness unto sin: but yield yourselves unto God, as those that are alive from the dead, and your members as instruments of righteousness unto God." Here we have the key statement in Scripture concerning consecration: *"as those that are alive from the dead."* We know that the old man did not rise from the dead. The wages of sin is death, and the sinful Adamic life was condemned and crucified in Christ on the cross (Rom. 6:6). But the recreated life, the new man in Christ Jesus, arose from the dead in His resurrection. ". . . you were also raised up with Him through faith in the work-

ing of God, who raised Him from the dead. And when you were dead in your transgressions and the uncircumcision of your flesh, He made you alive together with Him . . ." (Col. 2:12, 13, NASB).

It is this new life, our Christian life, the life that is already hid with Christ in God, that we are to yield, to consecrate, to set apart unto our Father. It is the only acceptable life—the life that He has already accepted in His beloved Son. In consecration we are carrying out our responsibility of responding to that which He has already done, of willing according to His will, of gladly yielding to Him that which already belongs to Him. In the matter of *life*, it is "yield yourselves unto God . . . and your members as instruments of righteousness" (Rom. 6:13). In the matter of *service*, it is "present your bodies a living sacrifice, holy, acceptable" (Rom. 12:1).

Consecration is based upon reckoning (Rom. 6:11). We turn *from* the old man by counting ourselves to have died unto sin and self. We turn *to* our position in the risen Lord by counting ourselves as new creations alive unto God in Christ Jesus. Abide above!

24 Identification and Growth

Positional truth is the basis of every sphere of our Christian life. But nowhere are we more dependent on the principle of position than in the understanding of our identification with the Lord Jesus in His death to sin and resurrection to God. As in all positional steps, identification is not experiential, but is a matter of placing our faith in the facts of the Word. Whereas justification has to do with *birth*, identification has to do with *growth*, which is to continue until we see Him face to face.

Position   When we received the Lord Jesus as our Saviour and thus were born into Him as our life, all that He *is* and all that He *has* became ours. Justification (His righteousness) was perhaps all that we could apprehend at the time, but that was only the beginning of an infinity of wonders into which we are to enter, now and throughout eternity. Because of our grace-given position in the Heir, we are "heirs of God, and joint-heirs with Christ" (Rom. 8:17).

All is held in trust for us in Christ, our new position, and becomes our condition as we are taken forward, step by step, in faith. When we are able to receive and appreciate the benefits of the riches of Romans 1-5, then He is free to take us into the reality of the wealth of Romans 6-8. When we are firmly established in the positional truth of Christ dying *for* our sins and rising again for our justification (Rom. 4:25), then we are prepared to see our position and enter into the benefits of our having died and risen *with* Him (Rom. 6:5).

Now, let us look at some of the positional truths concerning our identification with the Lord Jesus. "For if we have become united with Him in the likeness of His death, certainly we shall be also *in the likeness* of His resurrection" (Rom. 6:5, NASB). For us to be reborn, newly created in the risen life of the Savior, God had to free us from the penalty of sin and the nature of the fallen Adam. He accomplished this by placing us in Christ on the cross, by identifying each one of us, as future believers, with Him. Thus, when Christ died *to* sin (out of the realm and reign of the principle of sin), we as sinners died to sin in Him. Why should this be so difficult to comprehend when we understand clearly that the Lord Jesus died for every one of our sins (all future at the time) on that same cross? He was identified with our sin in order that we might become identified with His righteousness. "For he hath made him to be sin for us, who knew no sin; that we might be made the righteousness of God in him" (2 Cor. 5:21).

We know that the Lord Jesus rose again, once He had paid in full the wages of sin. Since we were identified with Him in His death, and thereby were freed from both the penalty and power of sin, we know that we arose with Him in His resurrection. It could not be otherwise. "Now if we have died with Christ, we believe that we shall also live with Him" (Rom. 6:8, NASB).

"For the death that He died, He died to sin, once for all; but the life that He lives, He lives to God" (Rom. 6:10, NASB). The Lord Jesus died to the power and reign of sin, and He rose again in the "power of an endless life" (Heb. 7:16). Identified with Him on the cross, we too died to sin's tyrannical dominion and "have been buried with Him through [spiritual] baptism into death: in order that as Christ was raised from the dead through the glory of the Father, so we too might walk in newness of life" (Rom. 6:4, NASB).

God provides the facts before He calls for faith. Early in Romans 6 we are asked, "Know ye not" that all who were identified with the Lord Jesus were identified in His death (v. 3)? In verse 6 Paul says, "Knowing this, that our old self was crucified with *Him*" (Rom. 6:6, NASB). It is not until the facts of our identification with Christ are understood that we are admonished to exercise faith. In this way there is no effort or struggle to consider, because we *know*.

Yes, it is in the clear light of identification with Christ in His death and resurrection that direction is given to "consider yourselves to be dead to sin, but alive to God in Christ Jesus" (Rom. 6:11, NASB). It would be utterly impossible for our Father even to suggest that we count ourselves as having died to sin and become alive to Him in Jesus if it were not already true of us! Nor could He ever call on us to consecrate ourselves to Him "as alive from the dead" (Rom. 6:13) if He had not already made us "new creations" in the risen Christ (2 Cor. 5:17).

However, true as our identification with the Lord Jesus is, if we are not fully aware of the facts we will derive little benefit from them in our daily life. And that is where we need them. Moreover, unless we realize our need of the separating (sanctifying) power of our death and life in Him, there will be no motivation for our faith to reach out and receive. To dwell on a positional fact is to see it clearly, to believe it, to count on it, to receive and appropriate the practical reality of it with thanksgiving. "Rooted and built up in him, and stablished in the faith, as ye have been taught, abounding therein with thanksgiving" (Col. 2:7).

> Death and judgment are behind us,
>   Grace and glory are before;
> All the billows rolled o'er Jesus,
> There they spent their utmost power.
> Jesus died, and we died with Him,
>   Buried in His grave we lay,
>   One with Him in Resurrection,
> Now "in Him" in Heaven's bright day.

The gracious Spirit of truth revealed to us that the Lord Jesus died for our sins, and by faith in the facts we entered into the position of justification (which included our complete and eternal salvation). When the Holy Spirit reveals to us the truth of our Lord Jesus having died to sin, and our identification with Him in that death and resurrection, by faith in the facts we acknowledge our position—we reckon ourselves to have died to sin and to be forever alive to God in Christ.

That which we reckon in our position becomes experiential in our condition. As we count ourselves to have died to sin on the cross, the effect of that cross is applied by the Spirit to the sinful self-life. "For we which live are alway delivered unto death for Jesus' sake . . ." (2 Cor. 4:11). Self is crucified, held in the place of death, as we are led into sacrificial paths for His glory. As self is thus dealt with by the cross, our condition reflects progressively the facts of our position in Christ. ". . . That the life also of Jesus might be made manifest in our mortal flesh" (2 Cor.4:11).

Condition   "But God be thanked, that ye were the servants of sin, but ye have obeyed from the heart that form of doctrine which was delivered you. Being then made free from [the power of] sin, ye became the servants of righteousness" (Rom. 6:17, 18). Our daily experience can be no more true than the doctrine we hold, and by which we are held.

The steps would be as follows: (1) We finally see and understand our *position,* our identification with Christ in having died to the dominion of sin and been made alive to God in Him. (2) We become aware of the need to be separated in our *condition* from self and to Christ. (3) We then exercise faith in the completed work of our *position* by reckoning upon the facts of our death and resurrection in Christ. (4) On the basis of this faith, the Holy Spirit is free to translate the truth of our position into our daily condition.

The Spirit of Christ is extremely practical in His operations. He uses everyday means in bringing our positional sanctification into our experience. As we reckon upon the fact of self's crucifixion, He conveys the effect of that finished work into our lives through daily circumstances. Due to our weakness and sinfulness, He is able to utilize situations and human relationships to show us what we are in ourselves. We are thereby faced with the choice: self, or Christ. If we count ourselves to have died to sin and self, the emancipation of the cross is experienced within. And as we abide in the Lord

Jesus, knowing ourselves to be alive to God in Him, He is free to manifest Himself more fully in our condition. This is spiritual growth. The "works" of the flesh are curtailed, the "fruit" of the Spirit is revealed. "For to me to live is Christ . . ." (Phil. 1:21).

". . . unless a grain of wheat falls into the earth and dies, it remains by itself alone; but if it dies, it bears much fruit" (John 12:24, NASB). This statement of the principle of life out of death applies primarily to the Lord Jesus Christ. He is the Grain of Wheat who refused to abide alone as God's only begotten Son, but gave Himself at Calvary to become the "firstborn, among many brethren" (Rom. 8:29). Since He died and rose again, thereby bringing forth "much fruit," and that harvest being after His kind, our lives as similar grains of wheat are based on the same principle of life out of death.

No matter how self-contained and comfortable our Christian life may be, there is bound to develop a deep heart-hunger to see others become grains of wheat. The Lord Jesus "shall see his seed . . . He shall see of the travail of his soul, and shall be satisfied" (Isa. 53:10, 11). His heart-hunger is expressed through Paul: "My little children, of whom I travail in birth again until Christ be formed in you" (Gal. 4:19). And the Spirit of Christ yearns in our hearts that the Lord Jesus may gain a rich and lasting harvest of golden grain through us.

This entire life-out-of-death process is directly related to our reckoning upon our position of life out of death. As we yearn to be used, to multiply, to be brought to harvest, the Holy Spirit takes us down into death in our experience. He "plants" or "buries" us in this difficult situation or that dark area and, as the old life is thus held in the place of death (inoperative), the new life grows up and is manifested not only in us, but in others through us. "So then death worketh in us, but life in you [others]" (2 Cor. 4:12).

Conversely, when we are self-centered and refuse the path of the cross, we think little of others and everything of ourselves. We scheme, fight, maneuver, and even pray to "abide alone." But the Lord Jesus has established the principle that "whosoever will save his life shall lose it [no fruit, no harvest]:

but whosoever will lose his life for my sake ['alway delivered unto death for Jesus' sake'], the same shall save it [shall see it multiplied and harvested in others]" (Luke 9:24).

Actually, the Holy Spirit patiently uses everything (and everyone) in His process of bringing us to the grain-of-wheat stage. When we are self-centered and carnal, He applies the appropriate pressures—perhaps in the physical body, the home, or the place of work—thereby, in time, causing us to hunger to be Christ-centered.

When we begin to see and hate the self-life for what it is, when we begin to see and love the Lord Jesus for who He is, then we become willing for the Holy Spirit to take self into death in order that Christ may be formed in us. "We are assured and know that [God being a partner in their labor], all things work together and are [fitting into a plan] for good to those who love God and are called according to [His] design and purpose. For those whom He foreknew—of whom He was aware and loved beforehand He also destined from the beginning (foreordaining them) to be molded into the image of His Son [and share inwardly His likeness], that He might become the first-born among many brethren" (Rom. 8:28, 29, Amplified).

25 Sin and Purged Conscience

Briefly, it can be said that due to the Fall man came into possession of a moral sense to distinguish right and wrong, known as conscience. Man's sinful condition, however, renders conscience an unreliable guide. Nevertheless, the Holy Spirit works on the conscience in bringing conviction of sin.

The Natural Man Due to such factors as heredity, social and religious training, and environment, the conscience of the unbeliever has an erratic range all the way from good to very bad. But either way, its ground of reference is wrong since it is centered in the self-life. ". . . When they measure themselves with themselves and compare themselves with one another, they are without understanding and behave unwisely" (2 Cor. 10:12, Amplified). At best, the unsaved are under legal bondage, ". . . they are a law to themselves. . . . They show that the essential requirements of the Law are written in their hearts and are operating there; with which their conscience (sense of right and wrong) also bears witness . . ." (Rom. 2:14, 15, Amplified).

Even when the unbeliever's conscience is clear, this state is often attained by a combination of rationalization and good works, resulting in self-righteousness. Hence his so-called good conscience is the very element that tends to keep him from seeing his need for God's righteousness and life. On the other hand, when his conscience is bad, he flees from God with a sense of despair because of personal unworthiness. It is only when the Holy Spirit convicts the mind, heart, and conscience concerning sin, whether of self-righteousness or of unworthiness, that the sinner can see his need of turning to Christ.

The Carnal Man   As far as his conscience is concerned, the carnal Christian is much the same as the unbeliever. By dint of self-effort to produce some good works for God, and the blind rationalization of comparing himself with supposedly weaker Christians, he is able sporadically to maintain some semblance of a good conscience. This very feeling, false as it is, tends to exaggerate his dependence on himself. "But he that glorieth, let him glory in the Lord. For not he that commendeth himself is approved, but whom the Lord commendeth" (2 Cor. 10:17, 18).

When the carnal believer's conscience is bad, he seeks to hide from God, and even attempts to place the blame for his sinfulness on others. Yet, the Holy Spirit often works through the conscience to turn such a person to the Lord Jesus for cleansing from unrighteousness and for spiritual growth. "Let us all come forward and draw near with true (honest and sincere) hearts in unqualified assurance and absolute conviction engendered by faith [that is, by that leaning of the entire human personality on God in absolute trust and confidence in His power, wisdom and goodness], having our hearts sprinkled and purified from a guilty (evil) conscience . . ." (Heb. 10:22, Amplified).

The Spiritual Man   The believer who rests in his position rather than his condition, who abides in his risen Lord in the presence of the Father, is growing spiritually. He is fully assured that "Christ also hath once suffered for sins, the just for the unjust, that he might *bring us to God*" (1 Peter 3:18, italics mine). By simply faith in the facts, he acknowledges his place in Christ who is his life, the One who, "when he had by himself purged our sins, sat down on the right hand of the Majesty on high" (Heb. 1:3). Knowing his sins to be purged once for all, his conscience is thereby clear, since "the worshippers once purged" have "no more conscience of sins" (Heb. 10:2).

The spiritually minded believer is conscious of sin *in* him, but he is fully assured that there is no sin *on* him; all of his sin has been laid on the Lord Jesus. Although his condition is needy, for he is indwelt by the principle of sin, he *lives* in his position in Christ. His constant resources for spiritual growth are received from on high. He knows his freedom to "come boldly unto the throne of grace" in order that he may "obtain mercy, and find grace to help in time of need" (Heb. 4:16).

When the growing believer sins, his conscience and his communion with the Father being thereby disturbed, he freely confesses his sin. He knows that the Lord Jesus "is faithful and just to forgive us our sins, and to cleanse us from all unrighteousness" (1 John 1:9). He also has recourse to the truth that when he does sin he has "an advocate with the Father, Jesus Christ the righteous" (1 John 2:1). Hence a pure conscience and communion are restored and maintained, and he is free to continue his fellowship with the Father and the Son. He has learned that "if we walk in the light . . . we have fellowship one with another, and the blood of Jesus Christ his Son cleanseth us from all sin" (1 John 1:7).

Condition   The condition-centered Christian has no other recourse but to fight against indwelling sin, and thus seek to control self as best he can. Added to this intolerable burden is the frustrating fact that God does not seem to help him in this endeavor. He is immersed in the defeat of Romans 7. He battles here below, only to lose; he should rest above, where he is sure to win.

One of the chief reasons so many believers are spiritually ill (as well as mentally and physically) is a guilty, oppressed conscience. They are laboring under the burden of their unrighteous condition, rather than resting in the liberty of their righteous position. Sad to say, there aren't many of God's people today who know anything at all about a "pure," a "perfect," conscience. Countless Christians, including those who are awakened and hungry to grow, are bound by a bad conscience. They are honestly aware of their sinful condition, but are only vaguely aware of their perfect position.

This chapter has to do with the basic reason for the guilty conscience, which is the indwelling principle of sin. The next chapter will deal with the product of that principle, sins committed. First the cause, then the effect. There is a tremendous paradox in the Christian who, although redeemed by the Lord Jesus Christ from the penalty and tyranny of sin, nevertheless is rendered spiritually helpless and useless by an overwhelming burden of guilt.

We are thinking of the hungry-hearted Christian who is awakened to the sin of self, since he is the only one who is ready (prepared by the Holy Spirit) to be freed from this guilty condition. Awareness of need is the primary motivation for intelligent faith. Is this not the cry of the honest, struggling, guilt-ridden believer?: ". . . I do not understand my own actions—I am baffled, bewildered. I do not practice or accomplish what I wish, but I do the very thing that I loathe [which my moral instinct condemns]. . . . However, it is no longer I who do the deed, but the sin [principle] which is at home in me and has possession of me" (Rom. 7:15, 17, Amplified). Here is the progressing believer who sees his condition, but not as yet his position.

Position   There is but one place in which faith can rest, and that is in our Lord Jesus, where the Father has positioned us. And it is only in that abiding place that our conscience can be clear with regard to indwelling sin. Our guilt cannot be relieved through removal of the sin within, because that principle will be present as long as we reside in our unredeemed body. Nor is there hope of relief through improvement of self, since in the flesh there dwells no good thing to improve.

There was also the problem of a guilty conscience prior to Calvary. Then, into the holy place made with hands "went the high priest alone once every year, not without blood, which he offered for himself, and for the errors of the people . . . which was a figure for the time then present, in which were offered both gifts and sacrifices, that could not make him that did the service perfect, as pertaining to the *conscience*. . . . But Christ being come an high priest . . . by a greater and more perfect tabernacle, not made with hands . . . neither by the blood of goats and calves, but by his own blood he entered in once into the holy place, having obtained eternal redemption for us" (Heb. 9:7, 9, 11, 12).

Yes, our Lord Jesus "appeared to put away sin by the sacrifice of himself" (Heb. 9:26). ". . . we are sanctified through the offering of the body of Jesus Christ once for all. . . . But this man, after he had offered one sacrifice for sins for ever, sat down on the right hand of God. . . . For by one offering he hath perfected forever them that are sanctified" (Heb. 10:10, 12, 14). As new creations in Christ Jesus, we have been redeemed from the penalty of indwelling sin; further, we have been sanctified (separated) from the domination of that same principle of sin. We have sin in us, but not on us; always indwelling, but never imputed!

It is essential to know how definitely and thoroughly God dealt with this principle of sin, especially since its presence within us is so burdensome. ". . . God sending his own Son in the likeness of sinful flesh, and for sin, condemned sin in the flesh" (Rom. 8:3). The principle of sin has not been forgiven, it has not been cleansed; neither has it been improved, nor removed. But thanks be to God it has been condemned by the crucifixion of the Cross. In His flesh, our Lord Jesus condemned the sin in our flesh. Thus condemned, there can now be no condemnation for us.

"There is therefore now no condemnation to them which are in Christ Jesus. . . . For the law of the Spirit of life in Christ Jesus hath made me free from the law of sin and death" (Rom. 8:1, 2). It is due to this blessed fact that our conscience finds peace, and is purged from the guilt of indwelling sin.

It should not be difficult for us to make the correct choice between the consciousness of our condition, and the revelation of our position. If, because of feelings and lack of scriptural knowledge, we put more stock in our condition than our position, we will continue to labor under the intolerable burden of a defiled conscience. But if we agree with God concerning His condemnation of the old man, there is a perfectly peaceful conscience for us in the matter of indwelling sin. It is the infinite difference between our telling Him what we are in ourselves (condition), or heeding His testimony as to what we are in His Son (position). The former means guilt and enslavement, the latter freedom and growth.

At Calvary, when our Lord Jesus was made to be sin for us, He was crucified and thereby sin was condemned. At the same time, He took each potential believer as a sinner down into that death. Then He brought us up out of death, as new creations, in His resurrection life. Now and forever, the only position we have as believers is before our Father in His risen Son, cut off (sanctified) from our old relationship to indwelling sin by our death and resurrection in Him.

Once for all, the Lord Jesus has separated us in death and resurrection from both the guilt and the power of indwelling sin. "But now once at the consummation [of the ages] He has been manifested to put away sin by the sacrifice of Himself" (Heb. 9:26, NASB). "For both he that sanctifieth and they who are sanctified are all of one . . ." (Heb. 2:11). Resting in this position not only purges our conscience from all guilt concerning the self-life, but also gives us increasing freedom from its domination.

Why not acknowledge and thank Him for this wonderful position, purchased at infinite price and so freely given? Anything we do short of resting in Him as our position, anything we attempt to do beyond that rest, is to slight the perfection of His life and work. "For you have died and your life is hidden with Christ in God" (Col. 3:3, NASB). "How much more shall the blood of Christ, who through the eternal Spirit offered himself without spot to God, purge your *conscience* from dead works to serve the living God?" (Heb. 9:14 italics mine).

26 Sins and Conscience

"We have been sanctified through the offering of the body of Jesus Christ once for all" (Heb. 10:10, NASB). It is because of His work on the cross that our conscience is at peace despite indwelling sin. Once we know our conscience to be purged concerning the ever-present principle of sin, we can rest in our Father's gracious provision for the sins we commit—but not until. The fact of sin within can in no way keep us from resting and rejoicing in our risen Lord, abiding in the very presence of our Father. He Himself, after condemning sin in the flesh, "raised us up with Him, and seated us with Him in the heavenly *places,* in Christ Jesus" (Eph. 2:6, NASB).

Advocate   When we are at rest concerning sin, through abiding in the risen Lord, we are established and ready to receive His answer to the problem of *sins committed.* There are two factors that come into play when we have sinned: Christ's advocacy (this chapter); our confession (next chapter). His advocacy is the foundation for our confession.

"My little children, these things write I unto you, that ye sin not. And if any man sin, we have an advocate with the Father, Jesus Christ the righteous" (1 John 2:1). An advocate is one who speaks in support of another. Our Lord Jesus has entered heaven, "now to appear in the presence of God for us" (Heb. 9:24). As our High Priest, He is in God's presence on our behalf; He is there as our propitiation, our atonement.

"But this man, after he had offered once sacrifice for sins forever, sat down on the right hand of God" (Heb. 10:12). He is seated because, as far as our acceptance and position before God are concerned, there is nothing more required either to do, or say. ". . . by his own blood he entered in once into the holy place, having obtained eternal redemption for us" (Heb. 9:12).

As our Advocate, the Lord Jesus is before the Father, maintaining us in fellowship with Him. There, in our position, we are "perfected forever" (Heb. 10:14). Here, in our condition, indwelt by the principle of sin, we are often overcome by its power. Nevertheless, by the ministry of the Spirit our condition is being perfected, or matured.

When we sin in word, thought, or deed, consciously or unconsciously, our heavenly Advocate speaks to the Father on our behalf. His faithful intercession is justly founded on His perfect work and Person, and thereby our right of position in our Father's presence is forever maintained. Although our sins are never imputed to us, they do defile us and hinder our fellowship with the Father.

Even though God fully and justly accepts the atonement of His Son on our behalf, He in no way passes over or tolerates our sins. He has not only provided His Son as our Savior, but also as our Advocate. "If any man sin, we have an advocate with the Father, Jesus Christ the righteous" (1 John 2:1). Further, He has given us the responsibility and privilege of confessing our sins. ". . . He that is washed [atonement] needeth not save to wash his feet [confession] . . ." (John 13:10). For, "if we confess our sins, he is faithful and just to forgive us our sins, and to cleanse us from all unrighteousness" (1 John 1:9).

Not only do we have an Advocate in heaven before the Father, but we also have an Advocate within our spirit. The word "Comforter" in John 14:16 is rendered "advocate" in 1 John 2:1. We need, and have, a dual advocacy! When we sin, Jesus intercedes for us on the ground of His having borne the judgment of that very sin. The indwelling Spirit acts on our conscience to produce confession. Thereby we have the assurance of the sin having been forgiven, the unrighteousness cleansed, and our fellowship with the Father completely restored.

"So too the (Holy) Spirit comes to our aid and bears us up in our weakness; for we do not know what prayer to offer nor how to offer it worthily as we ought, but the Spirit Himself goes to meet our supplication and pleads in our behalf with unspeakable yearnings and groanings too deep for utterance. And He Who searches the hearts of men knows what is in the mind of the (Holy) Spirit—what His intent is—because the Spirit intercedes and pleads [before God] in behalf of the saints according to and in harmony with God's will" (Rom. 8:26, 27, Amplified). "He restoreth my soul: he leadeth me in the paths of righteousness for his name's sake" (Ps. 23:3).

The fact that we need constant advocacy before our Father in no way detracts from the truth of our perfect and eternal standing in the Lord Jesus. The Word makes it clear that each of us, at the moment of our new birth, is fully accepted in the Beloved. We are complete in Him, perfectly and forever forgiven, justified, sanctified, and glorified—through His death, resurrection, and ascension—never to come into judgment, but have passed from death to life as new creations in Christ Jesus. Before God, we are not in the flesh (the fallen, first Adam race), but in the Spirit (the new, Last Adam creation). Having died unto sin, self, Satan, the law, and the world, we are now and forever alive in our risen Lord "after the power of an endless life" (Heb. 7:16).

Condition   Although we are not in the flesh as to our position, we are in the body pertaining to our condition. While we are complete in Christ who is our life, as new creations in Him we have to be matured in the midst of the pressures and exigencies of everyday experience. Moreover, all is carried on in this "body of death" which is indwelt by the principle of sin. Therefore, we need the two faithful Advocates who undertake to fulfill God's purpose in and through us, despite the power of the world, the flesh, and the devil.

The negative and positive aspects of our spiritual growth could be summarized in these words: (1) We are to consider ourselves to have died to sin, thus giving the Holy Spirit freedom to apply the finished work of the cross to indwelling sin, so that it may be progressively held inoperative. (2) At the same time, we are to consider ourselves (as new creations) alive to God in Christ Jesus, abiding in Him as a branch in the True Vine.

Praise the Lord that, if and when we do sin in thought, word, or deed, consciously or otherwise, "we have an advocate with the Father, Jesus Christ the righteous: and he is the propitiation for our sins" (1 John 2:1, 2). His advocacy has nothing whatsoever to do with our eternal standing, nor is it the placating of an angry, vengeful God (He already bore the wrath due our sin). But in His personal reconciliation on the cross and righteous presence before God, He makes it possible for our Father justly to show us mercy despite our sins.

The chasm between our perfect position and our imperfect condition is bridged by His advocacy and cleansing. Our only source of life and growth is in Chirst. From that completed source our condition is gradually developed. Our progress on earth is dependent on our fellowship with Him in heaven. Because of sins committed, that fellowship must be restored by Christ's advocacy and our confession. As we mature spiritually, there are fewer sins to be confessed. How futile to seek to deal with sins in any other way than through His advocacy and our confession!

There are those who, for one reason or another, by-pass the identification truths of Romans 6, and rely rather on confession and cleansing for dealing with the problem of sin. But there is no real spiritual progress unless the source of sins is dealt with continually by the Spirit's application of the cross. He carries on that ministry as we consider self having been crucified. Apart from this, there is nothing but the endless struggle of the treadmill—sinning, repenting, confessing, but then sinning again and again. On this erroneous basis there is no dealing with the source that relentlessly produces the sins.

Rather, we are to learn to rely on the cross to deal with the sin principle, as we abide in the risen Lord for our spiritual growth. Then, if we do sin, we depend on our Advocate in heaven to reestablish our fellowship with the Father, and our Advocate within to repair the spiritual damage by means of conviction, leading us to repentance and confession.

While living in this world it is heartening to realize that we neither have to ask nor to plead for His intercession. Both our Advocates are unceasingly interceding for us. "Wherefore he is able also to save them to the uttermost that come unto God by him, seeing he ever liveth to make intercession for them" (Heb. 7:25). The fact that we commit sins despite such faithful ministry does not reflect on the worth or effectiveness of the intercession, but on *our* faithfulness. We fail to count on our death to sin and our life in Christ.

If it were not for the constant intercession of our heavenly Advocate, our faith would surely fail when we are overcome, or when we willingly submit to the tyranny of sin and self. Think of what happened when Simon Peter denied his Lord: ". . . Simon, Simon, behold, Satan hath desired to have you, that he may sift you as wheat; but I have prayed for thee, that thy faith fail not: and when thou art converted [restored], strengthen thy brethren" (Luke 22:31, 32).

The Lord Jesus did not pray that Peter might not sin, but, having fallen, that his faith would respond to His Lord's advocacy. His faithful intercession kept Peter from self-centered despair, giving him grace for true repentance, deep sorrow for his sin, purity of conscience, and restoration of fellowship.

Position   At rest in our position in the Lord Jesus, we can depend on the Holy Spirit to take us through all that is required for our growth in the purpose of God. "Inasmuch, then, as we have in Jesus, the Son of God, a great High Priest who has passed into Heaven itself, let us hold firmly to our profession [confession] of faith. For we have not a High Priest who is unable to feel for us in our weaknesses, but one who was tempted in every respect just as we are tempted, and yet did not sin. Therefore let us come boldly to the throne of grace, that we may receive mercy and find grace to help us in our times of need" (Heb. 4:14-16, Weymouth).

We must face the fact that there is going to be constant need, even as we are most fully learning to hate (reject) self and love the Lord Jesus. In that God is "just, and the justifier of him which believeth in Jesus" (Rom. 3:26), He is free to utilize even our failures as He develops our condition. ". . . all things work *together* for good to them that love God . . ." (Rom. 8:28). In all that we go through we are taught more fully to reject self via the cross, and to abide in Christ via our position. At the same time, we are to count more on His advocacy and rejoice in the privilege of our fellowship with the Father. Moreover, we thus become better fitted to understand and minister to our weaker brethren, knowing full well what they are going through. ". . . when thou art converted [restored], strengthen thy brethren" (Luke 22:32).

If we turn for our position of rest to fight against sin, and work to improve our condition, we have stepped off the rock of grace, into the swamp of self-effort. But as we turn from self to abide in our Lord at the right hand of the Father, we find that He has dealt with both the principle of sin, and our sins.

We can rest in the fact that His work of atonement is never repeated, as His Word assures us: " 'And their sins and offences I will remember no longer.' But where these have been forgiven no further offering for sin is required" (Heb. 10:17, 18, Weymouth). We depend on the fact that His work as Advocate is never interrupted, "seeing he ever liveth to make intercession for them" (Heb. 7:25).

"Since therefore, brethren, we have confidence to enter the holy place by the blood of Jesus, by a new and living way which He inaugurated for us through the veil, that is, His flesh, and since we have a great priest over the house of God, let us draw near with a sincere heart in full assurance of faith, having our hearts sprinkled clean from an evil conscience . . ." (Heb. 10:19-22, NASB).

27 *Sins and Light*

"But if we [really] are living and walking in the Light as He [Himself] is in the Light, we have [true, unbroken] fellowship with one another, and the blood of Jesus Christ His Son cleanses (removes) us from all sin and guilt . . ." (1 John 1:7, Amplified).

What is this light in which we have been placed, in which we are to live and walk? "And this is the message . . . which we have heard from Him and now are reporting to you: God is Light and there is no darkness in Him at all—no, not in any way" (1 John 1:5, Amplified). Since our Father is Light, our Lord Jesus is Light also. "For God, who commanded the light to shine out of darkness, hath shined in our hearts, to give the light of the knowledge of the glory of God in the face of Jesus Christ" (2 Cor. 4:6).

While here on earth, the Lord Jesus said, "I am the light of the world" (John 8:12). Nevertheless, the full extent of that light was kept almost totally obscured by His humanity. For a brief moment, while on the Mount of Transfiguration, He allowed the true light within to be manifested. "And [He] was transfigured before them: and his face did shine as the sun, and his raiment was white as the light" (Matt. 17:2). Peter wrote later that he and the others "were eyewitnesses of his majesty" (2 Peter 1:16). At present, our Lord Jesus is in glory, "on the right hand of the Majesty on high" (Heb. 1:3). It is in His light that we are to abide and walk, for "now are ye light in the Lord: walk as children of light" (Eph. 5:8).

Every Christian is positionally in the light, but until he learns to abide and walk in that light he can only struggle on in the darkness of sin and self. "For once you were darkness, but now you are light in the Lord. . . . For the fruit—the effect, the product—of the Light . . . [consists] in every form of kindly goodness, uprightness of heart and trueness of life" (Eph. 5:8, 9 Amplified). Our blood-bought position is in the light of our Father's presence.

Condition The healthy babe in Christ begins well, whether or not he knows anything at all concerning his position in the light. Being a child spiritually, he is handled as such by the Father. He feels that the Lord Jesus is very close to him and is leading him by the hand. He is filled with the joy of the Lord, and loves Him with all his heart. Although he is looking to the Lord Jesus, he is still self-centered because of ignorance regarding his position in Him. He is taken up mainly with what Christ has done, is doing, and will do *for him;* he is, in turn, seeking to live and work *for* the Lord. For the most part, he is emotionally motivated and therefore affected by his condition rather than his position.

Later, during the believer's spiritual adolescence, the Lord begins His reversal of all this. The emphasis in the life is to be shifted from dwelling on what Jesus Christ has done to rejoicing in who, what, and where He is; from being happy and active, to being like Him; from living and working for Christ, to living in and working through Him; from what the believer is in himself, to what he is in Christ and what He is in the believer. From condition to position—"not I, but Christ."

Of necessity, the transitional process from a condition-centered to a position-centered life is extremely painful. "Now no chastening [child-training] for the present seemeth to be joyous, but grievous: nevertheless afterward it yieldeth the peaceable fruit of righteousness unto them which are exercised thereby" (Heb. 12:11). "For whom the Lord loveth he chasteneth . . ." (Heb. 12:6).

In spite of the believer's good beginning, and in the midst of his joy and activity for the Lord, self begins to creep back into the picture. The indwelling principle of sin once more asserts its tyrannical power, and the world regains its attraction. Peace and love tend to weaken and drain away. The "quiet time" quietly dies. Study of the Word becomes burdensome work. The conscience is defiled; sins are no longer confessed, but excused. The eyes are off the Lord, the struggle with self is on—simply because condition has been given precedence over position.

Now the faltering believer becomes keenly aware of self, and only vaguely aware of the Son. Desperately upset about his failing condition, he struggles to improve himself, all the while begging God to give him relief and "victory." This is the vantage point Satan has been waiting for. He slyly leads the believer to compare the present condition with the happy, carefree days gone by, and to question every realm of belief, thus shaking all reliance on the Word and the Lord. He ruthlessly puts the wavering Christian on the defensive in every aspect of his life and walk. He applies downward pressure, and fills the heart with the gnawing remorse of self-condemnation.

When the believer allows the Enemy to spread the choking smog of self-accusation over his life, the realization of his righteousness in Christ is dimmed. The goal of Satan is to lure the believer back onto the ground of condemnation, in order to negate the benefits of his resurrection with Christ and his union with Him in the heavenlies.

Those who are not established on the "no condemnation" ground of Romans 8:1 make very little spiritual progress. They go just so far and then bog down; their fruit falls before it ripens. But the destroying power of the Enemy is rendered null and void when the believer rests in the truth that "the law of the Spirit of Life in Christ Jesus hath made me free from the law of sin and death" (Rom. 8:2).

Although the Holy Spirit, as Convictor, puts the heart in an agony of conviction of sins, He never points downward. While Satan's accusation results in self-consciousness, Holy Spirit conviction leads to Christ-consciousness. When He convicts the heart and conscience concerning sins, He leads the believer to the self-judgment of confession. He then points upward to the remedy for sins committed—the blood that has opened the way to the peace and life of our position in the light of

God's presence. "Having therefore, brethren, boldness to enter into the holiest by the blood of Jesus" (Heb. 10:19).

The Enemy spurs the failing one to self-effort by holding the impossible standard of perfection over the very imperfect believer's head. He agitates continually for immediate and complete rectification of the failing condition. But the patient Holy Spirit, on the other hand, allows time for development, graciously reminding of the ever-available and finished work of the shed blood for our cleansing from all unrighteousness throughout the process of growth. He gently leads the faltering believer from self-centeredness and darkness to Christ-centeredness and light. To bring this about, the Spirit of truth presents positional truth: "If [since] ye then be risen with Christ, seek those things which are above, where Christ sitteth on the right hand of God" (Col. 3:1). "For you have died and your life is hidden with Christ in God" (Col. 3:3, NASB).

Position   The awakened Christian who is not resting in his position becomes discouraged by his condition. Therefore, confession of his sins is sporadic and he has little or no assurance of being cleansed from all unrighteousness. He is out of fellowship with the Father and the Son, and finds himself convicted by the Holy Spirit whom he is grieving. He is also under the domination of sin and self, as well as the condemnation of the devil. He is utterly wretched, with his sins accumlated as a cloud obscuring the light of his position of freedom and fellowship in his risen Lord.

But it is the history of Satan always to overstep himself. His most apparent victories all contain the seed of his own defeat. The very need generated by the believer's failure is the Spirit's preparation for his seeing and abiding in his blessed position of light. His faith is to be focused on the fact that God has already given him a position in His presence; what is more, He has already established him in that position! "I have blotted out, as a thick cloud, thy transgressions, and, as a cloud, thy sins: return unto me; for I have redeemed thee" (Isa. 44:22).

The honest but still self-centered believer is oppressed and hindered by the darkness of his sinful condition. Nevertheless, in the midst of his downward trend, the Holy Spirit is presenting the truth so as to overwhelm him by the light of his righteous position. "And ye shall know the truth, and the truth shall make you free" (John 8:32). Not only is he free from the penalty of sin, but also from its power to bring forth sins. The believer is bound until, in spite of his sins, he rests in the truth concerning those sins.

What, then, is the specific truth concerning our sins? In our condition, we are totally unacceptable for the Father's presence and fellowship. But position is what counts with God, and it must come first with us! "Giving thanks unto the Father, which *hath* made us meet [suitable] to be partakers of the inheritance of the saints in light: who *hath* delivered us from the power of darkness, and hath translated us into the kingdom of his dear Son: in whom we *have* redemption through his blood, even the forgiveness of sins" (Col. 1:12-14, italics mine). ". . . The blood of Jesus Christ his Son cleanseth us from all sin" (1 John 1:7).

Every believer, regardless of his present condition, is in the very presence of the Father; we are in Christ, at the right hand of the Majesty on high. The source of our Christian life is in the light above, in Christ risen. It is there we are to abide; it is that completed standing which alone will affect the growth of our daily state. "And, having made peace through the blood of his cross, by him to reconcile all things unto himself; by him, I say, whether they be things in earth, or things in heaven. And you, that were sometime alienated and enemies in your mind by wicked works, yet now hath he reconciled in the body of his flesh through death, to present you holy and unblameable and unreproveable in his sight" (Col. 1:20-22).

We are not to be influenced by our feelings and our condition, but rather by His written Word. In spiritual growth, the eye of faith is slowly transferred from our own point of view to His, from condition to position. By means of intelligent faith in the scriptural facts, we are to turn boldly from sinful darkness to rest in His holy light. "The entrance of thy words giveth light . . ." (Ps. 119:130). "But now in Christ Jesus ye who sometimes were far off are made nigh [reconciled to His

presence] by the blood of Christ. For he is our peace . . ."
(Eph. 2:13, 14). "For he hath made him to be sin for us, who
knew no sin; that we might be made the righteousness of
God in him" (2 Cor. 5:21). Since we are born into Christ, who
is our righteousness, our Father is able to accept us fully into
His presence, just as we are. Our right to the light is our
eternal position, in spite of our present condition.

Our walk is the result of the source of our life. If we attempt
to walk as Christians in dependence on our own resources,
there is self-centeredness, self-righteousness, and darkness.
But when we walk in dependence on the Source of our life in
the light of God's presence, there is Christ-centeredness, His
righteousness, and "the LORD shall be thine everlasting light"
(Isa. 60:20).

In our estimation, which is looming larger—our sins, or
His blood shed for those sins? Are we viewing our sins from
His side, or ours? Are we letting God be God in this matter?
It is for us to think God's thoughts after Him. He has graciously and justly placed us in His Son, the very Light of earth
and heaven. Can our sins come between our Father and His
glorified Son who is our life? Never! He has borne them all in
His own body on the tree. He is our risen Advocate, Jesus
Christ the righteous. By means of His atoning blood, He
maintains eternally our relationship with the Father in
unbroken integrity.

Though our sins can in no way affect our position in the
light, or alter His thoughts of love toward us, they can and
do affect *our* thoughts and attitude toward our Father. They
can never cloud His view of our Advocate, but they can and
do obliterate *our* vision of His advocacy. They immediately
hinder our communion and fellowship with the Father and
the Son. The dark cloud of guilt and conviction of sin settles
down on our heart and conscience, unless we learn to judge
ourselves and willingly confess our sins before God. "For
if we would judge ourselves, we should not be judged"
(1 Cor. 11:31).

28 *Sins and Confession*

"If we confess our sins, he is faithful and just to forgive us our sins, and to cleanse us from all unrighteousness" (1 John 1:9). God the Father is free to forgive our sins because the Lord Jesus has already dealt with their source, the principle of sin. He condemned it in His flesh on the cross (Rom. 8:3). Confessing our sins, therefore, has nothing to do with condemnation, but with cleansing and communion.

Condition The believer who is not aware of his perfect position before God, who does not realize that the Father has already placed him in the light of His presence, is more aware of his self-centered condition than his Christ-centered position. Hence he does not actually accept the benefit of his position in the light when he does confess his sins. He does not *feel* forgiven and cleansed of all unrighteousness, and soon gives up confessing. Thereafter he flounders in darkness and guilt. This is the predicament of all too many believers today.

In the early days of their Christian life, most believers are quite faithful in confessing their sins to the Father. But, because they are yet babes, there is very little scriptural knowledge of what God has done about the indwelling source of those sins, and before long there are more sins committed than confessed. This accumulation of unconfessed sins brings guilt to the conscience, and the believer finds himself out of fellowship with the Father. Not only that, but he is experiencing chastisement. To make matters worse, he now seeks to hide from the light. He forgets that the purpose of light is not to punish and condemn the sinner, but to reveal sins so that they may be confessed and freely forgiven.

Another common error is that of praying for forgiveness, instead of heeding the Word, confessing the sins, and receiving the assurance of forgiveness. One may pray for forgiveness for months, and still not receive the assurance of it. Many admit sin in general, instead of confessing sins in particular. Assurance of forgiveness and cleansing are the sure result of honest and specific confession of sins committed in thought, word, and deed. There may be repentance and brokenness, but this is the result of confession and cleansing, not the cause. "If any man sin," there is immediate recourse to confession, and to Christ's advocacy and shed blood for complete forgiveness and cleansing. "If we *confess* our sins, he is faithful and just to forgive . . ." (1 John 1:9).

Position When we rest in our position in Christ, we find that we are in the light. We know that our sins have been purged once for all and therefore our conscience is cleansed. At the same time, we are very much aware that although we abide in the risen Lord Jesus, our everyday Christian life is carried on in a sinful world. There are sins committed as we grow, because we take our eyes off the Lord Jesus and foolishly rely on self; a defiled conscience and broken fellowship are the result. We also know that the remedy is to confess our sins, thereby to receive cleansing from all unrighteousness and restoration of a clear conscience and blessed fellowship.

Our present experience is greatly inferior to our eternal position, no matter what the stage of our spiritual growth. The development of our condition is *toward* our finished position, and at the same time *from* that completed source. The discrepancy between our position and our condition, manifested by our many failures in growth and service, is justly taken care of by means of our confession and His cleansing. Our need is further met by Christ's faithful advocacy, whereby our postion and fellowship are maintained throughout the progress of our spiritual growth. By these means our Lord ever keeps us dependent on Himself, and at the same time fully confident in Him. Needy, but bold.

Abiding and walking in the light keeps us honestly aware of our sins, while also enhancing our appreciation of His grace. The realization of our sins does not cripple us, because His cleansing frees us. The light that reveals our sins manifests the Son, enabling us honestly to face both without fear. Where we are most detected, there we are most protected. On this basis, the sins that are committed are immediately dealt with, and we are able to continue in fellowship and growth. The only alternative is self-confidently to struggle with sin, to fail, and thereby to be hindered in our development.

Our Father's counteraction is the ministry of the indwelling Spirit of life. To have our sins so freely forgiven does not make us lax as to our walk. For one thing, with the forgiveness there is often His faithful chastisement. A good conscience is cherished too much for it to be lost by license. We admit that "we all often stumble and fall and offend in many things" (James 3:2, Amplified), but there need be no fear of facing up to each offense and confessing it. The light that reveals our sins ever reveals our perfect position in the Lord Jesus. For us, "the darkness is past, and the true light now shineth" (1 John 2:8).

Confession and cleansing enable us to rest before God without guile. Our attitude becomes, "Search me, O God, and know my heart: try me, and know my thoughts: and see if there be any wicked way in me . . ." (Ps. 139:23, 24). There is no pretension of being without sins; rather, we want them clearly revealed so that they may be confessed and thereby kept from breaking our all-important fellowship with the Father. We are faithfully taught the lesson not to attempt to hide our sins and refrain from confession. "When I kept silent about my sin, my body wasted away through my groaning all day long. For day and night Thy hand was heavy upon me . . ." (Ps. 32:3, 4, NASB). Guilt and chastisement do their thorough work, and we learn to appreciate the fact that God's way of confession is imperative.

All because of our position in the Lord Jesus, and in spite of our condition in ourselves, our Father is able to say to us,

"For I know the thoughts that I think toward you . . . thoughts of peace, and not of evil, to give you an expected end" (Jer. 29:11). "Blessed is he whose transgression is forgiven, whose sin is covered. Blessed is the man unto whom the LORD imputeth not iniquity, and in whose spirit there is no guile" (Ps. 32:1, 2). "Therefore being justified by faith, we have peace with God through our Lord Jesus Christ: by whom also we have *access by faith into this grace wherein we stand,* and rejoice in hope of the glory of God" (Rom. 5:1, 2, italics mine).

As we grow, we learn to stand in our standing of grace, abiding in the risen Lord Jesus, and walking in the light of the Father's presence and fellowship. We appreciate the fact of our position as we experience failures in fighting against sin. We express our growing hatred of self by freely confessing our sins, which amounts to judging ourselves for submitting to indwelling sin. We admit our responsibility for walking (or drifting) beyond the realm of light, into the shadows of sin and self. "For if we would judge ourselves, we should not be judged. But when we are judged, we are chastened of the Lord, that we should not be condemned with the world" (1 Cor. 11:31, 32).

Standing in the light, we are not only aware that our sins have been cleared away by the blood, but we realize that we as sinners have also been put away by the death of the cross. We count ourselves to have died to sin, and now to be alive as new creations in Christ Jesus. As such, we confess our sins as they are revealed in the light, and we are thereby made free from self-occupation—free to be fully occupied in fellowship with the Father and the Son.

To turn from the darkness and death of self to the light and life of Christ is not to give up the fight and give in to sin. Not at all! It is fighting "the good fight of *faith*" (1 Tim. 6:12), it is entering into the benefits of the fact that the fight has already been fought and won for us by Another. This transition from bondage and defeat to freedom and victory is the faith-move from condition to position. "For he that is entered into his rest, he also hath ceased from his own works, as God did from his" (Heb. 4:10).

The Holy Spirit brings us through this transition by a very

simple process. He allows us to struggle with sin and self until we learn the futility of it. Then it is that He shows us that the Lord Jesus has already done for us what we can never do. It is from "O wretched man that I am! who shall deliver me from the body of this death?" to, "I thank God [He has already accomplished it] through Jesus Christ our Lord . . ." (Rom. 7:24, 25). It is from the bondage of the "law in my members, warring against the law of my mind, and bringing me into captivity to the law of sin which is in my members," to the liberty of "the law of the Spirit of life in Christ Jesus [which] hath made me free from the law of sin and death" (Rom. 7:23, 8:2).

Fellowship "God is faithful, by whom ye were called unto the fellowship of his Son Jesus Christ our Lord" (1 Cor. 1:9). The root word for fellowship and communion is *common.* Our communion with the Father and the Son, having fellowship one with another, is to have common thoughts, affections, and purposes. It is a oneness of heart and mind. It is to "love the Lord thy God with all thy heart . . . and with all thy mind . . ." (Luke 10:27). As we study His Word in dependence on His Spirit, we are in communion with His thoughts. As we love the Lord Jesus, we are loving the One whom the Father loves with all His heart.

Free from self-condemnation, free from a guilty conscience, free in the faithful advocacy of the Lord Jesus, free in the confession of our sins and cleansing from all unrighteousness, we are in the light of His presence to worship Him, commune with Him, and grow in Him. "But we all, with open face beholding as in a glass the glory of the Lord, are changed into the same image from glory to glory, even as by the Spirit of the Lord" (2 Cor. 3:18). It is the look that justifies, but it is the gaze that sanctifies.

Having died in Christ to sin, Satan, law, and the world, we are freed and born anew, made new creations in the Lord Jesus. Abiding in Him in the light of the Father, we are at liberty to gaze on Him in the full love of hearts and minds that are free from the palling darkness of unconfessed sins and a defiled conscience. No nervous, anxious, or restless self-effort; just quiet rest in Him, knowing that our "life is hid with Christ in God" (Col. 3:3). By the ministry of the Spirit of Christ within, the life of the Lord Jesus is manifested increasingly in our everyday walk.

Our Father's purpose for us is that we become conformed to the image (character) of His Son. To that end, all things are being "worked together" (Rom. 8:28, 29). In our position in Christ, our Father has already perfected us, made us complete in Him. In our walk, He by His Spirit is fashioning us after that blessed pattern, "that the life also of Jesus might be made manifest in our mortal flesh" (2 Cor. 4:11).

"He that saith he abideth in him ought himself also so to walk, even as he walked" (1 John 2:6). In the first place, the Lord Jesus walked in the light, in fellowship with His Father. ". . . the Son of man which is in heaven" (John 3:13). Secondly, He walked in full dependence on the Holy Spirit. "Then was Jesus led up of the Spirit into the wilderness . . ." (Matt. 4:1). ". . . who through the eternal Spirit offered himself without spot to God . . ." (Heb. 9:14). Likewise, our life is hid with Christ in God, and we walk in the light of God's presence during our earthly course. Our dependence is expressed as we "walk in the Spirit," that we may not "fulfill the lust of the flesh" (Gal. 5:16). We are to ". . . worship in the Spirit of God and glory in Christ Jesus and put no confidence in the flesh" (Phil. 3:3, NASB).

One of the Father's means of teaching us the Spirit-dependent walk in the light is to let us flounder in the darkness of self. The Lord Jesus also patiently waits to show us that all our sins have been cleansed by His blood. Coupled with our sins is the crushing weight of an evil conscience, which is often endured for years. And He continues to wait for us to acknowledge our position in Him in the light, so that we may rest in what He has already done about our sins. "Let us draw near with a sincere heart in full assurance of faith, having our hearts sprinkled clean from an evil conscience . . ." (Heb. 10:22, NASB).

"How much more shall the blood of Christ, who through the eternal Spirit offered himself without spot to God, purge your conscience from dead works to serve the living God?"

(Heb. 9:14). Laboring under a load of unconfessed sins, we are disqualified from fellowship with our Father, as well as from usefulness to others; we are, rather, a burden to all. It is such believers whom He urges to "come boldly unto the throne of grace, that we may obtain mercy, and find grace to help in time of need" (Heb. 4:16). The need is ever present, the work is forever done! He has placed us in His Son, having "made us sit together in heavenly places in Christ Jesus" (Eph. 2:6). All that is required is that we confidently abide where we have already been placed.

We are not to abide in our present condition, counting on help from Him in heaven for our walk and service. Just the opposite! He has shown us our position in order that we may abide in our risen Lord, in the light and presence of the Father. It is from that vantage point that we become involved in the needs of this world. In John 3:13 our Lord Jesus referred to Himself as "he that came down from heaven, even the Son of man which is in heaven." He shared heavenly life in a world of need. If He is to do the same and more today, through us, we must abide in heaven as we sojourn on earth. Only life lived in the light of glory can overcome the world of darkness.

In summary, (1) we count ourselves to have died to sin, and to be alive to God in the Lord Jesus (Rom. 6:11); (2) we accept our position in the light when we know ourselves to be new creations in our risen Savior (Eph. 2:6); (3) we enjoy His blessed fellowship as we judge ourselves in confession of our sins (1 John 1:7, 9). Then it is that our Lord can work through us in the lives of others, "to open their eyes, and to turn them from darkness to light, and from the power of Satan unto God, that they may receive forgiveness of sins, and inheritance among them which are sanctified by faith that is in me" (Acts 26:18).

Keep Looking Down

"For you have died and your life is hidden with Christ in God" (Col. 3:3, NASB).

Part Three
THE GROUND OF GROWTH

29 Our History in the First Adam

In this opening chapter of Book Three we will trace our history in relation to the first Adam: the ruin we received from Adam by inheritance, and the remedy we received from God by the cross. We cannot become what we already *are* in Christ, until we know what we *were* in Adam. Therefore it is important that we personalize the facts: this is *my* history!

Everything in Adam is the ground of sin and death; everything in the Lord Jesus is the ground of growth and life. Our responsibility is to keep off the old ground, and to live on the new ground—our position in Christ.

The First Adam To know what we were in Adam we must discover what Adam was, since he is the head of the human race into which we were born. Thus we can understand the nature and condition of the life we inherited from him, the life that continues to indwell us as believers.

Adam sinned and entered death—separated from God, the source of life. Through him we were born into sin, death, judgment, and condemnation. "Wherefore, as by one man sin entered into the world, and death by sin; and so death passed upon all men . . ." (Rom. 5:12). And death not only came into the world and the race, but it reigned as king. "By one man's offence death reigned by one. . . . Therefore as by the offence of one *judgment came* upon all men to condemnation" (Rom. 5:17, 18).

Let us note three basic aspects of our relationship to that representative man. (1) Our position of sin (Adam-source); (2) our nature of sin (Adam-nature); (3) our personal sins (Adam-practice). To know the facts concerning the position and condition of our old life in Adam is to possess a vital key to spiritual growth. Ignorance or neglect here means certain defeat throughout one's Christian life.

Our Position of Sin

Because of our fallen progenitor each of us was born into a doomed humanity. As David wrote, "In sin did my mother conceive me" (Ps. 51:5). In Adam, we were declared to be "dead in trespasses and sins," because "in Adam all die" (Eph. 2:1; 1 Cor. 15:22). The result of our position in Adam, our source, is that we are dead to God, and alive to sin.

Our Nature of Sin

Our position of sin resulted in a sinful being, or life, and therefore the propensity of that life is sinful. In Adam, we are "*by nature* the children of wrath" (Eph. 2:3; italics mine). In this condition we are natural, fleshly, carnal, separated from God. "The natural man receiveth not the things of the Spirit of God: for they are foolishness unto him: neither can he know them . . ." (1 Cor. 2:14).

This fallen nature never changes, much less improves. "That which is born of the flesh is flesh" (John 3:6). The Adamic nature is self-centered (the sin of sins), therefore totally against God and that irreparably. "For they that are after the flesh do mind the things of the flesh. . . . Because the carnal mind is enmity against God: for it is not subject to the law of God, neither indeed can be. So then they that are in the flesh cannot please God. . . . I am carnal [in Adam], sold under sin" (Rom. 8:5, 7, 8; 7:14).

Our Personal Sins

The natural product of a sinful nature is sins. The practical result of our congenital condition is stated in Scripture: "all have sinned, and come short of the glory of God" (Rom. 3:23). We grew up to be sinners in practice, and that by choice, hence we were desperately in need of a Savior.

If by careful study of the above we allow the Holy Spirit to impress us with the awful truth concerning our history in Adam, we will be better able to appreciate the wonderful remedy our Father has provided.

The Con-　　　We must continue to think in terms of our
demned Adam　personal history. Now we want to see exactly
　　　　　　　　what our Father did to rectify this terrible
relationship and condition.

Our Position of Sin

God did not forgive the principle of Satan-injected sin that dealt the death blow to the human race through Adam. He does not forgive sin any more than He forgives Satan. On the Cross, in the person of His Son, our Father once and forever dealt with the principle of sin, thereby canceling our position of sin.

"For he hath made him to be sin for us, who knew no sin." "God sending his own Son, in the likeness of sinful flesh, and for sin, condemned sin in the [His] flesh" (2 Cor. 5:21; Rom. 8:3). Far from being forgiven, sin was judged and condemned in death.

Our Nature of Sin

Our sinful life and nature were not forgiven, but likewise were taken into the judgment death of the Cross. All that we inherited from Adam suffered this same fate. "Knowing this, that our old self was crucified with Him" (Rom. 6:6, NASB). Had it been possible for God to forgive our old nature, it could then have been restored, or reinstated.

Our Personal Sins

Our sins were forgiven—past, present, and future—by His shed blood on Calvary. "Who his own self bare our sins in his own body on the tree." "Having made peace through the blood of his cross." "Unto him that loved us, and washed us from our sins in his own blood" (1 Peter 2:24; Col. 1:20; Rev. 1:5).

141

Adam Relationship Terminated   At last we can see ourselves at the very end of our history in Adam. On the one hand we look at the Cross, and on the other hand we look into the tomb. We might ask a few questions as to God's wonderful work in severing us from Adam.

Why?—"The wages of sin is death" (Rom. 6:23). Representative Adam sinned, therefore everything Adamic was condemned to death.

When and Where?—All of God's dealings with sin were accomplished in and by His Son, on the Cross of Calvary.

How?—On the Cross the Lord Jesus was identified with our sin, and our sinful nature, our "old man" being thus condemned and crucified with Him. At the same time, in His substitutionary work of redemption, He paid the penalty of our sins.

Thus His death on our behalf completely freed us, as individual believers, from Adam and all Adamic penalites and consequences. This enabled God to justly include us in Christ's death *to* sin. "We have been planted together in the likeness of his death. . . . For in that he died, he died unto sin once" (Rom. 6:5, 10).

Having by His death borne the condemnation of sin and paid all its penalties, our Lord Jesus died unto, out from, the realm and responsibilities of sin. Stripped of our relationship to Adam by and in that death—we having died in Christ unto the old—we can now see ourselves in His tomb, ready to be identified with Him in His resurrection life and divine nature.

Let us prayerfully think through these truths concerning our history in Adam, going over them until the Holy Spirit makes the picture clear.

* * * * *

The first step to my becoming free of the old man in daily experience is to know that I was separated once for all from that life by crucifixion and burial. The ultimate in deliverance—death.

30 Our History in the Last Adam

Our history in the Last Adam, our risen Lord Jesus, begins on the only basis for resurrection life—death. Our relationship to the first Adam rendered us dead *in* sin, but our death with Christ made us dead *to* (in relation to) sin—the one condition for newness of life.

In Christ Buried   There, in the tomb, we must see ourselves as dead to Adam, but not yet alive in Christ.

Our individual identity has not changed, but our relationship to the fleshly Adam has, thank God! "Therefore we have been buried with him." "In Him you were also circumcised with a circumcision made without hands, in the removal of the body of the flesh by the circumcision of Christ [on the cross]; having been buried with Him" (Rom. 6:4, NASB; Col. 2:11, 12, NASB).

Death, our ruin, has been made the very means of our triumph over it. "Death is swallowed up in victory. . . . Thanks be to God, which giveth us the victory through our Lord Jesus Christ" (1 Cor. 15:54, 57).

In Christ Risen   His death and burial having done its liberating work on our behalf, we can now begin to look up—from death to Adam fallen, to birth into Christ risen. When the Lord Jesus burst the bonds of death, He took us with Him in His glorious resurrection life.

"Just as Christ was raised from among the dead by the Father's glorious power, we also should live an entirely new life. For since we have become one with Him by sharing in His death, we shall also be one with Him by sharing in His resurrection" (Rom. 6:4, 5, Weymouth). Now, safely and forever on resurrection ground in Him, we can study (1) our new position of life; (2) our new nature of righteousness; and (3) our new walk of fruitfulness.

Our New Position of Life Whereas our old position in the first Adam made us dead to God and alive to sin, our new position in the risen Last Adam makes us alive to God and dead to sin. "For you have died, and your life is hidden with Christ in God" (Col. 3:3, NASB). Formerly our Judge, now by means of His Son's death and resurrection He is free to be our Father, and we His sons. "Beloved, now are we the sons of God. . . ." "And because ye are sons, God hath sent forth the Spirit of his Son into your hearts, crying, Abba, Father" (1 John 3:2; Gal. 4:6).

Our New Nature of Righteousness In our co-resurrection with Christ, our Father gave us a new life with a new nature which can only bring forth righteousness. "Blessed be the God and Father of our Lord Jesus Christ, which, according to his abundant mercy *hath begotten us again* unto a lively hope by the resurrection of Jesus Christ from the dead" (1 Peter 1:3).

The old life is not *changed*, but *exchanged* for that which is *altogether new*. Paul's clearest description of this is given in 2 Corinthians 5:17 and 18: "Therefore if any man be in Christ, he is a new creature; old things are passed away; behold, all things are become new. And all things are of God, who hath reconciled us to himself by Jesus Christ. . . ."

Our Father sees each of us as completely new in His Son. We have been forever freed from our relationship to the first Adam with its reign of sin and death. And He wants us to see ourselves from His point of view—new creations in Christ Jesus!

It might be helpful for us to consider further the fact that in this death-to-life transition our personal identity is kept intact. We remain the same individual while acquiring a new position, life, and nature in the risen Lord Jesus. The Father maintains the identity of each believer throughout the process of the Cross, the tomb, and the Resurrection.

"And *you*, that were sometime alienated and enemies in your mind by wicked works, yet now hath he reconciled in the body of his flesh through death, to present you holy and unblameable and unreproveable in his sight. . . . And *you*, being dead in your sins and the uncircumcision of your flesh, hath he quickened together with him, having forgiven you all trespasses" (Col. 1:21, 22; 2:13, italics mine).

In Christ Ascended

Being identified with the Lord Jesus in His death to sin and His resurrection into life, we are also in Him in His ascended life at the Father's right hand. Born from above, we are to abide above.

"But God, who is rich in mercy, for his great love wherewith he loved us, even when we were dead in sins, hath quickened us together with Christ, (by grace ye are saved;) and hath raised us up together, and made us sit together in heavenly places in Christ Jesus: that in the ages to come he might shew the exceeding riches of his grace in his kindness toward us through Christ Jesus" (Eph. 2:4-7).

Our New Walk of Fruitfulness   As newly created believers, we are in the Lord Jesus in the heavenlies, while at the same time we are in the Spirit of Christ here on earth. The Comforter is our environment in this sin-cursed world. "But ye are not in the flesh, but in the Spirit, if so be that the Spirit of God dwell in you" (Rom. 8:9). He it is who ministers the life of the Lord Jesus in us as our new life, and who develops the characteristics of that life in and through our new nature.

On the one hand, He applies the finished work of the Cross to the life of the flesh within. "Walk in the Spirit, and ye shall not fulfill the lust of the flesh" (Gal. 5:16). On the other hand, He causes the fruit of the Spirit to grow in our new life. "The fruit of the Spirit is love, joy, peace, longsuffering, gentleness, goodness, faith, meekness, temperance" (Gal. 5:22, 23).

A close look at Galatians 2:20 may further clarify the distinction between what we were in the first Adam, and who we now are in the Last Adam. "I have been crucified with Christ; and it is no longer I who live, but Christ lives in me: and the life which I now live in the flesh I live by faith in the Son of God, who loved me, and delivered Himself up for me" (Gal. 2:20, NASB).

There are vital distinctions here that, when seen, make a world of difference. (1) I, the old man in Adam, have been crucified with Christ; (2) it is no longer the old I that lives, but Christ lives in me, the new creation; (3) the life which I, the new man, now live in the flesh (body), I the new man live in faith; (4) this faith is in the Son of God, who loved me as a lost individual and gave Himself up for me, a sinner.

The oft-quoted words, "Not I, but Christ," tend to give the believer the impression that he as a person is crucified, and out of the picture, and now there is only Christ as his new life. He is wont to feel that he must somehow get himself out of the way, that Christ may be all. Granted, the old self must go down—but the new self must grow up.

It is true that He is our risen life, but it is also true that His is the life and nature of *our* newly created life. "For to *me* to live is Christ." "Christ, who is *our* life" (Phil. 1:21; Col. 3:4, italics mine). We are not to become lost in Him, but He is to be found in us. "That the life also of Jesus might be made manifest in our mortal flesh" (2 Cor. 4:11). He lives in *me*, not instead of me; He is the source and motivation of my Christian life.

*   *   *   *   *

I am to realize and rest in the fact that it is *my* being, *my* personality, which is enlifed by the human-divine life and nature of the Lord Jesus. I am the same person, but with a new life in union with His life. By the ministry of the indwelling Holy Spirit *I* will grow in grace and increasingly be conformed to His image.

31 *Diametric Differentiation*

Let us distinguish yet further between the old life and the new. One important distinction is that sooner or later the healthy believer realizes that he is not alone in his body. The condemned Adam-nature from which he was delivered at the Cross is nonetheless in residence, and as sinful as ever.

Unless we see the extent to which the Cross separated us from the old, we will not be able to keep clear of the enslaving flesh and walk freely in the Spirit. Our Father positionally separated us from the Adam-life by our crucifixion, death, burial, resurrection, and ascension life in the Lord Jesus Christ.

One might ask why our Father, after condemning the old man in the death of His Son, should allow that crucified life and nature to reside in His re-created and risen ones. God has perfect reasons for everything He does. We can list a few here for consideration.

(1) To reveal the depths of sinfulness from which we were saved.

(2) To teach us to count ourselves dead to the old, and alive in the new.

(3) To teach us to abide in the Lord Jesus—above.

(4) To teach us to walk in the Spirit—below.

(5) To glorify the Father and manifest the life of the Lord Jesus despite a fallen nature, body, and world.

(6) To give us good cause to watch for His appearing.

(7) To give us a greater appreciation of eternal glory.

In that there are two distinct natures seeking expression by means of our as-yet-unredeemed body, we must keep them separated in our thinking. In itself the old nature is ever strong to do evil; only by the Spirit is the new nature strong to bring forth righteousness.

The Spirit and The sinful nature dooms the sinner, and
the Old Nature defeats the believer. The growing Christian is sadly aware of the many ramifications of the flesh that fester within. "Now the works of the flesh are manifest, which are these: adultery, fornication, uncleanness, lasciviousness, idolatry, witchcraft, hatred, variance, emulations, wrath, strife, seditions, heresies, envyings, murders, drunkenness, revelings, and such like . . ." (Gal. 5:19-21).

The progressing believer not only discovers the characteristics of the fallen nature, but he comes to know and experience its overpowering strength, despite the fact that he is a new creation in Christ. The fallen life within is undergirded by the power of sin, the body, and the world. "I see another law in my members, warring against the law of my mind, and bringing me into captivity to the law of sin which is in my members" (Rom. 7:23).

In time, the defeated believer realizes that the Holy Spirit is the one who is commissioned to deal with the old man. "This I say then, Walk in the Spirit, and ye shall not fulfill the lust of the flesh. For the flesh lusteth [striveth] against the Spirit, and the Spirit against the flesh: and these are contrary the one to the other: so that ye may not [marg.] do the things that ye would" (Gal. 5:16, 17).

Although He could do so, the Spirit does not deal with the fleshly life by means of His own strength. He doesn't have to. He depends on what God has already done about the old man. And so should we. The key to deliverance from the works of the Flesh is not strength, as we utlimately learn. Freedom comes by means of explicit faith. As we reckon on Calvary's crucifixion of the Adam-life, the Holy Spirit applies the finished work to that life thereby holding it in the position of death, inoperative.

The Spirit and While the Spirit draws on the death of the
the New Nature cross to render the old nature powerless, He ministers the life of Christ to render the

new nature productive. He works according to the principle of life out of death. "For we which live are alway delivered unto death for Jesus' sake, that the life also of Jesus might be made manifest in our mortal flesh" (2 Cor. 4:11).

Only the believer who has repeatedly gone down in defeat under the relentless power of the Adam-nature can appreciate the necessity of walking in dependence on the Holy Spirit. It is the faithful Spirit who gives growth to our new-creation life, slowly manifesting the very image of its Source. This growth is evidenced by the fruit of the Spirit as set forth in cluster form in Galatians 5:22 and 23.

We might give some thought to the first segment of that fruit of the Vine, which is *love*. Obviously this love is that of the Lord Jesus; resident in His nature, and therefore in our new nature. We are to behold this love, as well as all the other characteristics of His life, in order that we may intelligently depend on the Spirit for their development in us. We can look at His love in 1 Corinthians 13:4-13.

"[Love] suffereth long, and is kind; [love] envieth not; [love] vaunteth not itself, is not puffed up,

"[Love] doth not behave itself unseemly, seeketh not her own, is not easily provoked, thinketh no evil;

"[Love] rejoiceth not in iniquity, but rejoiceth in the truth;

"[Love] beareth all things, believeth all things, hopeth all things, endureth all things.

"[Love] never faileth. . . .

"And now abideth faith, hope, [love], these three; but the greatest of these is [love].

"Follow after [love]" (1 Cor. 14:1).

Before considering briefly how to follow after love, we must understand how we are not to walk. What are some of the characteristics of the old nature that we are to shun? It does not suffer long; it is unkind; it envies, vaunts itself, and is usually puffed up. It behaves itself unseemly, seeks its own, is easily provoked, and thinks evil.

This Adam-life within rejoices in iniquity, and does not rejoice in the truth; it refuses to bear all things, believe all things, hope for all things, endure all things. Quite the contrary. And it always fails! Why be occupied at all with that foul brood?

How are we to follow after love? We are to see where God has positioned us, and live there. By means of crucifixion and resurrection our Father has released us from the old life that cannot love, and brought us into union with the life of the Lover. "Your life is hid with Christ in God." "God is love" (Col. 3:3; 1 John 4:8).

As new creations in Christ we no longer have to yield to indwelling sin; the cross has freed us from its power. But we are responsible to abide in Him by faith, in order that His love and righteousness may be manifested to this needy world. Much of the *how* to escape the old and become established in the new is embodied in Romans 6:11-13 (NASB).

(1) "Consider yourselves to be dead to sin, but *alive to God* in Christ Jesus."

(2) "Therefore let not sin reign in your mortal body that you should obey its lusts."

(3) "And do not go on presenting the members of your body to sin as instruments of unrighteousness; but present yourselves to God *as those alive from the dead,* and your members as instruments of righteousness to God."

* * * * *

I make choices daily as to what ground I am on: either to be dominated and defeated by indwelling sin, or to be freed and growing in the Lord Jesus Christ. There can be no neutrality. The Lord Jesus has made it very clear: "No man can serve two masters; for either he will hate the one, and love the other; or else he will hold to the one, and despise the other. . . . He that is not with me is against me" (Matt. 6:24; 12:30).

32 *In-Law*

The believer will remain in bondage as long as he does not know that through the cross he has been delivered from the reign of the old man, the law, the world, and the Enemy. We have already discussed the Adam-life. In this chapter we will deal with the law, both as commandment and as a principle.

Purpose of the Law Strictly speaking, God's formal law was given to the nation Israel and to none other. The following points will clarify its place and purpose.

(1) Four hundred and thirty years before God introduced the law, He gave Abraham the covenant of promise. This covenant had to do with faith, and with Christ.

Faith—"Abraham believed God, and it was accounted to him for righteousness. . . . So then they which be of faith are blessed with faithful Abraham" (Gal. 3:6, 9).

Christ—"Now to Abraham and his seed were the promises made. He saith not, And to seeds, as of many; but as of one, And to thy seed, which is Christ" (Gal. 3:16). The Father's Old Testament expression of His one and only way of salvation was by grace through faith in the coming Messiah.

(2) Four centuries after Abraham received the covenant of promise, God presented the law to the Jews. "The law was given by Moses" (John 1:17). The law was not meant to replace the principles of promise, grace, and faith, but was brought in alongside. "The law, which was four hundred and thirty years after, cannot disannul, that it should make the promise of none effect. For if the inheritance be of the law, it is no

151

more of promise: but God gave it to Abraham by promise" (Gal. 3:17, 18).

(3) God's "law is holy, and the commandment holy, and just, and good" (Rom. 7:12). But it has to do with sin and death, not righteousness and life. "For by the law is the knowledge of sin" (Rom. 3:20). The law reveals man's condition and intensifies his need. "But sin, that it might appear sin, working death in me by that which is good; that sin by the commandment might become exceeding sinful" (Rom. 7:13).

(4) The law can have nothing to do with grace, or faith, or life. "No man is justified by the law in the sight of God. . . . The just shall live by faith. And the law is not of faith. . . . But before faith came, we were kept under the law, shut up unto the faith which should afterwards be revealed. Wherefore the law was our schoolmaster until [marg.] Christ, that we might be justified by faith" (Gal. 3:11, 12, 23, 24).

The Law and the Old Nature The law has to do with sin, and therefore it applies to the Adam-life, the old man.

(1) The ministry of the law is to judge and condemn all that came from Adam. "The law is not made for a righteous man but for the lawless and disobedient, for the ungodly and for sinners. . . ." "For when we were in the flesh [Adam], the [sinful impulses], which were [aroused] by the law, did work in our members to bring forth fruit unto death" (1 Tim. 1:9; Rom. 7:5).

(2) The fleshly Adamic nature will have nothing to do with God, nor can God have anything to do with it. He used His law to judge and condemn it to death. "For the mind set on the flesh is death . . . because the mind set on the flesh is hostile toward God; for it does not subject itself to the law of God, for it is not even able to do so" (Rom. 8:6, 7, NASB).

The Christian and the Old Nature The old man, whether Jew or Gentile, is under law. For the former, it is external, via command; for the latter it is internal, via principle. "For when the Gentiles, which have not the [external] law, do by nature the things contained in the law, these, having not the law, are a law unto themselves" (Rom. 2:14). The old nature is law-oriented; carnal, not spiritual.

The Christian who is mainly living by means of the old life, and thereby giving expression to the old nature, is carnal, fleshly. (The Latin word for carnal is *carnis:* flesh). Hence, whether by command or by principle, the law is predominant in his life. He is under law as a rule of life; he is in Romans 7.

Results of Law—Negative:

(1) The law says, Don't sin, so the old man struggles to keep from sinning. The law says, Do righteousness, so he struggles to be righteous. But the law does not give the Christian power over sin—it gives sin power over the Christian! "The strength of sin is the law" (1 Cor. 15:56). "I find then a law [indwelling principle], that, when I would do good, evil is present with me. . . . For the good that I would I do not: but the evil which I would not, that I do" (Rom. 7:21, 19).

(2) The Christian who is walking after the flesh is walking under law, and therefore is doomed to failure. Law applies to the fleshly life, but there is no good thing in that nature; it is neither subject to the law, nor can it be (Rom. 7:18; 8:7). The carnal believer is depending on fleshly means for deliverance from fleshly failure; he is looking for strength to the very source from which he is seeking deliverance.

(3) The Christian life becomes a burden, and a continuous up-and-down experience. There is little hunger for the Word of God. Prayer all but fades away. Sins are not honestly confessed, hence there is scarcely any true fellowship with the Lord. Instead of having a testimony and being a pattern, such a defeated believer becomes a detriment to others. What love he has is self-centered—there is none for the needy. Instead of manifesting the love of the new man in Christ, there is the opposite expression from the old man in Adam—unkindness, envy, unseemly behavior, and other works of the flesh.

(4) As to service, where there is any at all it is mainly by means of self-effort—whether it be preaching, teaching, or personal witness. Flashy gimmicks and neat little methods

are employed, but the flesh can only spawn more of its own kind. The problem is compounded.

From time to time there may be a bit of reviving in the life by means of dedication, but this usually results in deeper frustration and depression. There is no growth or fruitfulness for the believer in the legal realm. To such Paul says, "Ye are yet carnal: for whereas there is among you envying, and strife, and divisions, are ye not carnal, and walk as [natural] men?" (1 Cor. 3:3).

Results of Law—Positive:

Through all this legalistic and fleshly failure, the Father is working out His eternal purposes. He is using the principle of law to bring the believer to the end of Romans 7: "Oh, wretched man that I am!" Thus the Christian is prepared for the wonderful exchange of faith—that of turning from the old law-bound nature to his new life of grace in the Lord Jesus. By the Spirit he will be brought from the realm of the [old] law of sin and death into that of the [new] law of the Spirit of life in Christ Jesus (Rom. 8:2).

* * * * *

By various maxims, forms, and rules,
That pass for wisdom in the schools,
I sought my passions to restrain;
But all my efforts proved in vain.
But since my Saviour I have known
My rules are all reduced to One,
To keep my Lord by faith in view,
This strength supplies and motive too.

—John Newton

33 *Out-Law*

If a Christian is under the law as a "rule of life," he is laboring in a doleful, gray, alien land of self-righteousness—he struggles to produce. The believer who learns to walk in the Spirit of life in Christ Jesus has the joy of the Lord for his strength—he rests to receive.

Instead of our Father demanding *from* us according to the law, by grace He ministers *to* us from the One who is our life in glory. "And God is able to make all grace abound toward you; that ye, always having all sufficiency in all things, may abound to every good work" (2 Cor. 9:8).

The Law and the New Nature Our new nature is that of the risen life of the Lord Jesus Christ. The purpose of the law being to reveal sin and condemn the sinner, it has nothing to say to the new man in Christ Jesus. "For sin shall not have dominion over you; for ye are not under the law, but under grace" (Rom. 6:14).

(1) As each of us was separated from the Adam-life by means of the Cross and the tomb, we were delivered from the realm of law. We rose from the tomb into newness of life—out of the grip of law into the freedom of His resurrection. Now we are discharged from the law and have terminated all intercourse with it, having died to what once restrained and held us captive. So now we serve not under [obedience to] the old code of written regulations, but [under obedience to the promptings] of the Spirit in newness [of life]" (Rom. 7:6, Amplified).

(2) Law has to do with works—the works of the flesh. The new creation has to do with life—the life of the Son. Abiding in Him, our nature will grow and manifest the fruit of the

Spirit. "You have undergone death as to the Law through the [crucified] body of Christ, so that now you may belong to Another, to Him Who was raised from the dead in order that we may bear fruit for God" (Rom. 7:4, Amplified).

The Christian and the New Nature
Our Lord Jesus Christ, seated at the Father's right hand in glory, is not under law of any kind. His life is subject neither to commands nor to the principle of law. It is holy by nature. We, having been born into Him, now share His life. "For to me to live is Christ . . ." (Phil. 1:21).

(1) The wages of sin being death, the law by the execution of the death penalty exhausted its rights over the man in Adam. Having died to the law in Christ, the law no longer has any *claim* on the believer. He is now free from its reign. "When the commandment came, sin lived again, and I died—was sentenced by the Law to death." "For through the Law I died to the Law, that I might live to God" (Rom. 7:9, Amplified; Gal. 2:19, NASB).

(2) Being in Christ Jesus, the believer no longer has *need* for the law as a governing principle—he can now live by nature, effortlessly and naturally. "We are debtors, but not to the flesh—we are not obligated to our carnal nature—to live [a life ruled by the standards set up by the dictates] of the flesh" (Rom. 8:12, Amplified).

(3) When the believer sees his deliverance from the old, he can begin to walk in the freedom of the new. "Where the Spirit of the Lord is, there is liberty." "For, brethren, ye have been called unto liberty; only use not liberty for an occasion to the flesh . . ." (2 Cor. 3:17; Gal. 5:13).

Walking in Liberty
Some of the positive results are the following:
(1) Even when there is failure, the abiding believer learns from it and gains thereby. He knows that his Father is working all things together for his good, to conform him to the image of His Son (Rom. 8:28, 29). His reliance is neither on the law nor the flesh, but on the Holy Spirit,

"that the righteousness of the law might be fulfilled in us, who walk not after the flesh, but after the Spirit" (Rom. 8:4).

(2) Instead of struggle to keep from sinning, and self-effort to progress spiritually, he rests in Christ—the ground of growth. The Word of God is his daily sustenance; he feeds on it in reliance on its Author, the Spirit of Truth.

(3) Prayer is his cherished fellowship with the Father; he depends on the Spirit for this most vital aspect of his life. "The Spirit also helpeth our infirmities: for we know not what we should pray for as we ought: but the Spirit itself maketh intercession for us with groanings which cannot be uttered. And he that searcheth the hearts knoweth what is the mind of the Spirit, because he maketh intercession for the saints according to the will of God" (Rom. 8:26, 27).

(4) Having learned to hate the old life, he willingly judges himself. He confesses his sins fully and without fear because he loves and trusts his Advocate and Redeemer, the Lord Jesus Christ.

(5) In his growth he is more and more free from the influence of indwelling sin and the old life, the law, and the surrounding world. He is at rest concerning himself, but burdened for others. His service is from the heart and in the Spirit—a sharing of *life*. He does not have to resort to human methods and fleshly means to win others and help them grow in grace and in the knowledge of the Lord Jesus. He allows the Holy Spirit to control and work through him by means of life—the life of the Lord Jesus.

(6) Underlying whatever service the Spirit may lead him into, his most important and effective ministry is simply to *be*—for to him to live is Christ. He becomes an "example (pattern) for the believers [and the lost], in speech, in conduct, in love, in faith and in purity" (1 Tim. 4:12, Amplified). His attitude is that of Paul, "Stand fast therefore in the liberty wherewith Christ hath made us free, and be not entangled again with the yoke of bondage [law]" (Gal. 5:1).

* * * * *

My liberty from the old is infinite in the Lord Jesus—limited only to the glory of my Father, and to the good of others.

34 The World and Its Prince

Continuing the consideration of that from which Christ has freed us, this chapter will deal with two of our deadly enemies, the world and Satan.

The World   Satan is the god and prince of this present evil world system (John 12:31; 2 Cor. 4:4). The world is the chief weapon by which he ever seeks to cripple the Christian. "For all that is in the world, the lust of the flesh, and the lust of the eyes, and the pride of life, is not of the Father, but is of the world." "The whole world lieth in wickedness" (1 John 2:16; 1 John 5:19, NASB).

The Worldly Christian

It is in the environment of this world that the Adam-nature is at home and flourishes. The believer who is dominated by the old nature is bound to be worldly. He feels that he can live for God effectively on a carnal level. He imagines that such a manner of life and service will attract the world to the unworldly Savior.

Others go to the opposite extreme by attempting to live for God through legalistic measures. But this is resorting to the wrong realm of life. "If then you have died with Christ to material ways of looking at things and have escaped from the world's crude and elemental notions and teachings of externalism, why do you live as if you still belong to the world?— Why do you submit to rules and regulations? [such as], Do not handle [this], Do not taste [that], Do not even touch

[them], referring to things all of which perish with being used. To do this is to follow human precepts and doctrines.

"Such [practices] have indeed the outward appearance [that popularly passes] for wisdom, in promotion self-imposed rigor of devotion and delight in self-humiliation and severity of discipline of the body, but they are of no value in checking the indulgence of the flesh—the lower [old] nature. [Instead, they do not honor God] but serve only to indulge the flesh" (Col. 2:20-23, Amplified).

Fleshly means are futile, whether utilized to win the world, or to avoid the world.

> Whatever passes as a cloud between
> The mental eye of faith and things unseen,
> Causing the brighter world to disappear,
> Or seem less lovely, or its hope less dear,
> This is our world, our idol, though it bear
> Affection's impress, or devotion's air.

The Christ-centered Christian

The risen Lord Jesus is the abiding place and environment of our new nature, and it is in that life we are to walk, "for our citizenship is in heaven" (Phil. 3:20, NASB).

It is there, abiding above, that we fellowship and grow; and it is from there that we minister here in this lost and needy world. Although we are in this world, we are not of it; we are primarily here in order for God to be glorified in us and the Lord Jesus to be manifested through us for the sake of others. "Conduct yourselves properly (honorably, righteously) among the Gentiles, so that although they may slander you as evil doers, [yet] they may be witnessing your good deeds [come to] glorify God" (1 Peter 2:12, Amplified).

To escape from the reign and corroding influence of the world we must count on the work of the cross, by which we were crucified to the world, and the world crucified to us (Gal. 6:14). The source of our Christian life is neither in the worldly nature, nor the worldly system; we are to look to another world for all our resources. "If [since] then you have been raised up with Christ, keep seeking the things above, where

Christ is, seated at the right hand of God. Set your mind on the things above, not on the things that are on earth. For you have died and your life is hidden with Christ in God" (Col. 3:1-3, NASB).

Satan   Both the cross and the risen Lord Jesus separate us from the reign of Satan. At Calvary we died out of his kingdom of darkness and death; in the resurrection we were born into the Son's kingdom of light and life. "Giving thanks unto the Father, which hath made us meet to be partakers of the inheritance of the saints in light: who hath delivered us from the power of darkness, and hath translated us into the kingdom of his dear Son" (Col. 1:12, 13).

Resist

Satan would seek to bluff us out of our position of safety. But we are to "be sober, be vigilant; because your adversary the devil, as a roaring lion, walketh about, seeking whom he may devour: whom resist steadfast in the faith. . . ." "Neither give place to the devil." "Submit yourselves therefore to God. Resist the devil, and he will flee from you" (1 Peter 5:8, 9; Eph. 4:27; James 4:7).

Our resistance to the Enemy is on the basis of faith, faith in the work of the cross in which he was doomed and his power broken. Through our reckoning, his defeat at Calvary is applied and we are made to triumph.

Satan, although dangerous, has been defeated. "For this purpose the Son of God was manifested, that he might destroy the works of the devil." "Forasmuch then as the children are partakers of flesh and blood, he also himself likewise took part of the same; that through death he might destroy [make of no effect] him that had the power of death, that is, the devil" (1 John 3:8; Heb. 2:14).

Stand

We are to stand in our position, "hid with Christ in God," that we may be "strong in the Lord, and in the power of his might" (Col. 3:3, Eph. 6:10). We do not have to wage war with the devil to obtain our position, nor do we have to fight him either to maintain it or to retain it. We simply stand where we have been placed, abiding above, resisting his assaults and fiery darts through faith in the Victor who defeated him and all his cohorts. At the cross the Lord Jesus "spoiled principalities and powers, he made a shew of them openly, triumphing over them in it" (Col. 2:15). We humbly walk in the train of His triumph.

Rest

Many believers, not knowing of, nor abiding in, their position in the triumphant Lord Jesus, attempt to war against and defeat the devil and his demons. Before long Satan looms larger and stronger in their eyes, while the Lord Jesus seems to become smaller and weaker.

Soon they imagine there are demons on every hand, possessing nearly everything and everybody. They become obsessed with their "warfare," and before long begin to experience defeat and breakdown in the physical, mental, moral, and spiritual realms.

If Satan can get the believer to become more aware of him than of the Lord Jesus, the inevitable result is a triumphant foe and a defeated Christian. Our responsibility is to steadfastly resist the Enemy by quietly resting in our impregnable position in Christ. "For in him dwelleth all the fullness of the Godhead bodily. And ye are complete in him, which is the head of all principality and power." "Let us therefore cast off the works of darkness, and let us put on the armour of light" (Col. 2:9, 10; Rom. 13:12).

Our Father often uses the Enemy as a foil, to teach us to handle our weapons of defense. We are told to "put on the whole armour of God, that ye may be able to stand against the wiles of the devil" (Eph. 6:11). Actually, the Lord Jesus is our armor—"put ye on the Lord Jesus Christ, and make not provision for the flesh" (Rom. 13:14). Satan cannot touch Him, nor can he touch us in Him.

Even when our Father chooses to let our Satan's chain a

bit, the Enemy's worst only proves to be God's best for the believer who stands his ground in Christ. Satan thought he was destroying the Lord Jesus on the cross, and now he attempts to do the same with the believer. But all he gets is a mouthful of ashes, his Calvary defeat. All he gets is judgment, "because the prince of this world is judged" (John 16:11).

* * * * *

I am thankful that the cross has closed my history as related to the world and its prince. I was a slave to the world, but now it is crucified to me, and I to it (Gal. 6:14). I was a slave to Satan, but now my Father has made me a partaker of the inheritance of the saints in light, and delivered me from the power of darkness (Col. 1:12, 13).

35 Transplantation

We would seek to encourage the believer by explaining the way in which our Father uses the old sinful life to establish us in the new righteous life. By faith we stand in the work of the cross for the Spirit's opposition to all that would hinder our growth, and by faith we abide in the Lord Jesus for the Spirit's accomplishment of that growth. We stand, and He works.

Downward Progress Before we can "grow up into him in all things, which is the head, even Christ" (Eph. 4:15), there must be a growth downward; a sturdy root system must be established. Naturally and spiritually, the underlying development comes first. The superstructure is dependent on a solid subterranean foundation.

Usually the believer is awakened and enhungered for true spiritual growth by an increasing awareness of the virulence and power of the old nature. Most Christians struggle for years in the vain attempt to control indwelling sin. The result is an up-and-down, defeated spiritual life.

A portion of 2 Corinthians 4:11 can give us valuable light here: "Alway delivered unto death." One of the most effective but heartrending applications of this death in the life of the believer is his realization of the sinfulness and strength of the flesh. The story of the reign of this death-dealing nature overcoming the believer is entitled "Romans 7."

Sooner or later the Christian discovers that, despite the fact he is a new creation in Christ, he does not have the strength to overcome this sin nature that would ruin his life and testimony. On and on goes the losing battle, year after weary year. "For I fail to practice the good deeds I desire to do, but the evil deeds that I do not desire to do are what I am [ever] doing" (Rom. 7:19, Amplified).

Liberating Light   But in time, God's time, the Holy Spirit begins to enlighten the failing believer as the real truth about the reign of sin. "Now if I do that I would not, it is no more I [as a new creation] that do it, but sin that dwelleth in me" (Rom. 7:20). This enlightening is the beginning of the end of the reign of sin in the believer.

The awakened Christian realizes that he does not have to submit to the indwelling source of sin, and that it is now an alien realm to him. He has a new sphere of life in which to abide. He can submit to the old source, he can choose to walk in its ways, he can by carelessness be overcome by its power—but he need not, and should not.

Some of the believer's sinful cooperation with the old nature is due to his inability to distinguish clearly between the workings of the old and those of the new. But sad failure teaches him to recognize, and repudiate, the old man for what it is. His realized need develops his discernment and appreciation of the Lord Jesus' life within.

Turning Point   The Holy Spirit uses the pressure and process of death within to prepare for the development of the resurrection life. The believer sees that the sin and carnality so often experienced is being produced by the old nature—certainly not by the new.

He begins to value his freedom to reject the sin-producing nature via the work of the cross, to reckon himself to have died to the old man. Death now separates the old from the new. "For we are the circumcision [separated from the flesh], which worship God in the spirit, and rejoice in Christ Jesus, and have no confidence in the flesh" (Phil. 3:3).

This should be an encouragement: Our growing hatred of the works of the flesh ultimately causes us to stand clear in our liberated position in Christ. He gives us freedom by means of the cross, and growth by "the law of the Spirit of life." Now we know who is who! "That which is born of the flesh is flesh; and that which is born of the Spirit is spirit" (John 3:6).

The old man will never change. It will ever be sinful and produce nothing but death, hence it must neither be cultivated nor coddled. We are to have nothing to do with the old, and everything to do with the new. "For neither is circumcision [now] of any importance, nor uncircumcision, but [only] a new creation [the result of a new birth and a new nature in Christ Jesus]" (Gal. 6:15, Amplified).

Everything apart from our new life has been fully dealt with and condemned at the cross. Thank God, we are new creations in Christ Jesus! Old things are passed away (in death), and all things are become new (in Christ)—these are the two basic truths that we are to lay hold of. We have been freed from the old and can turn from it to give our full love and attention to Him who is the source of the new (2 Cor. 3:18).

It is normal for the believer to want to grow up in the Lord Jesus, to become more like Him. But he does not at first realize how much his upward development depends on a deep and solid root system. This the Spirit accomplishes by making us aware of the fleshly life within, and the sin of our alliance with it.

By such negative means He brings us to the place of humility. Thus we learn the necessity of complete dependence on the Spirit of God, the Son of God, the Word of God, and our heavenly Father who is the Husbandman. We are being rooted and grounded for growth.

Upward Progress When the Holy Spirit has our root system well enough established, when we begin to exercise faith in the dying of the old life by the cross, and when we learn enough of the sin and danger of trafficking with the Adamic life, *then* it is that He turns our faith to the True Vine. "And hath raised us up together, and made us sit together in heavenly places in Christ Jesus" (Eph. 2:6).

In general, Christians focus on the death of the Lord Jesus— He died for me. But for the growing believer, His life must be the focal point of faith—"Christ, who is our life." His is a "justification of life" (Col. 3:4; Rom. 5:18).

Emphasis on His death gives assurance of the new birth, but what the believer needs is growth. Growth comes from life, resurrection life. "That I may know him, and the power of his resurrection" (Phil. 3:10). My position is in Him at the Father's right hand, and it is there that I find life and fellowship. Christians who dwell mainly on His death know little of life— His life.

Looking on Him as our life, the Holy Spirit enables us to exchange the old for the new. "And have put on the new man, which is renewed [recreated] in knowledge after the image of him that created him." "That ye put on the new man, which after God is created in righteousness and true holiness" (Col. 3:10; Eph. 4:24). In this risen position, hidden and resting in the Lord Jesus, I am on the ground of growth, free to grow up in Him. "My little children, of whom I travail in birth again until Christ be formed in you" (Gal. 4:19).

> Dead and crucified with Thee, passed beyond my doom;
> Sin and law forever silenced in Thy tomb.
> Passed beyond the mighty curse, dead, from sin set free;
> Not for Thee earth's joy and music, not for me.
> Dead, the *sinner* past and gone, not the sin alone;
> Living, where Thou art in glory on the Throne.

*   *   *   *   *

If I selfishly cultivate the old ground there will be nothing but a grim harvest of wood, hay, and stubble, "for he that soweth to his flesh shall of the flesh reap corruption . . ." (Gal. 6:8).

If I sacrificially cultivate the new ground there will be an eternal life-giving harvest, for, "unless a grain of wheat falls into the earth and dies, it remains [just one grain; never becomes more but lives] by itself alone. But if it dies, it produces many others and yields a rich harvest" (John 12:24, Amplified).

36 The Process of Conformation

While the ground of growth is celestial, the realm of the development and manifestation of that growth is terrestrial. We are to abide in our Lord Jesus there, in order to grow and become fruitful here—branches in the inverted Vine.

In the foregoing chapters we have sought to establish the ground of truth on which we are to stand. Now we need to see how that truth is made practical in our daily life and service. But let us first mention three of the principal reasons why many believers fail to live in the new life that is theirs in Christ.

Lack of Knowledge
The most prevalent factor is that many Christians do not know the truth concerning their union with the Lord Jesus in His death, burial, resurrection, and ascension. All know about His substitution *for* them, but too few realize their identification *with* Him. This is mainly due to the fact that the identification truths have long been a neglected teaching in schools, churches, and homes.

Misapplied Knowledge
There are others, less numerous, who do know their participation in this aspect of the work of the Cross. However, after reckoning upon their identification with Christ, they set about to produce its results by self-effort.

It is not readily understood that only the Holy Spirit can make experiential in us that which is already true of us in Christ. It is His specific ministry to apply the death of the Cross to the old man, and develop the life of the Lord Jesus in the new man. Our responsibility and privilege is to exercise faith in the facts of our identification and to walk in (dependence on) the Spirit of life in Christ Jesus (Rom. 8:1, 2). "Walk and live habitually in the (Holy) Spirit—responsive to and controlled and guided by the Spirit; then you will not gratify the cravings and desires of the flesh" (Gal. 5:16, Amplified).

Unbalanced Knowledge Still others are saying in their hungry hearts, "I know now that I died to the old nature on the cross of the Lord Jesus, and I confidently reckon upon that liberating truth. But I am not so clear about the second half of the reckoning, I seem to know more about the work of the Cross than I do about my new life in the risen Christ."

Be encouraged! Take one thing at a time. The Cross comes first: death to the old precedes the manifestation of life in the new. The years of struggle and failure have not been wasted, but have been governed by His loving hand to prepare the hungry heart for the blessed exchange. By means of His processing there comes a time when the failing believer begins to realize that living in and relying on the old nature is *sin*, not just a disappointing inconvenience.

Living in the old Adam-life is illegal cohabitation; it is spiritual adultery. The believer has been "married to another, even to him who is raised from the dead, that we should bring forth fruit unto God" (Rom. 7:4). He has to learn that in the old fleshly nature "dwelleth no good thing," and that even its so-called "righteousnesses are as filthy rags" (Rom. 7:18; Isa. 64:6).

Exchange This all-important realization provides the necessary hatred of the old man, and the desire not for change but for *exchange*. The horrible old relinquished for the holy new! But what about this life in Christ Jesus? In Him we are totally recreated, not just new creatures. Remember that in the tomb we were *dead.* Then in Christ risen we were totally regenerated, not just renovated. A butterfly is a new creature, not a new creation. But our new life and nature are a completely new creation of God. "All things are become new. And all things are of God" (2 Cor. 5:17, 18).

Knowing the Old   When the Christian's knowledge of Christ as his new life is insufficient or in error, he more or less abides in the old nature because that is the best he knows. How tragic! His mind and his life are centered in that sphere. Is that not where most believers are today? They are woefully aware of the sinfulness of the old life within, but they are hung up there. Even so, the Holy Spirit sees to it that this realm of existence becomes unbearable.

The work of the Cross has enabled them to be free from the domination of the old man, yet they are still paying attention to it. The more they dwell on that source the more it is activated—and its one by-product is "no good thing," nothing but sin. They must let the truth of their position overwhelm the feelings of their condition.

Knowing the New   When the old life within becomes intolerable, it is time to become acquainted with the new. "O unhappy and pitiable and wretched man that I am! Who will release and deliver me from [the shackles of] this body of death? O thank God!—He will! through Jesus Christ . . ." (Rom. 7:24, 25, Amplified).

There is the key—knowing the new! It was not for nothing that John said, "And this is life eternal, that they might know thee, the only true God, and Jesus Christ, whom thou hast sent." Nor that Paul exclaimed, "That I may know him . . ." (John 17:3; Phil. 3:10).

How do we come to know Christ as our very life? It is by the Word, and that by the Spirit. The Lord Jesus said, "I am . . . the truth." He said to His Father, "Thy word is truth." And He said of the Holy Spirit, "When he, the Spirit of truth, is come, he will guide you into all truth" (John 14:6; 17:17; 16:13).

If we leave the realm of the Spirit-wrought-and-taught Word of truth in an effort to know Christ more personally, some seeming "angel of light," some denizen of the dark, or an overheated imagination will have us thrilling over a "Jesus" who is not the Christ. Many today are thus led astray.

Then too, for many Christians their knowledge of God, and their attitude toward Him, are based on and controlled by circumstances—and/or their personal condition—rather than by the Word of God. They judge Him by what they feel He is doing for them, or seemingly is not doing for them. Self-centered, they complain and flounder from failure to failure.

But when our knowledge of our Father is Bible-based, we are able to evaluate our circumstances and personal condition in the light of who He is. Then there is rest and joy in Him no matter what the situation may be. To know Him is to trust and love Him. Calvary is the proof of His love for us, even if there were no other indication or if all other indications were to the contrary. "Whom he did predestinate, them he also called: and whom he called, them he also justified: and whom he justified, them he also glorified. What shall we then say to these things? If God be for us, who can be against us? He that spared not his own Son, but delivered him up for us all, how shall he not with him also freely give us all things?" (Rom. 8:30-32).

It is natural for the believer's mind to become fixed on the old nature within, because that has always been his life. But now it is sin to do so. He has a new life and nature, and a renewed mind. And he has been freed from the old so that he can dwell on and abide in the new. To think in the realm of the old brings forth sin and death. To think on the new results in righteousness and life.

Paul, in the Word of Truth, exhorts us, "Finally, brethren, whatever things are *true*, whatever things are *honest*, whatever things are *just*, whatever things are *pure*, whatever things are *lovely*, whatever things are of *good report*; if there be any *virtue*, and if there be any *praise*, *think on these things*" (Phil. 4:8, italics mine). Actually, all of these "things," in their highest essence and reality, are centered in the life of our Lord Jesus Christ.

*   *   *   *   *

As I rely on what the cross has already done with the old man, I am free as a new man to become intimately acquainted with the Lord Jesus. I am thereby resting in the very process that conforms me to His image.

37 *He Is Our All*

Think of the closer-than-breathing, bone "of his bones" (Eph. 5:30) relationship of life we have with the very Creator and Sustainer of the universe. Although He is seated in glory at our Father's right hand, He is not far off—His life is in us where we are, and our life is in Him where He is. Absolute oneness. "He that is joined unto the Lord is one spirit [with Him]." "For we are his workmanship, created in Christ Jesus. . . . Now in Christ Jesus ye who once were far off are made nigh . . ." (1 Cor. 6:17; Eph. 2:10, 13).

He Is Our Head When we see Jesus Christ as the sovereign Lord of the universe, we acknowledge Him to be the ruler of our personal lives and our circumstances. He is our Head; we are His body on earth. Our Father "hath put all things under his feet, and gave him to be the head over all things to the church, which is his body, the fullness of him that filleth all in all." "He is the head of the body, the church: who is the beginning, the firstborn from the dead; that in all things he might have the preeminence. For it pleased the Father that in him should all fullness dwell" (Eph. 1:22, 23; Col. 1:18, 19).

He Is Our Intercessor The better we know the Lord Jesus in His glory, the more fully will we depend on Him as our personal Intercessor. "Wherefore he is able also to save them to the uttermost that come unto God by him, seeing he ever liveth to make intercession for them." "Who shall lay any thing to the charge of God's elect? It is God that justifieth. Who is he that condemneth? It is Christ that died, yea rather, that is risen again, who is even at the right hand of God, who also maketh intercession for us" (Heb. 7:25; Rom. 8:33, 34).

When the believer sins, his relationship to the Father is not affected, but his fellowship with Him is impaired. It is for this self-induced exigency that we need the Lord Jesus at the Father's right hand as our Advocate and Intercessor. He is Jesus Christ the righteous, our defender in heaven against all the accusations of the Adversary. Since we have been "made the righteousness of God in him" (2 Cor. 5:21), He justly and continually clears us from all charges. And because He "of God is made unto us . . . righteousness" (1 Cor. 1:30), He is never our prosecutor.

When we fail to confess our sins, or to judge ourselves in the matter of sin, we must be chastened. When our Father's child-training is applied, it is always well deserved and for our good. Our Lord Jesus bore all the wrath against sin on the cross, therefore we grow by means of the chastening. "Now no chastening for the present seemeth to be joyous, but grievous: nevertheless afterward it yieldeth the peaceable fruit of righteousness unto them which are exercised thereby" (Heb. 12:11).

There are many Christians who feel that confession of sin is unnecessary. They reason that if their sins are already fully forgiven, why bother to confess them? It is true that we need not ask for forgiveness when we sin; rather, we are free to thank Him for that forgiveness provided at Calvary and received in Christ. But it is necessary to honestly confess our sins, thus siding with Him against ourselves, else how can we enjoy true fellowship with the One who is holy and hates sin perfectly?

The primary ministry of the Holy Spirit is to reveal to us the Lord Jesus as our new life, and to occupy our minds and hearts with Him. When we step down into the old life and consequently sin, the Spirit is grieved and must occupy us with ourselves until our honest confession of sin to the Father brings restoration of fellowship.

Yes, frank and immediate confession of sin is vital. Think for a moment of someone who observes a loved one sinning against him. Wounded, but ever loving, he forgives and says nothing. Meanwhile the loved one, although knowing there is forgiveness, does not confess his sin. Forgiveness is there, love is waiting. But now where is the fellowship and integrity of this relationship?

"But if we walk in the light, as he is in the light, we have fellowship one with another, and the blood of Jesus Christ his Son cleanseth us from all sin. If we say that we have no sin, we deceive ourselves [not Him], and the truth is not in us. If we confess our sins, he is faithful and just to forgive us our sins, and to cleanse us from all unrighteousness" (1 John 1:7-9).

He Is Our Life By now we should be seeing more clearly the wonderful truths concerning the fact that the Lord of Glory is our Life, and that we are, as individuals, new creations in Him. There is but one place, one position, where we are to abide, and that is in Him where He is. The resources and motivations of our daily lives are in the Son who is seated at the right hand of the Father. The expression of our new lives here is the indwelling life of Jesus manifested in our mortal flesh.

Our position and our resources as new creations are certainly not in the old man. Our death on the Cross now and forever separates us from the reign of sin, and we are free to reckon on that fact. Our mind does not have to dwell on and become involved with the indwelling sinful nature—death is there; life is in the Lord Jesus.

We are looking in the wrong direction, whether we dwell on the old man and are pulled down in depression and defeat by its sinfulness, or conversely consider that nature to be quite harmless and good. We have to slip past the Cross and violate our identification with Him in His death to sin, in order to traffic in that realm. Paul asks, "How shall we who died to sin still live in it?" (Rom. 6:2, NASB).

Our position as new creations is not in this sin-cursed world. We are traveling through it, but not abiding in it. How is it that the growing believer can rest and be at peace in the midst of this world of death, free to hold forth and share the

Word of life? It is simply because his anchorage and source of life is in another Person in another world. Keep looking down!

The death of the Cross stands not only between us and the old nature, but also between us and this world system. "But may it never be that I should boast, except, in the cross of our Lord Jesus Christ, through which the world has been crucified to me, and I to the world" (Gal. 6:14, NASB).

There is nothing here for us to rely on; there is everything there for us to depend on. On earth, death; in glory, life. "For if while we were enemies we were reconciled to God through the death of His Son, it is much more [certain], now that we are reconciled, that we shall be saved [daily delivered from sin's dominion] through His [resurrection] life" (Rom. 5:10, Amplified).

If today the roots of your life are in the old nature, and therefore in the world, absorbing the poison and death of those cross-condemned sources, it is time to move! There is a quiet and restful abiding place just where our Father has positioned us. Our communion is with the Father and the Son, where they are.

Is it not time to hide from the old by hiding in the new? In that attitude of faith and walk of fellowship our Lord Jesus will have another life through which to reach and replenish others. Therefore, "if any one preaches, let it be as uttering God's truth; if any one renders a service to others, let it be in the strength which God supplies; so that in everything glory may be given to God in the name of Jesus Christ, to whom belong the glory and the might to the Ages of the Ages. Amen" (1 Peter 4:11, Weymouth).

* * * * *

Fellowship with the old life results in nothing but sin, and chastening; fellowship with the Lord Jesus results in love, and life for others.

38 *That I May Know Him*

Our object in sharing these truths of the Word is that we may be turned *from* all that God condemned *to* a deep personal knowledge of our Lord Jesus Christ. Truth can be very impersonal and ineffective if its ultimate purpose is not realized. What we need is the Spirit's application of the full-orbed work of the Cross. This will enable us to avoid the sin within and without, and to give our complete attention and love to the Lord Jesus. Anything short of this will satisfy neither Him nor the hungry heart.

We must remember that it is by learning to know the Lord Jesus that we know our Father. "Have I been so long a time with you, and yet hast thou not known me . . . ? He that hath seen me hath seen the Father. . . . Believe me that I am in the Father, and the Father in me . . ." (John 14:9, 11).

We are not to know the Lord Jesus in order to emulate Him as our example. Rather we are to behold Him in the Word and allow the Spirit of God to conform us to His image. Not imitation, but conformation. If we flounder in the old man and pay attention to his clamorings, the hateful works of the flesh will inevitably be manifested for all to see and suffer from.

Our Lord Jesus said, "Learn of me" (Matt. 11:29). His infinite glory must not discourage us from pursuing our privilege of knowing Him intimately. His divine majesty is unfolded in order to display His divine mercy. To encourage the reader's further study, let us behold Him from several different viewpoints.

His Life as Creator   The Word sets forth Christ as He was prior to His humiliation here on earth, in the glory He had with His Father before the world was (John 17:5). There He is seen as Creator, in one aspect of His life. God does nothing directly, but all through His Son and by His Spirit. That is why it was in the Lord Jesus that He created us anew. "For by him [Christ] were all things created, that are in heaven, and that are in earth, visible and invisible, whether they be thrones, or dominions, or principalities, or powers—all things were created by him, and for him" (Col. 1:16). Thus we can come to know Him as *Creator*.

His Life on Earth "The fruit of the Spirit" is developed in us as we behold Him in His earthly walk and work. For actual growth, there is to be an entering into His life via the Word—feeding on Him, appropriating Him.

(1) Consider the Lord Jesus as He lovingly shares His life with the up-and-out religious leader, Nicodemus, and the down-and-out woman of Samaria. Listen closely to Him. Observe His tender concern for these individuals who represent the extremities of the spectrum of human need. Note how faithfully and effectively He applies the truth to their hungry hearts; not by method, but by nature: a ministry of *life* (Study John 2:23-3:21; 4:5-26.)

(2) Pay close attention to Him as He calls His first four disciples, and especially note the way He ministers to Peter. (Study Luke 5:1-11.) Spend time with Him as He shares and applies His wonderful parables by the sea. (Study Matthew 13:1-58.) Enter into His restful attitude as He in turn gives rest to the tossing tempest and the tempest-tossed. (Study Mark 4:35-41.)

(3) Stand with Him as He commissions the Twelve; observe Him; listen to what He shares with them. (Study Matthew 9:36-11:1.) All of this teaches us who He is and what He is like. Feed on Him as He feeds the four thousand, and hear Him reveal Himself as the Bread of Life. (Study Mark 8:1-9; John 6:22-71.)

(4) How touchingly His character is depicted in His parable of the Good Samaritan. (Study Luke 10:25-37.) And nowhere is He more explicitly manifested to us than in His fellowship in the Bethany home. (Study Luke 10:38-42; John 11:1-46.)

And what of His humble yet ever majestic service to the Twelve during the Last Supper? How our love is drawn out to Him there! (Study Luke 22:7-30.)

These are but a few of the specific instances in the Word by which we can come to know Him more intimately. Thus we realize something of the life the Holy Spirit is developing within *our* hungry hearts.

His Life in   The Holy Spirit does not limit us to the
Glory   earthy, nor to the earthly life of the Lord
                     Jesus. Knowing Him in His humility is
preparation for knowing Him in His glory. Remember the Lord Jesus' prayer, "Father, I will that they also, whom thou hast given me, be with me where I am; that they may behold my glory . . ." (John 17:24). We are to behold Him as He was and know Him as He is, so that we may be like Him here and now.

We come to know Him as He is from the vantage point of our position in Him at the Father's right hand, and this ever by means of the Word. Our Father "hath raised us up together, and made us sit together in heavenly places in Christ Jesus" (Eph. 2:6). By intelligent and confident faith we are to abide above in our life-source. "If then you have been raised up with Christ, keep seeking the things above, where Christ is, seated on the right hand of God. Set your mind on the things above, not on the things that are on earth. For you have died and your life is hidden with Christ in God" (Col. 3:1-3, NASB).

As we behold His glory there, we are conformed to His humility here, "that the life also of Jesus might be made manifest in our mortal flesh" (2 Cor. 4:11). Abide above to grow below. The Lord Jesus set the pattern: "He that came down from heaven, even the Son of man which is in heaven" (John 3:13). It is true that the source of our Christian life is in His glory, but *that* aspect of our lives will not be revealed until His appearing. "The glory which thou gavest me I have given them." "When Christ, who is our life, shall appear, *then* shall ye also appear with him in glory" (John 17:22; Col. 3:4).

First humility, then glory; first the Cross, then the crown. Is it not worth waiting for? We are "heirs of God, and joint-heirs with Christ; if so be that we suffer with him, that we may be also glorified together. For I reckon that the sufferings of this present time are not worthy to be compared with the glory which shall be revealed in us. For the earnest expectation of the creation waiteth for the manifestation of the sons of God" (Rom. 8:17-19).

What a comfort, as we study to know Him better in His glory, to be assured that the Father will honor Paul's faithful intercession on behalf of each one of us!: "That the God of our Lord Jesus Christ, the Father of glory, may give unto you the spirit of wisdom and revelation in the knowledge of him; the eyes of your understanding being enlightened; that ye may know what is the hope of his calling, and what the riches of the glory of his inheritance in the saints" (Eph. 1:17, 18). Whose inheritance?

His Life as Ruler and Sustainer Not only did our Lord Jesus create and redeem, but He ever upholds that which is His. Not only is He the Sustainer of the universe He created, but He also coordinates and directs all within the realm and to the consummation of His Father's eternal purposes—and that includes each of His own. "God . . . hath in these last days spoken unto *us* by his Son, whom he hath appointed heir of all things, by whom also he made the worlds; who, being the brightness of his glory, and the express image of his person, and upholding all things by the word of his power, when he had by himself purged *our* sins, sat down on the right hand of the Majesty on high" (Heb. 1:1-3).

The late Dr. Wm. Graham Scroggie made this observation that gives us further reason for rejoicing in the Lord Jesus and having no confidence in the flesh (Phil. 3:3):

> Our understanding of Nature, and our interpretation of History, are both partial and faulty; yet, if we are Christians at all, we must believe that back of both is the Divine Thinker, the Infinite Wisdom, and the Almighty Power, Who is the Son of God our Redeemer and Life.
>
> Things have not been started and then left to run on their own material or moral momentum, but all things are under the

constant control of the Divine Creator, in Whom all things have their center of unity, Who appoints to everything its place, Who determines the relation of things to one another, and Who combines all into an ordered whole, so that this Universe is a cosmos and not chaos.

It is not law ultimately which rules this Universe, but God our Father, and He rules it through His Son our Saviour. Human history is not in the grip of fate, but in the hands of Him Who was pierced for *us* on Calvary.

His Life Our Ground of Growth The ground of the first Adam is that into which we were born and in which we grew. It is there that the world, the flesh, and the devil would keep us in bondage. It is the ground of carnality, sin, and death—off-limits to the new creation in Christ.

The ground of the Last Adam is that into which we have been reborn and are to abide. It is there that the Father, Son, and Holy Spirit would have us grow and mature. It is the ground of spirituality, righteousness, and life—the Father's one abiding place for the believer.

As we take our rightful stand on the resurrection side of the Cross, setting our minds and hearts on the Lord Jesus via the Word, the Holy Spirit will establish us in Him above. On that ground of growth, we will "grow in grace, and in the knowledge of our Lord and Saviour, Jesus Christ. To him be glory both now and for ever. Amen" (2 Peter 3:18).

39 Summation

The following quotation from a message by Norman F. Douty seems to sum up what we have been seeking to share.

When we say that Christ's life has come into us to displace ours, what do we mean? We do not mean that this life of the Lord Jesus has come in to displace our personality. When I speak of our fallen life, I do not mean the human personality as such. I mean the poison which permeates our personality, the poison of sin which has degraded and defiled and distorted our humanity.

It is not that this new life of the Lord Jesus comes in to take the place of our personality, to take the place of our faculties created by God, but it comes in to take the place of the sinful life which is operating in our personality and employing our faculties. The vessel is the same, but the contents are different—the same vessel, the same person, the same faculties, but the contents different. No longer this sinful element, but the very holy nature of the Lord Jesus Christ filling, interpenetrating, permeating.

Our Father is not seeking to abolish us as human beings and have the Lord Jesus replace us. He is seeking to restore us as human personalities so that we may be the vehicle through which Christ will express Himself. Therefore you find that whenever God gets hold of a man, instead of abolishing his personality, He makes it what He intended it to be.

Redemption is the recovery of the man, not the destruction of the man. And when the Lord Jesus in us is brought to the place He is aiming for, there will not be an atom of the old life left, but the *man* will be left—glorified in union with the Lord Jesus Christ.

Part Four
THE REALIZATION OF SPIRITUAL GROWTH

40 *Principles of Reckoning*

The purpose of the section entitled "The Green Letters" was to set forth the truths of identification, as well as some of the basic principles by which God brings us into their reality.

As a sequel to the "Letters," this study deals with the essential principles having to do with our *reckoning* on the identification truths. It is an attempt to answer the question, "*How* do I reckon?"

To facilitate our understanding of the subject, we will define at the outset the three basic elements of the reckoning that counts.

Principles According to Webster, a principle is "the law of nature [or the method] by which a thing operates." The *how* of reckoning is based on principles. Our Father works according to His spiritual principles to fulfill His purpose in our lives. For example: He brings us into the reality of our identification on the basis of *the principle of knowledge* (know the scriptural truths), *the principle of faith* (reckon on the truths known), and *the principle of time* (yield to His lifetime processing for growth in the truths known and reckoned on).

Identification The truths of identification are those facts
With Christ in the Word that reveal our identification with Christ in His death to sin, and our subsequent re-creation in His resurrection. As foreknown believers, our Father judicially placed us in His Son on the cross—so that we died in Him to sin, and are now alive in Him to God.

Reckon   The word means "to regard as being, to count as true." Romans 6:11 calls upon us to count upon the truths of our identification with Christ: "Consider yourselves to be dead to sin, but alive to God in Christ Jesus" (NASB). We count on the truth that is made known to us; we exercise faith by resting on the facts.

It may be helpful to observe that there is a *pattern* throughout our spiritual development. Whether it was realized or not, we began to "reckon" at the very beginning of our Christian life. As lost sinners, we were convicted of our need and shown in the Word that the Savior died on the cross to redeem us. By His grace we reckoned on the truth, and received Him as our personal Savior.

With hearts full of love and zeal, we became active for the Lord as the new life began to emerge. All went well for a time, possibly several years. Then, imperceptibly, a deadly declension set in. We had been so busy enjoying the new experience and activities that we inadvertently began to neglect the Source of all true life and service—both the written and the Living Word. The inevitable result was the reassertion of the enslaving influence of sin, self, law, and the world. Almost before we realized it, we were defeated, heartsick, and wretched.

Finally, after years of failure in both life and service, we were prepared to see something of the wonderful truths concerning our identification with the Lord Jesus Christ in His death and resurrection. We saw that He not only freed us from the guilt and penalty of sin, but also from the power and domination of *the principle of sin.* Here we see the pattern of the experience of "babes in Christ": we believed, we struggled, we failed.

Now, what of the pattern of our adulthood, when we come to the place of reckoning on the identification truths? Just as in our counting on the justification truths for the initial steps of birth and babyhood, so in our reckoning on the identification truths for growth: we start immediately to work for the Lord in testifying of our new experience. We want everyone to know of our new joy and freedom through reckoning.

Not only do we seek out opportunities to share and teach these new-to-us truths, but, where necessary, we *make* openings. We are surprised to discover that few, if any, fellow believers prove to be receptive. As a matter of fact, many become antagonistic, and some even accuse us of falling into error. There are times when we limp home not quite as sure or enthusiastic about it all as when we started.

Then too, we begin to grow careless about our reckoning. We forget about the liberating truths for longer and longer periods of time. Once again we are relying more on our experience than we are on our Source (the risen Christ) and the means (reckoning) of receiving His abundant life. And what is the sure result of concentrating on experience rather than truth? Defeat! Thus the pattern is completed: our failure in the identification realm parallels our failure in the earlier justification phase.

At just this point many believers begin to waver in their hope and expectation of freedom from the old life and abundant growth in the new. Their confidence in the truths of identification begins to wane. How many defeated Christians have exclaimed bitterly, "I *tried* Romans 6, but reckoning didn't work for me!"

Most discouraged people turn back to the futile struggles of Romans 7 as a result of this seeming failure. Some even follow the alluring experience-centered errors of the so-called "holiness" groups. But whatever it may be, all outside the realm of Spirit-taught and Spirit-ministered identification truth results in compounded failure and bondage. "Having begun in the Spirit, are ye now made perfect [mature] in the flesh?" (Gal. 3:3).

Patterns spring from principles. There is a definite and essential principle underlying this pattern of seeing the truth, reckoning on it, experiencing the good of it for a time, and then—failure. Therefore, take heart, fellow believer, for our Father is ever working according to His principles, patterns, and purpose for us.

When the Holy Spirit brings us to a new and higher plateau of truth in the process of our growth, we see, we reckon on, we appropriate that which we understand. But the important thing to remember is that this is only the beginning of a new spiritual plane. At the outset of our reckoning on the identification truths, all is exciting and wonderful, and we are given a taste of the reality of these facts we are counting on. However, tasting is not eating. This initial experience is but a *token* of all that lies ahead in the long, slow, growing process. Our early enthusiasm makes it all seem clear and simple, but there are infinite depths and heights in every realm of truth into which He intends to bring us and establish us. This will require both time and eternity.

Hence, the Holy Spirit allows us to fail after our eager beginning. He applies *the principle of need* in every phase of our advance. The calculated failure is used to cause us to move beyond the early infant enthusiasm to the place where we have to dig in and settle down on the explicit truth of the Word. Before we can grow in any aspect of truth, we must be established in the knowledge of it. In every area of our spiritual development, it is one thing to begin on a new plateau, but it is quite another thing "through faith and patience [to] inherit the promises" (Heb. 6:12).

Our immaturity was understandable during the "milk-of-the-gospel" stage of our Christian life, but now it is time to face up to adulthood. We have partaken of the meat of identification. "Strong meat belongeth to them that are of full age, even those who by reason of use have their senses exercised to discern both good and evil" (Heb. 5:14). In our need and desperation we grasp a truth, but our initial knowledge is insufficient to enable us to persevere in it. To cause the truth to take hold of us and become a living part of our life, the Holy Spirit removes the token experience from us—but the knowledge of the truth is retained. By this means we are to be *established in the truth*, that we might "grow in grace, and in the knowledge of our Lord and Saviour Jesus Christ" (2 Peter 3:18). The first taste of identification awakens our heart hunger for its practical fulfillment. "I follow after, if that I may apprehend that for which also I am apprehended of Christ Jesus" (Phil. 3:12).

It will help us to bear in mind that *the principle of time* underlies all of God's dealings with us. Growth takes time! "The God of all grace, who hath called us unto his eternal glory by Christ Jesus, after that ye have suffered a while, make you perfect [mature], stablish, strengthen, settle you" (1 Peter 5:10).

41 *Three Steps in Reckoning*

Everything that has to do with our Christian life, including the longed-for freedom from the power of sin and self, is *in* our Lord Jesus Christ. Through our spiritual birth in Him, we know Him in His person to be the very *source* of our life. "For ye are dead, and your life is hid with Christ in God. . . . Christ, who is our life" (Col. 3:3, 4).

Now, failure in reckoning is certainly not failure of the truths reckoned on. Never! Without the Scriptures we would have absolutely nothing. Our authoritative Bible is the only means in the universe by which we can ever know anything rightly and personally of the Father, the Son, and the Holy Spirit. Sad to say, even with the revealed Word, there is little enough of this all-important spiritual knowledge among believers today.

We should remind ourselves that the written Word was designed specifically by God to bring us to know the Living Word. Never for a moment is the written revelation to be bypassed, or slighted in any way. We are to study, meditate, and count on it through the ministry of the Spirit of Truth, in order that we may know the Lord Jesus. He is our all, *by means of the Word.* "His divine power hath given unto us all things that pertain unto life and godliness, through the knowledge of him that hath called us to glory and virtue: whereby are given unto us exceeding great and precious promises: *that by these* ye might be partakers of the divine nature." "By him all things consist. And he is the head of the body." "For in him dwelleth all the fullness of the Godhead bodily" (2 Peter 1:3, 4; Col. 1:17, 2:9).

Surely, it can be affirmed that the written Truth, authored

and administered by the Holy Spirit, is the "vehicle" by which the Father and the Son come to us, and we to them. Still, as to reckoning on the specific identification truths centered in Romans 6, nearly all of us *stop* at the written Word. It is as though we stand there, with a deathgrip on a handful of truth, repeating with conviction: "I believe this is true, and I reckon, reckon, reckon!"

Much of the failure of our reckoning is due to *erroneous expectation*. We are delivered by belief only in the liberation truths! Certainly we must believe and appropriate these truths, but the actual liberation comes as the result of our intimate, personal fellowship with the Lord Jesus through the Holy Spirit. Simply put, the principle is: *liberation is in the Liberator*.

The reckoning that counts is made up of three essential steps. Most believers stop at the first, many stop at the second, but none can know the true results of reckoning apart from reliance on all three factors. Our freedom from domination by the sinful Adamic life was completed *positionally* through our identification with the Lord Jesus on Calvary. There we shared His death to sin, and from there we entered into His life to God. From this eternal position in Christ, our *experiential* freedom and growth are carried out as we: (1) Know, and reckon on, the identification truths; (2) Abide, and rest, in our Liberator; (3) Depend on, and walk in, the Spirit. Not just the first step, not even the first and second, but all three comprise the walk of reckoning!

1. Know and Reckon   When we first realize our identification with the Lord Jesus 6:1-10, we begin to count on these wonderful truths as we are encouraged to do in verse 11. Often there is a definite crisis in the life at this time, as some emancipation from bondage is experienced. But it isn't long before most "reckoners" go into spiritual shock; they do not understand that this initial taste of liberation is but a strengthening vision, a brief time of knowing something of what lies ahead. Our Lord removes fluctuating experience so that eternal truth, clear and steady, may be our basis. We are not to rely on *experiences* for growth and maturity, no matter how wonderful and stimulating they seem to be.

As we learn more of the truth on which we are reckoning, our knowledge becomes a set heart-attitude: I have died to sin; I am alive in Christ to God (Rom. 6:11). Although our initial reckoning may bring blessing, its primary purpose is to foster *the two-fold process of growth*: "alway delivered unto death . . . that the *life* also of Jesus might be made manifest in our mortal flesh [body]" (2 Cor. 4:11, italics mine).

2. Abide and Rest   Each of us must become aware of our union of life in the risen Lord; we are a branch in the True Vine. By means of this awareness we learn to abide. We simply rest where we have been newly created—in Christ. "Abide in me, and I in you. As the branch cannot bear fruit of itself, except it abide in the vine; no more can ye, except ye abide in me. I am the vine, ye are the branches: He that abideth in me, and I in him, the same bringeth forth much fruit: for without me ye can do nothing" (John 15:4, 5). Not only is the written Word to be counted on, but the Living Word is to be rested in.

3. Depend and Walk   The liberating principle is fully embraced by including the final step: walking in dependence on the Holy Spirit. Deep within our spirit He abides forever, and there, through our study, He teaches us the truth of our position. Then, as we reckon on the truth taught, He applies the crucifixion of the Cross to the old man, and ministers the life of Christ to the new. "Walk in [depend upon] the Spirit, and ye shall not fulfill the lust of the flesh." "For the law of the Spirit of life in Christ Jesus hath made me free from the law of sin and death" (Gal. 5:16; Rom. 8:2). Our reckoning becomes effective as we count on the Word, abide in the Lord, and walk in the Spirit.

Another subtle reason why our reckoning flounders in the midst of these steps is that our *motives* are centered in self. We know and count on identification for *our* liberation; we abide and rest in Him for *our* growth and peace; and we seek to depend on and walk in the Spirit for *our* empowering and fruitfulness. Is it any wonder we have to be child-trained and led into a Christ-centered attitude? The Father's purpose in justifying us in Christ and identifying us with Him is that we might be "conformed to the image of his Son"—"that *God* in all things may be glorified through Jesus Christ" (Rom. 8:29; 1 Peter 4:11).

The following example from the experience of Jacob illustrates God's method of *centering our hearts in Himself.* In this instance, He accomplished the spiritual by means of the physical.

The wily, self-centered Jacob had taken the correct steps, and he was "in the land." But he still had to be turned from Jacob, to God. He needed to be rendered helpless in himself, to become wholly dependent on God. The long night of the Father's dealings ("He touched the hollow of his thigh; and the hollow of Jacob's thigh was out of joint") was coupled with Jacob's trusting and tenacious wrestlings with God ("I will not let thee go, except thou bless me"). Through the merciful chastening of God, Jacob finally came to see his need. "And he blessed him there . . . and he halted upon his thigh." God blessed Jacob by crippling him in himself, thereby enabling him to limp the remainder of his life in blessed dependence on God; he was God-centered. He was brought all the way from Jacob, the supplanter, to Israel, a prince with God. "Thy name shall be called no more Jacob, but Israel: for as a prince has thou power with God and with men, and hast prevailed" (Gen. 32:24-29).

It is through this same *principle of strength out of weakness* that we are developed in the "not I, but Christ" life. "For my strength is made perfect in [your] weakness" (2 Cor. 12:7, 9).

42 Knowledge of Reckoning

Knowledge of scriptural truth should precede spiritual growth. For example, in the early chapters of Paul's epistles doctrinal truth is presented, while the latter chapters deal with the practical results of the truth set forth. We must first know what the triune God has done, before we can count on Him to "do." "That the God of our Lord Jesus Christ, the Father of glory, may give unto you the spirit of wisdom and revelation in the *knowledge* of him"; "For it is God which *worketh* in you both to will and to do of his good pleasure" (Eph. 1:17; Phil. 2:13).

There is a crippling tendency among believers today to deprecate head knowledge of the truth, and even doctrine itself. Emphasis is being put on so-called heart knowledge gained by means of experience. This, however, is to place condition before position, which is the opposite of God's scriptural pattern. Truth reckoned on fosters the only healthy and abiding spiritual experience. For faith to function, there must be Spirit-given knowledge of the Word.

The Spirit of Truth ministers truth to us by means of our mind—the spiritual mind that relies on Him. This head knowledge gives us the facts on which we exercise faith or reckon. In time, through deeper understanding and a quiet assimilation of the truth, there is both head knowledge and heart knowledge: we not only believe, but now we know experientially. Paul had believed on the Lord Jesus for many years before he wrote, "That I may *know* him" (Phil. 3:10). Likewise, he urges us to "Meditate upon these things; give thyself wholly to them; that thy profiting may appear to all"

(1 Tim. 4:15). For, as a man "thinks within himself, so he is" (Prov. 23:7, NASB).

Some people belittle head knowledge because they see many Christians who seem to know so much Scripture yet whose lives fail to "adorn the doctrine" (Titus 2:10). Doubtless there is some justification for this reaction, but it should be realized that one's knowledge of truth is always in advance of his growth in that truth. Many believers know truth in which it will take them a lifetime (and eternity) to grow.

Further, there are those on every hand who know *about* truth, having grasped and even memorized Scripture by means of the natural mind. Such knowledge will never become living experience. In the final analysis, we are not to decide about spiritual matters by observation of other believers. It is the Holy Spirit who must teach us by means of the Word, "comparing spiritual things with spiritual" (1 Cor. 2:13).

Paul states that there are some who have "a zeal for God, but not in accordance with knowledge" (Rom. 10:2, NASB). Ideally, head knowledge precedes heart knowledge. However, neither one is preeminent above the other—both are essential for *healthy growth* and *effective ministry.* Heart knowledge alone cannot progress beyond the fluctuating feelings and emotions of babyhood. It can exhort, emotionalize, and share experiences and blessings, but it cannot lead others to establishment in the truth. To share effectively, we must be brought to maturity of both head and heart knowledge.

We are to reckon and stand on certain truths for our *foundation.* Linked with these are other truths on which we are to reckon and rest for *growth.*

Foundation   There can be no growth unto maturity without an established foundation. By knowledge of the Word we are anchored and rooted in the eternal foundation of our Christian life: (1) *Born anew in Christ*: "Born again, not of corruptible seed, but of incorruptible, by the word of God, which liveth and abideth forever" (1 Peter 1:23). (2) *Accepted in Christ* (our Father is able to accept us fully in His Son): "To the praise of the glory of his grace, wherein he hath made us accepted in the beloved"

(Eph. 1:6). (3) *Eternally secured in Christ*: "Your life is hid with Christ in God" (Col. 3:3). (4) *Positioned in Christ*: "God . . . hath quickened [enlifed] us together with Christ . . . and hath raised us up together, and made us sit together in heavenly places in Christ Jesus" (Eph. 2:4-6). It is futile to seek to grow by means of these truths—they are foundational. But it is imperative that we grow on this imperishable foundation.

Growth   Once we receive the head knowledge and heart knowledge by which we are established on our foundation in Christ, the question of growth in Him is all but settled. The deeper truth, the spiritual master key to all growth and maturity, is the fact that we are not only founded in Him, but that we are *complete in Him*. "For in him dwelleth all the fullness of the Godhead bodily. And ye are complete in him" (Col. 2:9, 10). As the Holy Spirit gives us the knowledge of our position in Christ, we are prepared to know Him as our *Life* (Col. 3:4). To reckon himself "alive unto God in Christ," the branch must know the True Vine as his complete source of life. "Of him are ye in Christ Jesus, who of God is made unto us wisdom, and righteousness, and sanctification, and redemption" (1 Cor. 1:30). To reckon on the truth is to rest in, and receive the fruit of, the truth.

Can we now see where the failure began in our Christian walk? We had the knowledge of the justification truths for our new birth, and on this "milk of the gospel" we sought to grow and serve. But there was defeat, because the foundation truths are for beginning only. Further knowledge was our need. We had simply *gone beyond our teaching!* We knew the Lord Jesus as our Foundation, but not as our Life.

The same problem exists in many of our early attempts to reckon on the identification truths. We seek to reckon ourselves dead to sin without being established in the knowledge of the Cross. The failure is further compounded by our seeking to reckon ourselves alive to God in Christ without first being established in the knowledge of Him as our risen Life. We must be established in the knowledge of our foundation and source, if we are to become established in our reckoning and growth.

Three Pillars of	There are three pillars of knowledge having
Knowledge	to do with *position* on which the Christian
	life is to be secured and matured.

The First Pillar

The knowledge of our birth, acceptance, and security in the Lord Jesus Christ is the first pillar.

The Second Pillar

The knowledge of His Cross as our Cross is the central pillar. The Cross of Calvary is not only the central fact of the universe, but also of the life of the believer. As we see our identification with Christ in His death to sin, we know His Cross to be our Cross. We know self to have been crucified there; we know ourselves to have been cut off from Adam and freed from the power of sin. Only from this pillar of knowledge can we reckon ourselves dead to sin in our daily walk.

The Third Pillar

The knowledge that we are alive, and complete, in our risen Lord places us securely on the third pillar. Now our reckoning can be fully established, as we count ourselves to be alive to God in Christ. Now His life can be manifested in us by the growing fruit of the Spirit. This is the practical fulfillment of the very purpose of God for us: that we be conformed to the image of His Son.

43 Spirit-Applied Reckoning

"The Helper, the Holy Spirit . . . He will teach you all things. . . . He shall glorify Me; for He shall take of Mine, and shall disclose it to you" (John 14:26; 16:14, NASB).

"The Helper, the Holy Spirit." The Lord Jesus chose the perfect designation in introducing the Holy Spirit as our Helper or Comforter. Even in our sin, He comforts us. True, He convicts us of sin—and Holy Spirit conviction can be intense—but He does so in order to point us to the Blood that ever cleanses us from all sin, and to the Lord Jesus who is the propitiation for our sins, the One who ever lives to make intercession for us (1 John 1:7; 2:1, 2; Heb. 7:25). The enemy condemns us when we sin, and seeks to crush us under the weight of guilt. But the Comforter does not condemn; He convicts so that we might confess and be cleansed from all unrighteousness (1 John 1:9).

When it comes to reckoning, we need the Holy Spirit as our Comforter more than ever. We are quite surprised when we begin to realize how much suffering is involved in reckoning. We cannot reckon ourselves "to be dead indeed unto sin" without experiencing the deep, inner crucifixion of the cross as it is applied to the self-life. The dual truth on which the Spirit has us reckon is that which He makes experiential in our lives: (1) We count on having died to sin, and are "alway delivered unto death" as the outworking of that position of death; (2) we count on being alive to God in Christ, and the Spirit causes "the life also of Jesus to be made manifest in our mortal flesh" (2 Cor. 4:11).

All spiritual growth entails a life-long *process.* We have an infinite Lord as our life, to whose image we are being conformed by the Eternal Spirit. Our dire need causes us to long for and expect immediate emancipation and newness of life as a result of our reckoning. To a degree, the Spirit complies with this expectation during our early encounter with identification. But He must bring us into the process of growth.

Consider the pattern of the Mount of Transfiguration experience. Although Peter, James, and John were given the glorious privilege of beholding the Lord Jesus transfigured, each one had to come down from the Mount—the Lord Jesus and Peter going to crosses, James to the sword, and John exiled to lonely Patmos. The same principle applies to us. We are given a glimpse of the glory and reality of the truth reckoned on, and then we are taken into God's processing so that the truth may be as real *in* us as it is *to* us.

Through His purposeful dealings with us, our objective reckoning on the truth becomes subjective experience in our lives. As we count on our old man having been crucified at Calvary, and our having died to sin on the Cross, we become progressively Cross-centered Christians. As we count on our new life in the Lord Jesus, we develop into Christ-centered Christians. The path of the Cross is the path of growth.

In our failures, we learn more of what *self* is and thereby come to hate the natural, Adamic life. Then it is that we are taught to glory in the Cross, by which we are freed from the old life's influence, as well as the grip and lure of this *world*. "God forbid that I should glory, save in the cross of our Lord Jesus Christ, by whom the world is crucified unto me, and I unto the world" (Gal. 6:14). Reckoning is the only means of escaping the entanglements of this world. It takes the separation of the Cross, and our abiding in Christ.

As the Holy Spirit applies the Cross within, He takes us through difficulties and chastenings. We must face up to the fact that the Cross has only suffering and death as its ministry. But when we realize that "alway delivered unto death" means the daily crucifixion of self, we begin to glory in the resultant freedom. "Now no chastening [child-training] for the present seemeth to be joyous, but grievous: nevertheless afterward it yieldeth the peaceable fruit of righteousness unto them which are exercised thereby" (Heb. 12:11). If we are going to receive the benefit of the Cross, we must go through the suffering of the Cross. That is where we come to know and appreciate the Holy Spirit as our Comforter. He comforts us in the very crucifixion He applies, and we learn to glory in the Cross that crucifies. The work of the Cross causes us to "rejoice in Christ Jesus, and have no confidence in the flesh" (Phil. 3:3).

"He will teach you all things." It is often the case that hungry believers, needy as they know themselves to be, are more eager for experience than they are for revelation. They want a minimum of truth and study, with a maximum of results. But the more experience-centered these believers become, the less truth-established they will be. The penalty of this wrong emphasis is self-centeredness instead of Christ-centeredness.

This sad and selfish condition develops when *we* endeavor to handle and control the truth that we see. But the truth of the Word does not respond to self. "The natural man receiveth not the things of the Spirit of God . . . neither can he know them, because they are spiritually discerned" (1 Cor. 2:14). As we study, we are to rest in the Spirit of life in Christ. The Lord Jesus said, "The Spirit of truth . . . will guide you into all truth" (John 16:13). There are those who even go so far as to attempt to use the Spirit. They want Him to give them "power," and many other self-centered "experiences" and "blessings." The Holy Spirit does not respond to such unholy aspirations.

"He shall glorify Me: for He shall take of Mine, and shall declare it to you." In all the vital work of the Holy Spirit in the Body of Christ, His intention and purpose is to glorify the Son in the individual members. The Lord Jesus prayed to His Father, "I pray not for the world, but for them which thou hast given me; for they are thine. And all mine are thine, and thine are mine; and I am glorified in them" (John 17:9, 10).

How is He glorified in redeemed sinners? Our new birth means that each one of us is a new creation in Christ, at which time the Comforter enters our spirit to abide forever (John 14:16). Spirit to spirit joined, we are "partakers of the divine nature." At birth we are "babes in Christ," but as we grow in Him we develop in likeness of life—thus glorifying the Son.

The Holy Spirit receives the life of Christ and brings Him into our regenerated spirit. For that life to develop within, He reveals to us the Lord Jesus in the Word. Thus, feeding on Him in the Scriptures under the illumination of the Spirit of Truth, the new life in Christ grows and is made manifest in our mortal body. We grow in Him as we allow the Holy Spirit to show Him to us. "We all, with open face beholding as in a glass the glory of the Lord, are changed into the same image from glory to glory, even as by the Spirit of the Lord" (2 Cor. 3:18).

In the midst of finding out about ourselves, we are to be especially aware of what we are in our Lord Jesus Christ. While the Spirit must cause us suffering in the crucifixion of the self-life, He comforts us in our growth in the new life. "Take, my brethren, the prophets, who have spoken in the name of the Lord, for an example of suffering affliction, and of patience. Behold, we count them happy which endure. Ye have heard of the patience of Job, and have seen the end of the Lord; that the Lord is very pitiful, and of tender mercy" (James 5:10, 11).

As we turn from the old man by reckoning on the work of the Cross, we turn to the new man in Christ by reckoning on the work of the Spirit. Gradually, as we grow, there are less and less "works of the flesh" evident, and more and more of the "fruit of the Spirit" manifested in our daily walk (Gal. 5:19, 22).

What comfort there is in the faithful work of the Comforter! In the natural realm, a worm is changed into a butterfly—a different creature, but of the same order of life. In the spiritual realm, a believer is reborn—a totally "*new creation* in Christ Jesus" (2,Cor. 5:17, mg.). Therefore, we "yield ourselves into God, as those that are alive from the dead," and in dependence on the Comforter we "walk in *newness* of life" (Rom. 6:13; 6:4).

44 *Service and Reckoning*

Most of us have been warned at one time or another about "the barrenness of a busy life." Well-intentioned as the admonition may be, busyness does not necessarily produce a barren life. Rather, *barrenness of life produces busyness!*

The majority of active members in our sound churches today are primarily doers; their chief concern is to work for the Lord. But, service being the emphasis of their life, they are for the most part motivated by self. We must all learn, sooner or later, that the result of every form of self-effort is nothing but a barren waste, a spiritual Death Valley. Our growth is bound to falter and dry up when service is predominant in the life, especially in the formative years. Conversely, when *growth in Christ* is given first place, service will never suffer. Furthermore, our life work will be accomplished in His time and way—and that without physical, mental, or spiritual breakdown.

The tragedy of the church is that the service-centered believer has little or no concern for spiritual growth, other than enough development and training for what he considers to be fruitful service. Naturally altruistic, he is appalled at the thought of placing growth ahead of outreach. The activist rarely seems to become aware of the sin of self, of the necessity of the Cross in his life, or of God's purpose for him to be conformed to the image of Christ.

There are many believers who feel that the chief problem in our congregations is the existence of an overwhelming number of pew parasites. But, on the other hand, the vast army of busy-bee workers in our midst constitutes a comparable problem. Both doing nothing, and doing too much, are a hindrance to God's purpose. His will for the Christian is expressed in the word *being,* which in turn will result in effective *doing.*

The reason for this reversal of God's order is plain to see. The emphasis of the average sound ministry is on salvation and service. Get saved, and get busy! This makes the new birth everything, and service its by-product. With this approach, the individual has practically reached his goal at the outset. He is saved, and joins the church, then settles down to await his eternal reward. He attends sporadically, but must constantly be "attended to." On the other hand are those who do all the work, having little time or hunger to "grow in grace and in the knowledge of our Lord and Saviour Jesus Christ" (2 Peter 3:18).

Our Father's *ultimate purpose* in saving us is that we might be conformed to the image of His Son, not simply to keep us out of hell and get us into heaven. We have been born into Christ that He may be our *life,* not just our Savior. "And we know that all things work together for good to them that love God, to them who are the called according to his purpose. For whom he did foreknow, he also did predestinate to be conformed to the image of his Son" (Rom. 8:28, 29).

When we realize that we have been born into the Lord Jesus so that His life "might be made manifest in our mortal flesh," our heart hunger is brought into harmony with that of the Spirit for us: "changed into the same image from glory to glory, even as by the Spirit of the Lord" (2 Cor. 3:18). "Can two walk together, except they be agreed?" (Amos 3:3). Our burden for ourselves and others will be the same as the Holy Spirit placed on Paul's heart: "My little children, of whom I travail in birth again until Christ be formed in you" (Gal. 4:19). The emphasis of our life will be growth in Christ; the result of that growth will be fruitful and abiding service for His glory.

In our early years most of us place service far ahead of growth. It is true that there are "results" of a sort during this period, but the main lesson we learn in all this eager activity is how *not* to do things. We are quietly being taught and trained by the Spirit through failure. After a time, our soul-winning becomes more difficult; there are not as many "decisions" as there once were. Worse still, most of these decisions turn out to be just that, and nothing more. Our natural reaction is to place the blame on those with whom we deal, but the patient Holy Spirit finally enables us to face up to the fact that *we* are the hindrance. We are failures after all; we cannot serve acceptably.

It is usually this Spirit-planned failure in service by which we are brought to realize our need for growth and maturity. Then arises the heart burden to become conformed to His image, and have Him do His work through us. The extended Romans 7 failure in this realm also is the Spirit's means of bringing us to the responsibility of reckoning. Instead of struggle and work, resulting in failure, the pattern becomes reckon and rest, resulting in growth.

Certainly we seek to keep the lost from going to hell, by winning them to the Savior. However, our responsibility in service is not to force decisions, but to allow the Holy Spirit to beget healthy souls through the Word and the testimony of our lives. We are first to be *witnesses,* then soul winners. When the Lord Jesus is reigning and manifest in us, others will hunger for Him: "Sir, we would see Jesus" (John 12:21). When the Holy Spirit has convicted others of their need for the Savior, they will freely exercise "repentance toward God, and faith toward our Lord Jesus Christ" (Acts 20:21). Thus, they will not be badgered into a decision to get saved before they are convicted of being lost; neither will they be coming to Him to get, but to give. At his conversion, Paul, "trembling and astonished said, *Lord,* what wilt thou have me to do?" (Acts 9:6).

This pattern of service is outlined in the Word. In Acts 2:32, Peter said, "This Jesus hath God raised up, whereof we all are *witnesses.*" The Holy Spirit used witnesses to convict hearts concerning Christ. "Now when they heard this, they were pricked in their heart, and said unto Peter and to the rest of the apostles, Men and brethren, what shall we do?" (v. 37). When hearts were convicted of sin through the loving boldness of believers and the witness of the Word, and they reached out. "*Then* Peter said unto them, . . . Repent . . ." (v. 38). There was no actual soul-winning attempt until Peter's witness had effectively prepared hearts, then "the Lord added to the church daily such as should be saved" (v. 47).

When our witnessing and personal work is under the control of the Holy Spirit, the burden and aim of our outreach will be not only that others may be brought to the Lord Jesus, but that they may be built up in Him. "Rooted and built up in him, and stablished in the faith, as ye have been taught, abounding therein with thanksgiving" (Col. 2:7). For one thing, this will eliminate much of the heartache and devastation caused by so many falling by the wayside. When we have in mind the Father's ultimate purpose for each one, from the outset of our witnessing, there will be prayerful and careful Spirit-motivated preparation of hearts both *before* and *after* conversion.

The Lord Jesus is to be manifested in us for effective witnessing; He must be free to minister through us for fruitful soul-winning. Responsible service can be on no lesser basis. Others have every right to witness something *of* Him before deciding *about* Him. "Thanks be to God, who always leads us in His triumph in Christ, and manifests through us the sweet aroma of the Knowledge of Him in every place" (2 Cor. 2:14, NASB).

45 *Romans 6 Reckoning*

When we first encounter the identification truths, the most serious mistake we can make is to try to reckon *ourselves* to be dead. Surprising as it may be to some, the Word does not teach that we are to think this! Neither does it teach that the world, the flesh, and the devil are to be reckoned dead.

It is quite common for the awakened believer, one who is yearning for the liberation of the Cross in his life, to concentrate on reckoning himself to be dead. He is sincere about fully entering into this first aspect of Identification. Although he is still aware of the old life within, he feels that if he just reckons on his death in Christ intently and consistently he will in time come to the place where there is no longer any response to sin and self.

Others press this matter a step further, claiming that self is dead at the very outset of their reckoning it so. To uphold this claim, any subsequent manifestation of sin or self in the life is to them "just a shadow cast by the enemy"; they do not consider it to be sin. Also, these uprisings of sin within are considered to be simply "old habits seeking to reassert themselves," which they feel will soon be replaced by the development of new, righteous habits.

But this desired result cannot follow, as the entire principle is erroneous. Sad to say, the problem of faulty reckoning in this instance, due to a wrong interpretation, is mainly caused by an inferior translation in our beloved King James Version. In Romans 6:6 the word "destroyed" is used in reference to "the body of sin" (the law of sin in our members), thereby causing many to take for granted that self is dead and gone once they begin to reckon it so.

In the first place, the content of Romans 6 has to do with the tyrannical reign of *the principle of sin*—not its symptom, sins. The problem of sins has been dealt with at the source by the crucifixion of the cross. The King James Version's use of "destroyed" in verse 6 is far too strong for that particular Greek word. In the Greek it has reference to enslaving power, setting forth the fact that the old man has not been annihilated, but crucified; its power has been "annulled," "put down," "made without effect."

This same Green word (*katargethe*) is used in Hebrews 2:14, where at the Cross our Lord is said to have "destroyed" the devil. Rather, it is there that He broke the enemy's power—he certainly was not annihilated! in Romans 3:3 this word is translated "make without effect"; in 3:31, "make void"; in 7:2, "loosed"; and in 7:6, "delivered." Self has been crucified at Calvary so that it may be rendered powerless to enslave us; made without effect so that we may be delivered from the reign and tyranny of the indwelling principle of sin, that henceforth we should not have to serve sin.

Our King James Version has a tendency to lead one astray in the area of reckoning because of its failure to set forth our death with Christ in the *past tense*. In this version, the present tense is used in connection with these truths: concerning self, "our old man *is* crucified with him"; and concerning the believer, "he that *is* dead is freed from sin," and "if we *be* dead with Christ" (Rom. 6:6-8).

The new American Standard Bible, which is more accurate for study purposes, gives us the contrasting correction. In Romans 6:6, "our old self *was* crucified with Him"; verse 7, "he who *has died* is freed [released] from [the tyranny of] sin"; and verse 8, "if we have *died* with Christ." Thus the NASB makes it possible for us to reckon aright. In both versions, Romans 6:11 calls us to reckon ourselves *dead* unto sin, but *alive* unto God. The NASB enables us to see and understand that we *have died* to sin but are now *alive* in Christ. We are not dead, but very much *alive* as *new creations*.

The usual mistake made in reckoning is to stop at the wrong point. The purpose of reckoning is that we may abide in Christ, who is our life. The first half, "dead unto sin," is but the stepping stone into the Land. If we stop short there, we are stranded in midstream. True reckoning is to step out firmly, and to keep on going. We have died to the old Adamic source, but have been resurrected and are now alive in the new Source. *Death was the means, life is the goal.*

Although we are not to halt at the first half of our reckoning, neither are we in any way to regard that step as a superficial one. There can be no effective reckoning on our life in Christ until we are firmly established in the truth of our having died to the old. The steps to maturity cannot be skipped over. Spiritual growth comes by walking in the Spirit, and He establishes us in each successive realm in preparation for the next. We cannot rest in our risen Lord until we know we have been positionally released from Adam through death. Neither can we rest in the *process* of being experientially released from the domination of the Adamic life until we know and count on the fact that we are already loosed positionally.

True reckoning has its ultimate emphasis on the life side of the Cross; we count on our having died to sin in order to count on our being alive to God. Since we are new creations in Christ, death is forever past; we were brought out of it in Him at His resurrection. As for the old man within, we continually reckon that source to have been crucified, so that it may be held daily in the place of death. *We reckon; the Cross crucifies.*

Look carefully at Colossians 3:3: "For ye are dead, and your life is hid with Christ in God." However, we are not dead, but alive. Neither is self dead, but judicially crucified. We have forever passed beyond death. The NASB brings out the past tense: "For you have died, and your life is hidden with Christ in God." All the difference in the world! Once we see that our death to sin is in the past tense, completed, we are free to count ourselves *alive* to God in Christ Jesus, and to *live*—in the present tense!

The principle of life out of death is pictured both in our public baptism and in the Lord's Supper. Actually, our water baptism is to be a testimony of our reckoning. We count ourselves to have been baptized into (placed in union with) the Lord Jesus by the Spirit, and therefore we died to sin with

Him, were buried with Him, and arose in Him (Rom. 6:3, 4). The testimony of this reckoning is carried out in pictorial form by our being baptized in (placed in) water, which covers us in burial, from which we arise to "walk in newness of life." We are confessing that we died and were buried, as far as the old source of life is concerned, and now are risen as new creations to walk in the Spirit of life in Christ Jesus. Water baptism, therefore, holds less than its full meaning to the believer until he has apprehended the identification truths.

Water baptism testifies to our position: we have died to the old life, and are alive in the new. The Lord's Supper sets forth our experience (condition): we are being conformed to His death, so that His life may be manifested. We do not *leave* the influence of the Cross to live, but we continually receive the benefit of its emancipation for our walk in newness of life. To what are we testifying in receiving and assimilating the broken bread and the fruit of the vine? "For as often as ye eat this bread, and drink this cup, ye do shew *the Lord's death* till he come" (1 Cor. 11:26).

The testimony of our baptism is a once-for-all picture of our reckoning on the finished work, and represents our *position.* The Lord's Supper is a continuous picture of our being conformed to His death, and has to do with our *condition.* We confess that we are continually participating in His death, via reckoning, that His resurrection life may be increasingly manifested in and through our mortal bodies.

46 *Romans 7 Reckoning*

If believers knew more fully the deliverance of the first part of Romans 7, they would experience less of the defeat of the latter part! This vitally important chapter has to do mainly with *the principle of law.*

Positionally, in Christ, no believer is under law. "The law was given by Moses, but grace and truth came by Jesus Christ"; "For Christ is the end of the law for righteousness to every one that believeth" (John 1:17; Rom. 10:4). *Conditionally,* almost all believers are to some extent under the principle of law "as a rule of life." The all-too-general attitude is: I must love the Lord and others; I must maintain my testimony; I must witness and work for Him; I must resist self; I must stop this sinning. The feeling of constraint expressed in "I must" makes for Romans 7 defeat.

"The law is holy . . . just, and good" (Rom. 7:12). The purpose of God's law, both in command and principle, is to bring to light and cause us to face up to the fact of our sinfulness, weakness, and bondage. Its faithful ministry, negative though it be, is all-important. Law does not make us sinners; it is holy, and reveals to us that we are sinful. "By the law is the knowledge of sin" (Rom. 3:20).

Anything we seek to do, or keep from doing, in our own strength brings us under legal bondage. Any promises or vows we make to the Lord, any code of ethics or rules of conduct that we set up for ourselves or have placed on us, are on the basis of law and therefore result in failure and ever-deepening enslavement. The principle of law applies to the self-life, and can produce nothing but self-righteousness. Thus, the law convicts of our need of life in Christ.

The years of struggle and failure we experience are not only to prepare us for liberation from the tyranny of the principle of sin, but from the bondage of the principle of law. We are brought not only to the release of Romans 6, but to the deliverance of Romans 7. We exchange "the law of sin and death" for "the law of the Spirit of life in Christ Jesus" (Rom. 8:2).

We are given the key to the problem of law at the very door of Romans 7: *"Know ye not, brethren, . . . how that the law hath dominion over a man as long as he liveth?"* (v. 1). Exactly! All through the years of defeat, we have been slowly learning that the harder we tried to live the Christian life the deeper we came under the dominion of the law of sin. We tried to "be," we tried to "do," and there was nothing but failure year in and year out.

"For when we were in the flesh, the motions of sins, which were by the law, did work in our members to bring forth fruit [works] *unto death"* (Rom. 7:5). As long as we depended on our own resources, all we produced was sin; we hungered for life, and brought forth death. But in the midst of our wretched attempts to be delivered from the "body of this death" (Rom. 7:24), our faithful Father was teaching us what we had to know for our freedom in Christ: self is our greatest enemy, Christ is our only hope. "For to me to live is Christ" (Phil. 1:21).

With Paul, we came to recognize an internal law: when we would do good, evil was present with us. That is, we saw another law in our members, warring against the law of our mind, and bringing us into captivity to the law of sin which is in our members (Rom. 7:21, 23). All this has been specifically designed by the Spirit to bring us finally to the blessed condition of defeat where we cry from the heart, "O wretched man that I am! who shall deliver me from the body of this death?" (Rom. 7:24). Victory is found only through our realization of defeat: "I thank God through Jesus Christ our Lord" (Rom. 7:25).

First, we learn that our having died in Christ on the Cross gives us the ground for freedom from the power of sin. But unless we learn the answer to the bondage of the principle of law, we will be right back in the defeat of Romans 7, no matter how hard we reckon. Law reveals sin and produces bondage.

The answer to the principle of sin prepares us for the answer to the principle of law. Reckoning is the key to both, and both have to do with the death of the Cross and our life in Christ. *"But now we have been released from the Law, having died to that by which we were bound; so that we serve in newness of the Spirit and not in oldness of the letter"* (Rom. 7:6, NASB). As Paul tells us in verse 1, as long as we lived and walked in the self-life we were under the principle and dominion of law.

But thanks be to God, we not only died to the principle of sin in Christ on the Cross, but there we also died to (out from the dominion of) the principle of law! Further, we were not only thereby freed from the "oldness of the letter," but were joined to Him in "newness of spirit." *"Therefore, my brethren, you also were made to die to the Law through the body of Christ, that you might be joined to another, to Him who was raised from the dead, that we might bear fruit for God"* (Rom. 7:4, NASB).

Here again we must be reminded that the *power* for deliverance from the law does not reside in the fact that we have died to it, but in our *relationship* to the risen Liberator. "Christ the power of God" (1 Cor. 1:24). Unless we clearly reckon on our having died to the principle of law, we are constantly under the pall of failing to meet our spiritual obligations. On the other hand, when we rest in our risen Lord we are more aware of His sufficiency than we are of the claims of law on us, and we are able to walk in the "liberty wherewith Christ hath made us free" (Gal. 5:1). "Come unto me, all ye that labour and are heavy laden, and I will give you rest" (Matt. 11:28).

Each of us has "died to the Law" (Gal. 2:19, NASB), we were "discharged from the law" (Rom. 7:6), and we are now "not under the law" (Rom. 6:14). We are completely out of the realm of the principle and command of the law, and are forever on the ground of grace in our Lord Jesus Christ. "The Law came in, that the transgression might increase; but where sin increased, grace abounded all the more, that, as sin reigned in death, even so grace might reign through righteousness to eternal life through Jesus Christ our Lord" (Rom. 5:20, 21, NASB).

The Spirit of Truth is not only explicit and thorough in presenting the truth, but He is also exact and painstaking in preparing our hungry hearts for the appropriation of it. Most of His spiritual work He accomplishes in our lives through natural means, such as our careful, dependent study coupled with the vicissitudes of everyday life. The bondage of the principle of law finally brings us to its goal—the death of the Cross. Now we are able to understand that "Through the Law I died to the Law, that I might live to God. I have been crucified with Christ; and it is no longer I [self] who live, but Christ [my new life] lives in me [new creation]: and the life which I now live in the flesh [body] I live by faith in the Son of God, who loved me, and delivered Himself up for me" (Gal. 2:19, 20, NASB).

As we reckon on having died to the principle of law, and abide in our risen Lord, the Holy Spirit progressively carries out the will of the Father in our life. His perfect will becomes a *delight* to us, not a *duty.* "For what the Law could not do, weak as it was through the flesh, God did: sending His own Son in the likeness of sinful flesh and as an offering He for sin, condemned sin in the flesh, in order that the requirement of the Law might be fulfilled in us, who do not walk according to the flesh, but according to the Spirit" (Rom. 8:3, 4, NASB), "not after the law of a carnal commandment, but after the power of an endless life" (Heb. 7:16).

"Stand fast therefore in the liberty wherewith Christ hath made us free, and be not entangled again with the yoke of bondage" (Gal. 5:1); "for the law of the Spirit of life in Christ Jesus hath made me free from the law of sin and death" (Rom. 8:2). "Consider yourselves to be dead to sin [and law], but alive to God in Christ Jesus" (Rom. 6:11, NASB).

47 *Romans 8 Reckoning*

There is a Spirit-fostered hunger and longing in the heart of every growing Christian for *the heaven-on-earth walk of Romans 8.* The very purpose of reckoning is that we may live in this wonderful—and practical—realm of life in Christ. All that the Holy Spirit teaches us in Romans 6, and takes us through in Romans 7, combines to prepare us for the walk of Romans 8. This, in turn, brings us on to the blessed heights of Ephesians and Colossians.

Through the years, whether we realize it or not, the Holy Spirit is developing us "from glory to glory" (2 Cor. 3:18) along His prescribed path. Romans 6 is the *step* that deals with the principle of sin, and is the answer to its power. Romans 7 is the *struggle* (usually years in duration) that has to do with the principle of law, and brings the answer to its bondage. Romans 8 is the *walk* based on the principle of life in Christ as ministered by the Spirit of Life.

In studying some of the truths of this heart-satisfying eighth chapter of Romans, we must once more give special attention to the first verse. This is another instance where the King James Version might lead us into bondage, unless we study with care. "There is therefore now no condemnation to them which are in Christ Jesus, who walk not after the flesh, but after the Spirit" (v. 1). This text is actually stating that there is no condemnation for us *if* we do not walk after the flesh, and *if* we walk after the Spirit. Thus, our eternal safety would depend upon our present walk; this is law, rather than grace.

We can praise the Lord that the entire New Testament teaches differently—that we escape condemnation through our eternal position in Christ, not our present condition in ourselves. Once more we apply to the corrected new American Standard Bible: *"There is therefore now no condemnation for those who are in Christ Jesus."* We are free solely because of our redemption and position in Christ, apart from "conditions." The remainder of the King James Version's verse (the conditions), belongs in verse 4 of this chapter and has to do with something else, as we shall see later.

Notice how correctly and powerfully the truth is now revealed, as these first two verses fit together without the erroneous interpolation. "There is therefore now no condemnation for those who are in Christ Jesus. For the law of the Spirit of life in Christ Jesus has set you free from the law of sin and of death" (Rom. 8:1, 2, NASB).

There is actually a dual application in the truth of Romans 8:1 and 2. Concerning the future, the law of the Spirit of life in Christ has freed us from the eternal condemnation of the law of sin and death. As to the present, the Holy Spirit ministers the *life* of the Lord Jesus within for our daily walk, progressively freeing us from the power of sin and the deathly influence it spawns. "For if while we were enemies we were reconciled to God through the death of His Son, it is much more (certain), now that we are reconciled, that we shall be saved (daily delivered from sin's dominion) through His (resurrection) *life*" (Rom. 5:10, Amplified). We are saved from condemnation of sin because of His reconciliation; we are delivered from the power of sin because of His *life*.

Especially in our early years as believers, most of us have felt that it was our responsibility, with the Lord's help, to live the Christian life. Our unqualified failure in attempting to do so has been the Holy Spirit's means of showing us that we cannot "produce," nor are we meant to. Only the Lord Jesus can live His life through us; and He does this as we reject our own resources, to walk in reliance upon the Spirit of Life. "That the righteousness of the law might be fulfilled in us, who walk not after the flesh, but after the Spirit" (Rom. 8:4). This is the addition we noted in verse 1 of the King James Version. It belongs here as verse 4, not having to do with our redemption or condemnation, but with our walk and growth.

What it takes years for us to learn thoroughly is that the

Holy Spirit ministers *all*. By the Spirit we are sealed, we live, we grow, and we shall be raised (Eph. 1:13; Rom. 8:10; 2 Cor. 3:8; Rom. 8:11). It is especially important for us that He is the *Spirit of Life*. Even though we are alive in Christ Jesus, we have no power by which to live the new life; for that, as well as for everything else, we must rely on the Holy Spirit. (Incidentally, He should not be referred to as the "Holy Ghost.")

Too many Christians today are seeking to live for the Lord on the basis of *the principle of love*. Their thinking is, "He loved me and gave Himself for me, therefore the least I can do is love Him and give myself to Him." Such a motive is good, high, and altruistic; but it is neither the best nor the highest, nor is it spiritual. Our love is far too weak and vacillating for such an undertaking. *Self* will see to that! "For to will is present with me; but how to perform that which is good I find not. . . . For I delight in the law of God after the inward man: But I see another law in my members . . . bringing me into captivity to the law of sin" (Rom. 7:18, 22, 23).

There is only one true and adequate *motivating power* for living the Christian life, and that is the very life of the Lord Jesus—ministered within by the Spirit of Life Himself. This is not a motivation of love, but the *empowerment of life*. "For to me to live is Christ" (Phil. 1:21). It is not, "Only what is done *for* Christ will last," but rather, "Only what is done *by* Christ will last."

In Romans 8:6 we must again take a close look at our King James Version: "For to be carnally minded is death; but to be spiritually minded is life and peace." This particular translation runs counter to the actual teaching of the Word. For the believer to be "carnally minded" does not bring death, as all believers pass through a great deal of carnality as part of their growth. To be "spiritually minded" does not bring life, as all believers are alive in Christ.

Once more, the New American Standard Bible states the truth accurately: "For the mind set on the flesh is death; but the mind set on the Spirit is life and peace" (Rom. 8:6). Here, the Word is stating that the make-up, the bent, the life of the flesh, is nothing but death; whereas that of the Spirit is life and peace—the life of Christ, and the peace of God. Verse 7 further reveals the nature of the flesh: "Because the mind set on the flesh is hostile toward God; for it does not subject itself to the law of God, for it is not even able to do so."

The flesh in its entirety, all of self, is dead set against God and everything spiritual. "In my flesh dwelleth no good thing" (Rom. 7:18). The flesh is at absolute enmity with God, and can neither be reconciled nor redeemed. It took the death of the Son and our newly created life in Him to bring us to God. Our old source was not changed, but crucified; it was exchanged for the new creation in Christ Jesus. "For they that are in the flesh cannot please God" (Rom. 8:8).

We exchanged the position of death for the position of life. By means of our identification in the Lord Jesus on the Cross, we were "cut out of the olive tree which is wild by nature [Adam]," and were "grafted contrary to nature into a good olive tree [Christ]" (Rom. 11:24). How glorious to be a newly created branch grafted into the True Vine!

As the life of the Vine flows by the Spirit of Life, the fruit of the Spirit is increasingly manifested in the branch: "love, joy, peace, longsuffering, gentleness, goodness, faith, meekness, temperance: against such there is no law" (Gal. 5:22, 23). In the Vine, we are complete; in ourselves, we are being "completed" through the growth based on reckoning. We are gradually being conformed to the image of our Lord Jesus Christ (Rom. 8:29).

48 The Self-Life and Reckoning

To be perfectly scriptural, it must be said that the reckoning of Romans 6:11 has nothing whatsoever to do with the *self-life*. We are certainly not to reckon the old man to have "died unto sin," any more than we are to reckon him to be "alive unto God in Christ." The reckoning of this key verse applies to the "new creation in Christ Jesus."

It is as a "new man" in Christ that I am to reckon myself to have died to the principle of sin, and to be alive to God in Christ Jesus. While God knew me as a lost individual in Adam, He also foreknew me as a believer in Christ. At Calvary, He not only identified the Lord Jesus with my sins by making Him "to be sin for us" (2 Cor. 5:21), but He also identified me, the sinner, with the Lord Jesus. As Redeemer, He died there in payment *for* the penalty of my sins; as Life, He died *to* (out from the jurisdiction of) sin. In my identification with Him, the death of the Cross separated me from the power and tyranny of the principle of sin.

As Life, and having fully paid the penalty of our sins, the Lord Jesus arose from among the dead. Being identified with Christ, I, as an individual cut off from sinful Adam, was created anew in Him. Romans 6:11 calls on me, as a new creation in Christ, to reckon myself alive to God in Him, having died to sin at Calvary. By faith in these facts, I am to rest in my eternal position—alive in the risen Lord—looking on the death of the Cross as separating me from the influence of sin and self.

I am a new creation in the Last Adam. Judicially, the old things of the first Adam have passed away, both as to their penalty and their power. "The first man is of the earth, earthy;

the second man is the Lord from heaven. . . . And as we have borne the image of the earthy, we shall also bear the image of the heavenly" (1 Cor. 15:47, 49). My history in the earthy Adam having been brought to an end at Calvary, I now count on my relationship to the heavenly Adam to conform me to His image.

Our reckoning has to do with our position in Christ, not our condition in the body. Although the Adamic life is not the source of my Christian life, that source is still active in my mortal body. When I fail to reckon on, and abide in, the Lord Jesus as my new life, the old life expresses itself by "the works of the flesh" in my members. Paul's alternative to this is, "Do not go on presenting the members of your body to sin as instruments of unrighteousness; but present yourselves to God *as those from the dead,* and your members as instruments of righteousness to God" (Rom. 6:13, NASB). When we yield to sin and the old life, the result is unrighteousness; when we yield our "alive-from-the-dead" life to God, there is righteousness. "I beseech you therefore, brethren, by the mercies of God, that ye present your bodies a living sacrifice . . . unto God" (Rom. 12:1).

"But thanks be to God that though you were slaves of sin, you became obedient from the heart to that form of teaching [identification] to which you were committed, and having been freed from [the tyranny of] sin, you became slaves of righteousness. . . . But having been freed from [the power of] sin and enslaved to God, you derive your benefit [of the Spirit], resulting in sanctification" (Rom. 6:17, 18, 22, NASB). In reckoning, we are thereby yielding ourselves to our risen Lord, and the fruit of His life is manifested in us by growth in His image. When we fail to count on His life, the old Adamic source exercises its sinful influence and power throughout our being, making us carnal, self-centered believers.

Romans 6:6 (NASB) affirms that the Adamic source of life within was crucified on the Cross: "Knowing this, that our old self was crucified with him." We may have tried for years in our Romans 7 struggles to overcome and crucify self, but there was only miserable failure. Now we finally stop struggling, and begin to trust. We reckon on what was done with that source on Calvary, thereby enabling the law of the Spirit of life in Christ Jesus to free us from the law of sin and death.

When we have sinned, or are about to be overcome by the old man, it is *too late* then to reckon. No, our reckoning concerning self is to become our *heart attitude.* We know that the old source was crucified at the Cross, and we continually count on that fact—it is to be the set of our mind. We begin the day in that attitude of heart; we do not wait until a need arises. In this way, the influence of the Cross is more consistently applied to self, and our resultant emancipation becomes progressively confirmed.

"Christ suffered in the flesh—for us, was crucified for our sin. Therefore arm yourselves with the same purpose (suffer rather than to sin), for he whose mortal nature has suffered (in Christ's Person and been crucified) has done with sin—has obtained a ceasing from (the domination of) sin. So that he can no longer spend the rest of his natural life living by (his) human appetites and desires, but (he lives) for what God wills" (1 Peter 4:1, 2, Amplified). In reckoning, our attitude becomes one of a firm stand against self, cost what it may. *The price of birth is His death for us; the price of growth is our death with Him.*

It is difficult for us to realize and acquiesce to the fact that *suffering* is one of the main factors in our spiritual growth. In the first place, we are in union of life with a suffering Savior whose earthly ministry was expressed in sacrifice for others. Secondly, there is the suffering we go through when we fail to abide in Him, but walk in the flesh—the suffering of sin and its inevitable consequences. Thirdly, there is the suffering that results from our day-by-day emancipation from the influence of the self-life by means of crucifixion.

Our *hatred of self* is actually developed and strengthened during our miserable years of slavery to it. We never realize the necessity and value of Romans 7 failure while we are in its throes. It is normal and healthy to begin the Christian life victoriously, but in those infant days we know little or nothing about self, and little enough of the Lord Jesus. To rectify this deficiency, the Holy Spirit reveals the carnality of self—that we may ultimately grow into the maturity of Christ.

Through this practical revelation of the sinfulness of self we gain the knowledge of the holiness of Christ, and our need for counting on Him as our life. Until we thoroughly hate and distrust self, we are not fully able to love and trust the Lord Jesus. Conversely, the more we grow to love Him, the more clearly do we see self for what it is. All through our earthly life, the Holy Spirit will be allowing us to get into situations where we will discover ever deeper manifestations of the old source. For this reason He develops within us the proper "mind"—the mind to *suffer* in the flesh, rather than *yield* to the flesh.

This is the heart attitude we, as believers, need today. Many of us unwillingly reckon on the crucifixion of the old man, only to draw back from the Cross when we feel the bite of the nails. It takes a real *hatred* of the old life, coupled with a deep *hunger* for the new, to be able to glory in the Cross that crucifies.

But when we stand firm in the Lord Jesus, armed with a mind to suffer rather than sin, then it is we are yielded and willing to be "alway delivered unto death for Jesus' sake, that the life also of Jesus might be made manifest in our mortal flesh" (2 Cor. 4:11). We realize that the practical crucifixion of the Cross is freeing us from the life hated by both God and us, and all that matters is that the life of the Lord Jesus may be seen in and through us. "So then death worketh in us, but life in you" (2 Cor. 4:12). "Wherefore let them that suffer according to the will of God commit the keeping of their souls to him in well-doing, as unto a faithful Creator" (1 Peter 4:19).

49 Reckoning in Galatians 2:20

Nowhere does the believer go farther astray than by *reckoning self dead*! For, if the old man died at the Cross, it would mean he was annihilated. To reckon self to be dead results in the error of eradication. But every honest Christian knows only too well that the self-life is very much alive within. To err here is to cut the life-line to healthy spiritual development.

On the other hand, we are to view the old man as having been *crucified*: nailed to the cross, helpless, but 'not *slain*. (See Chapter 6.) "Our old man is crucified with him, that the body of sin [the law of sin in our members] might be "*katargethe*" (Rom. 6:6). This Greek word carries these meanings: "held inoperative," "annulled," "made without effect," "power broken," "put down."

As we reckon on that crucifixion, the Holy Spirit applies the effect of the Cross to self, holding it inoperative and thereby freeing us from its power. Our failure to reckon will release the old man from the Cross to resume his sinful reign in our members. There could not be this resumption if self were dead.

Galatians 2:20 (NASB) clearly delineates the two sources of life involved in our reckoning: "I have been crucified with Christ; and it is no longer I who live, but Christ lives in me; and the life which I now live in the flesh I live by faith in the Son of God, who loved me, and delivered Himself up for me." How important it is diligently to "study . . . rightly dividing the word truth" (2 Tim. 215). Unless *the principle of distinctions* is faithfully adhered to, our reckoning will be invalid and come to nothing.

"*I have been crucified with Christ.*" The identity of this "I" is clearly disclosed in Romans 6:6: "Our old man is crucified with him." Our sinful, Adamic source of life was crucified in Christ on Calvary. In our daily walk this self-life is not slain, but crucified—held in the place of death, rendered inoperative by the work of the Cross.

"And it is no longer I who live." "I" as the old creation, my history in Adam, ended at the Cross. For me as a new creation in Christ, the death of the Cross constitutes full separation from the reign of old life.

"But Christ lives in me." This refers to "me" as newly created in the risen Lord. "I am the vine, ye are the branches: He that abideth in me, and I in him . . ." (John 15:5). When our Father identified each of us with the Lord Jesus on the Cross, all the life that came from the fallen Adam source was crucified; we, as individuals, were taken down into His death and raised as new creations in Christ. "For if we have become united with Him in the likeness of His death, certainly we shall be also in the likeness of His resurrection" (Rom. 6:5, NASB).

Think for a moment of 2 Corinthians 5:17: "If any man be in Christ, he is a new creature [creation]: old things are passed away; behold, all things are become new." This speaks of our *position,* not our *condition.* Our condition will develop from this completed position by means of our reckoning faith. When we arose from the dead in Christ, we were created anew, cut off from the old source of life by the Cross, and joined to the new Source in the "power of an endless life." "Old things are passed away": the old man is passed away, as far as the new life is concerned—separated by the death of Calvary. "All things are become new": everything is new in Christ, for we are a completely new creation. It is not that the old life is changed, but crucified, and exchanged for the new life.

"And that life which I now live in the flesh [body] I live by the faith." This is the newly created "I" as a born-again believer in Christ risen; I now live by faith. *"The faith of the Son of God."* I count on Him, not upon self. *"Who loved me and gave himself up for me."* The Lord Jesus did not love the old man; He took him to the Cross! I am also to hate my (old)

life, and count it a crucified thing held in place of death by the Holy Spirit. The Lord Jesus loves the new "me," the branch in the True Vine.

The subject of our reckoning may be further clarified by separating *the three parts of the one heart attitude:*

(1) Identified with Christ, "we have become united with Him in the likeness of His death" (Rom. 6:5, NASB). We were spiritually baptized into His death by virtue of being identified with Him. "Know ye not, that so many of us as were baptized into Jesus Christ were baptized into his death?" (Rom. 6:3). This has reference to the true baptism of the Spirit. "For by one Spirit are we all baptized into one body" (1 Cor. 12:13). Water baptism by immersion is a pictorial testimony of this finished work. Knowing ourselves to have been identified with Christ, we are able to reckon ourselves to have died to sin.

(2) Reckoning that we died at the Cross in Christ is not reckoning ourselves to be dead now. We passed *through* death, and are forever alive as new creations in Him. God "hath quickened [enlifed, recreated] us together with Christ . . . and hath raised us up together, and made us sit together in heavenly places in Christ Jesus" (Eph. 2:5, 6). Being brought out of death in His resurrection gives us ground on which to reckon ourselves alive to God in Christ.

(3) As for the Adamic "law of sin which is in my members," we reckon on the fact that it has been crucified (not "destroyed"), its power over us as new creations "broken," and "rendered void." As we reckon on this truth, the Holy Spirit applies the crucifixion of the Cross to self, and we are progressively freed from its influence while walking in dependence on the Spirit. If we become careless, or choose to walk in the flesh and draw from the resources of self, the old man is at once free to bring forth "the works of the flesh" in our members. But as we increase in knowledge of the finished work, and allow the Cross to separate us in experience from the Adamic source while the Spirit develops the new life within us, we grow in the "not I, but Christ" walk.

There is further light on *the principle of distinctions* in Romans 7:19 and 20. Here, the mighty Paul is learning that in his own strength he is powerless against the indwelling law of sin. "For the good that I would I do not: but the evil which I would not, that I do. Now if I do that I would not, it is no more I that do it, but sin that dwelleth in me." Note the distinction between the two sources within—sins flowing from the old source, not the new. He also discovers that even as a new creation in Christ, he cannot by his own endeavors overcome indwelling sin.

The fallen Adam life within, the very embodiment of the principle of sin, can do nothing but sin. "For I know that in me (that is, in my flesh) dwelleth no good thing" (Rom. 7:18). The Last Adam, the very life of Christ within, cannot sin, and is manifested as "the fruit of the Spirit." "Whosoever is born of God doth not commit sin . . . and he cannot sin, because he is born of God" (1 John 3:9). As we reckon on the crucifixion of the *first Adam* source, the flow of indwelling sin is progressively cut off by the daily work of the Cross. And while we reckon on our new life in the *Last Adam,* the flow of His endless life is increasingly deepened by the Spirit of life in Christ Jesus.

The source of our Christian life is distinctly revealed in Romans 8:9: "But ye are not in the flesh, but in the Spirit, if so be that the Spirit of God dwell in you. Now if any man have not the Spirit of Christ [the Holy Spirit], he is none of his." God sees us as *"not in the flesh, but in the Spirit."* We are to reckon likewise. As individuals identified with the Lord Jesus, we were cut off from fallen Adam in His death, and created anew in Him in His resurrection. The source of our new life is the Last Adam, who indwells us by the Holy Spirit. This is *the principle of the two Adams* (sources).

Although as believers we are "not in the flesh, but in the Spirit," the self-life will flow (and grow) as long as we fail to reckon on the work of the Cross, and to abide in Christ. Contrariwise, as we walk in dependence on the Spirit, He will cause the indwelling life of the Lord Jesus to flow through us as "rivers of living water."

There is the allegory of the sea captain who, in mid-ocean, is charged with a capital offense, put in chains, and replaced by another. As the ship sails on, the chained one seeks to assert his old authority over the crew. Some of them might be foolish enough to respond, but there is no need to for he has been judicially deposed. It is now simply a matter of acknowledging the new captain, and refusing the threats and orders of the condemned one. The death sentence is not yet carried out beyond his being held in the place of death, his power broken, but he will be executed when the ship reaches port. In the meantime, he causes a lot of trouble.

Is this not a picture of the Adamic source, held in the place of death, replaced by the new Source at the helm of our ship? Our attitude toward the old man is to be this: "I reckon on the crucifixion of the cross as your undoing, and therefore refuse your reign over me. I count the Lord Jesus Christ as the Captain of my life." When we reach the heavenly port, the conflict will be over; in the meantime, we rest in Him.

50 *Reckoning in Philippians 3:10*

Philippians 3:10 involves reckoning. It is often quoted but seldom understood. It sets forth first the Christian's *goal*, then the means and process by which that goal is reached: "That I may know him, and the power of his resurrection, and the fellowship of his sufferings, being made conformable unto his death."

"That I may know him." The one reason for our existence as believers is to come to know the Lord Jesus Christ; and it is through this knowledge that we know our heavenly Father. Let it be repeated, and may it be heeded: "This is life eternal, that they might *know* thee the only true God, and Jesus Christ, whom thou hast sent" (John 17:3). This is to be personal, oneness-of-nature knowledge, not just knowledge *about* Him. Entering into this wonderful fellowship of union with Him is going to require the best of our attention here, and all of it in eternity.

The key to knowing the Lord Jesus here and now is the Word of God. We can learn about Him through our general study of the Scriptures, but we can only get to know Him personally by *feeding* on Him therein. In our devotions, we should concentrate on the Living Word as revealed in the written Word. In this quiet fellowship, we study Him in Scripture in dependence on the Spirit of Truth. We get to know Him as we meditate on Him in the Word, both as He was on earth and as He is in glory—observing His character (attitudes, actions, and reactions), listening to Him speak, speaking to Him, responding to Him, loving and trusting Him.

While we feed on Christ as the Bread of Life, and abide in Him as the True Vine, the faithful Holy Spirit is forming Him deep within the springs of our life, within our very spirit where He abides. Gazing on the Lord Jesus in the authoritative Word keeps us under the transforming influence of *the principle of assimilation*: "We all, with open face beholding as in a glass the glory of the Lord, are changed into the same image from glory to glory, even as by the Spirit of the Lord" (2 Cor. 3:18).

"*The power of his resurrection.*" We first know this mighty power of His resurrection and ascension when we see our scriptural *position* in our risen Lord. The foundation of all resurrection life is death. "For if we have been planted together in the likeness of his death, we shall be also in the likeness of his resurrection" (Rom. 6:5). "But God, who is rich in mercy, for his great love wherewith he loved us . . . hath quickened us together with Christ . . . and hath raised us up together" (Eph. 2:4-6). We are new creations in Christ Jesus by the power of His resurrection.

Our reckoning is to be based on our *position*. We count ourselves alive to God in Christ. Through our faith in this fact, the Holy Spirit makes this truth real in our *condition*, our growth. We abide in Him above, and He manifests Himself in us below. In reckoning, we are yielding; our faith rests on the fact that God has raised us together with the Lord Jesus, and this enables us to yield ourselves to God "*as those that are alive from the dead*" (Rom. 6:13).

Certainly, we cannot yield ourselves to God when we do not know we are *free* to do so. We are hopelessly taken up with the struggle for freedom, unless we are aware we have been cut off from the slavery of sin and self through our having died on the Cross. Until we know we are alive from the dead, we cannot yield to Him as such. We do not yield to become free, but *because* we are free in the risen Lord. Having died to the old, we are alive and free in the new. Count it so.

Finally, we will know the power of His resurrection when our physical bodies are changed, at the Lord's return. "If the Spirit of him that raised up Jesus from the dead dwell in you, he that raised up Christ from the dead shall also quicken your mortal bodies by his Spirit that dwelleth in you" (Rom. 8:11). "For our citizenship is in heaven, from which also we eagerly wait for a Savior, the Lord Jesus Christ; who will transform the body of our humble state into conformity with the body of His glory, by the exertion of the power that He has even to subject all things to Himself. Therefore, my beloved brethren whom I long to see, my joy and crown, so stand firm in the Lord" (Phil. 3:20, 21; 4:1, NASB).

We know the power of His resurrection in our position; we are realizing that power in our spiritual growth; we will forever know His mighty power in our resurrection bodies. "When Christ, who is our life, shall appear, then shall ye also appear with him in glory" (Col. 3:4).

"The fellowship of his sufferings." Suffering is the lot of all men, the privilege of all believers. The general thinking is that God is not blessing unless He keeps us from, or relieves us of, suffering. Far from it! There is no fellowship with, and growth in, the crucified Lord without suffering—physical, mental, and spiritual.

Fellowship with the Lord Jesus Christ is the source of our suffering. "If, when ye do well, and suffer for it, ye take it patiently, this is acceptable with God. For even hereunto were ye called: because Christ also suffered for us, leaving us an example, that ye should follow his steps" (1 Peter 2:20, 21). Paul is our *pattern* of suffering as a Christian. As soon as the apostle was saved, the Lord Jesus said, "I will shew him how great things he must suffer for my name's sake" (Acts 9:16). "Alway delivered unto death for Jesus' sake" (2 Cor. 4:11). Paul's sufferings (see 2 Cor. 11:23-28, for instance) came indirectly from the nail-pierced hands and spear-pierced heart of his Lord. *All* these things were working together for his good. Notice Paul's attitude! "I obtained *mercy,* that in me first Jesus Christ might shew forth all longsuffering, for a pattern to them which should hereafter believe on him to life everlasting" (1 Tim. 1:16). "If so be that we suffer with him, that we may be also glorified together. For I reckon that the sufferings of this present time are not worthy to be compared with the *glory* which shall be revealed in us" (Rom. 8:17, 18). "If we suffer, we shall also *reign* with him" (2 Tim. 2:12).

Our fellowship in His sufferings bears threefold fruit. In suffering we *learn something of the process of growth.*

"Knowing that tribulation worketh patience; and patience, experience" (Rom. 5:3, 4). He chastens (child-trains) us "for our profit, that we might be partakers of his holiness" (Heb. 12:10). In suffering we also *learn more of Him.* "For as the sufferings of Christ abound in us, so our consolation also aboundeth by Christ" (2 Cor. 1:5). And in suffering we *learn to appreciate the needs of others.* "Blessed be God . . . the God of all comfort; who comforteth us in all our tribulation, that we may be able to comfort them which are in any trouble, by the comfort wherewith we ourselves are comforted of God" (2 Cor. 1:3, 4).

"Being made conformable unto his death." We are "alway delivered unto death for Jesus' sake," and thereby are being "conformed to his death"—that we may be conformed to His image. As we take up our cross daily, this conformation is worked out in the two aspects of *death* and *life.* Self is dealt with by the crucifixion of Calvary; its power is broken by the death process within. As a result, the crucified life of the Lord Jesus is manifested in our mortal bodies. "Let this mind [attitude] be in you, which was also in Christ Jesus: who . . . made himself of no reputation, and took upon him the form of a servant . . . and being found in fashion as a man, he humbled himself, and became obedient unto death, even the death of the cross" (Phil. 2:5, 7, 8).

As we remain within the crucifying influence of the Cross, we are freed to abide in the life-giving influence of the Resurrected One. We are to be conformed to His death as the basis of our being conformed to the image of His life-out-of-death. In this alien world we are as pilgrims, crucified followers of our crucified Lord. "He said to them all, If any man will come after me, let him deny himself, and take up his cross daily, and follow me" (Luke 9:23).

51 Reckoning in Colossians 3

The first valid faith we exercised toward God was by means of reckoning. We counted on the Lord Jesus as our personal Savior, and were thereby saved. *The principle of reckoning is to have faith in a finished work.* Nowhere is this principle more explicitly revealed than in Colossians 3.

"If [since] then you have been raised up with Christ, keep seeking the things above, where Christ is, seated at the right hand of God. Set your mind on the things above, not on the things that are on the earth. For you have died and your life is hidden with Christ in God. When Christ who is our life, is revealed, then you also will be revealed with Him in glory" (Col. 3:1-4, NASB).

"If [since] then you have been raised up with Christ." Here, as always, Paul sets forth the doctrine before he presents the exhortation. He does likewise in Ephesians, revealing the wonderful fact that God "hath raised us up together, and made us sit together in heavenly places in Christ Jesus" (Eph. 2:6). This is the truth we need in order to reckon, so that we may abide in Him above and He may be manifested in us here below.

"Keep seeking the things above, where Christ is, seated at the right hand of God." Reckoning ourselves alive to God in Christ amounts to our taking our position in Him. Since the heavenly sphere is now our true position, it follows that we are to seek there the things of Christ—spiritual realities. Everything in heaven is centered in Christ, "For in him dwelleth all the fullness of the Godhead bodily. And ye are complete in him" (Col. 2:9, 10).

Our Father yearns for fellowship with His own. How can

His heart longing be satisfied apart from our feeding on the things of Christ, so that we may enter into oneness of mind and purpose with Him? To this end we have been made partakers of the divine nature.

Although we seek, and learn, *from* our risen position, yet the revelation comes *through* the Word. All, all depends on our knowledge of the scriptural facts. Through our Spirit-taught study of God's Word, we are given both the revelation of the truth, and its practical reality in our lives.

"Set your mind on the things above, not on the things that are on the earth." As we "eat of the old corn of the land" (Josh. 5:11), feeding on the Lord Jesus in heaven by means of the Word, we learn of Him and grow in Him. Our mind is set on the One in whom we live, not on self and this world to which we have died. "For where your treasure is, there will your heart be also" (Luke 12:34).

Dr. C. I. Scofield comments on Joshua 5:11 as follows: "The manna is a type of Christ in humiliation, known 'after the flesh,' giving His flesh that the believer might have life (John 6:49-51); while the *'old corn of the land'* is Christ apprehended as risen, glorified, and seated in the heavenlies. Occupation with Christ on earth, 'crucified through weakness,' tends to a wilderness experience. An experience befitting the believer's place in the heavenlies demands an apprehension of the power of His resurrection (2 Cor. 5:16; 13:4; Phil. 3:10; Eph. 1:15-23). It is the contrast between 'milk' and 'meat' in Paul's writings (1 Cor. 3:1, 2; Heb. 5:12-14; 6:1-3)."

The Holy Spirit ministers life exclusively from the true, heavenly Source, Christ. He is the Spirit of Christ, and He gives us the things of the glorified Lord. Even so, if we fail to reckon on our having died to sin at Calvary, the old earthy source within will continue to produce its stream of carnality. As our mind is set on things that are on the earth, we become increasingly earthbound and self-centered. When we set our minds on Christ and abide in Him as our risen life, we become increasingly conformed to His image.

"For you have died, and your life is hidden with Christ in God." In this one brief statement Paul compresses the entire finished work of Romans 6, the whole truth of our identifi-

cation with Christ. Upon these twelve one-syllable words our reckoning for growth is founded!

In this concise statement, Paul is dealing mainly with our relationship to the world and things earthly. Our having died on Calvary not only separated us from the reign of sin and self, but also from the deadly influence of this present world. By means of the Cross "the world is crucified unto me, and I unto the world" (Gal. 6:14).

"For you have died." The only way we can escape the influence of the earthly sphere, the very element in which the self-life thrives, is to count on our having died to it. The death through which we passed now stands between us and the world.

"And your life is hidden with Christ in God." Our Father not only has cut us off from the world system, but He has hidden us from its deadly power. We are in it, but not of it. Our life is anchored in, and maintained by, our risen Lord Jesus. The reason so many Christians are not living *from* their heavenly position in the Liberator is that they are not yet established in the truth of their freedom from the influence of the world.

There is a continuity of reckoning that must be followed; no step can be by-passed. Until we know and reckon on the truth of our having died *out of* the Adamic creation, we cannot exercise intelligent faith in counting that: (1) we are a new creation in Christ Jesus; (2) we are alive to God in Him; (3) our life is hidden with Christ in God. Established positionally, we will become established experientially.

When we learn to fix our mind on Christ and rest in Him in the heavenlies, we will not be oppressed by self, circumstances, and situations here on earth. Our spiritual position is not down here, praying and pleading for help from Him up there. Just the opposite! We do not go *to* Him for help, but we rest *in* Him as the All-sufficient One. We do not bring Him down to our level for our use; we abide in Him at His level, for His use.

"When Christ, who is our life, is revealed, then you will be revealed with Him in glory." Christ is our Christian life; therefore, as we grow spiritually we become more like Him. At

His second coming, we shall even have a glorious body like His. Our Father has already glorified us in Christ; our Lord's return will bring the manifestation of that finished work. "And whom he justified, them he also glorified" (Rom. 8:30). Count and rest on it. "For our citizenship is in heaven; from which also we wait eagerly for a Savior the Lord Jesus Christ; who will transform the body of our humble state into conformity with the body of his glory" (Phil. 3:21, NASB).

"*Ye have put off the old man*" (Col. 3:9). When was this accomplished? At Calvary! There we were separated from the old by our death in Christ. Now, experientially, we are cut off from the doings of the old man by reckoning on his crucifixion.

"*And have put on the new man, which is renewed in knowledge after the image of him that created him*" (Col. 3:10). The new man was put on when we were re-created in the Lord Jesus. This new nature is the very life of the One who is the express image of God. Therefore, our growth in the knowledge of Him results in the manifestation of His life.

For years we try to handle the problem of sin and self *directly*. On the negative side, we seek to suppress self, or crucify the old nature. On the positive side, we plead with God to change us for the better, and we try to be more Christ-like. But in it all, we never seem to emerge from Romans 7—total defeat.

Finally, we learn to meet the problem *indirectly*, by reckoning. We see in the Word that the old man has been effectively "put off" at the cross; and we also see that the new man has been "put on" through our resurrection in Christ. Instead of being taken up with the problem, we now set our mind and heart on God's answer: the crucifying cross and the risen Christ.

52 *The Rest of Reckoning*

"Leaving the elementary teaching about the Christ, let us press on to maturity [full growth]" (Heb. 6:1, NASB). As hungry and growing believers, we press on—but we do not press to "produce." The Holy Spirit instills within our being a determination that will not be denied, a hunger that must be satisfied. Our pressing on to His very best is fostered by the fact that we will never be satisfied in ourselves, but we will always be satisfied in Him. We are ever being drawn forward because of our realized need for freedom and growth. "This one thing I do, forgetting those things which are behind, and reaching forth unto those things which are before, I press toward the mark for the prize of the high calling of God in Christ Jesus" (Phil. 3:13, 14).

Thank God for our needs! They are the primary impetus toward His abundant life. Remember the wretchedness, agony, and frustration we knew, with very little hope or assurance that things would ever improve? We were overwhelmed by problems, and not yet aware of His answer to them. But we continued on in desperation, for deep within our spirit there was the constant yearning for freedom from struggle, and *rest in His life*. Our striving ebbed and flowed, but there was never a moment of rest. During our enslavement by sin and self, the faithful indwelling Spirit did not let us give up.

When the Holy Spirit has brought us into the depths of Romans 7, we have learned enough about self to acknowledge that it brings forth nothing but death (Rom. 7:24). Then it is that the Spirit centers our attention anew on the Lord Jesus, and we realize that He, not our futile struggling, has provided freedom from our bondage. "Who shall deliver me . . . ? I thank God through Jesus Christ our Lord" (Rom. 7:24, 25)! Thus, when our reliance is wrenched from self and every other broken reed, the Spirit has us prepared to *rest* on the written Word and in the Living Word. By means of the identification truths, the Spirit shows us the finished work of the Cross and our life in Christ, and we begin to *reckon.*

What a difference our new reliance on the truth makes! We press on with more determination than ever, and with an even greater hunger for His best. But now, the wonderful contrast is that in the midst of our pressing on, there is *rest*; the struggle is gone. We have entered into His rest because we know the facts; we know our position of freedom through the Cross, and life abundant in our risen Lord. Now we have the assurance that, as we reckon on the truths, the Holy Spirit will cause us to grow in them daily. There is rest in the midst of growth.

The Word presents an interesting paradox concerning this rest. "There remaineth therefore a rest to the people of God. For he that is entered into his rest, he also hath ceased from his own works, as God did from his. Let us *labor* therefore to enter into that *rest*" (Heb. 4:9-11). It is certain that there is no rest of faith as long as we struggle to "produce." And the hungry heart will not cease its striving until the truth of the finished work is seen and counted on. This is *the principle of rest,* by which we were born in Him, and by which we grow in Him.

The actual "labor" mentioned in verse 11 has to do with believing. It is quite an exercise to reckon that we died to sin and self, when we are keenly aware of their presence and manifestation in our life. It is also "labor" to believe we are new creations in Christ, when we are so definitely alive to the old man. The earlier reckoning, concerning our assurance of salvation and security in Christ, is preparation for the later reckoning in regard to identification.

Diligent reliance on the specific truth of the Word, in the face of all else to the contrary, is our only ground for rest. We cannot cease from self in any other way. We cannot even rest in Christ apart from counting on the revelation of God's Word.

No matter how far we progress in our growth, there will always be a degree of this "labor" involved—turning from the testimony of the temporal, to the eternal witness of Scripture. This especially necessary because self will never change; it will always be sinful, never possessed of one good thing. We must ever count on the *exchange* of the cross to separate us from the influence of self, freeing us to rest in the life of our Lord.

Knowing, and resting in, the finished work of our identification causes us to be neither slack, nor self-confident. Rather, knowing what He has done *for* us on the Cross, and *with* us in Christ, makes us all the more hungry and eager to know experientially what is already ours positionally. "Being confident of this very thing, that he which hath begun a good work in you will perform it until the day of Jesus Christ" (Phil. 1:6).

There is every scriptural reason about us to be perfectly confident in the Lord Jesus for our growth to maturity, and not to be discouraged by the length of time it takes or by the unchangeableness of self. We are "called according to his purpose. For whom he did foreknow, he also did predestinate to be conformed to the image of his Son" (Rom. 8:28, 29). "Faithful is he that calleth you, who also will do it" (1 Thess. 5:24). "For it is God which worketh in you both to will and to do of his good pleasure" (Phil. 2:13).

His dealings with us for our growth, especially as He makes us a "grain of wheat" to fall into the ground and die, may not be very "restful"; but our rest is in Him, and in the precise statements of His Word. We abide in Christ during the *processing* required for us to be brought to the fulfillment of His purpose; we do not fret and struggle because we are not mature the moment we see His standard for us in the Word.

There is another very important aspect of rest. This has to do with our *witness to others.* When we first begin to receive some of the benefit of reckoning, we are bent on teaching the truths of identification immediately. We know just the ones who need victory! It is easy to forget how long it took for us to come to the threshold of this realm of reckoning, and how thoroughly we had to be *prepared* before we were at all interested in the so-called "deeper truths." But we soon discover that there are very few believers who are responsive.

It is wise to remain comparatively quiet about the liberating truths for the first year or so following our awakening. After a period of reckoning and deeper study, we will not only know better what to share, but how, when, and with whom. Our teaching should be in the attitude of sharing. "If thou put the brethren in remembrance of these things, thou shalt be a good minister of Jesus Christ, nourished up in the words of faith and of good doctrine, *whereunto thou hast attained*" (1 Tim. 4:6).

Once we begin to reckon, some of us make the mistake of seeking to straighten out our pastor and the church along these lines. But our testimony must first be observed by others, and then heard. Only hungry, prepared hearts can receive. Often, barriers are raised by premature teaching; these may take years to remove, and sometimes they are never overcome. It is best to go slowly—at His pace—and make progress that abides.

Actually, the pulpit is not the ideal medium for sharing the truths of identification. No matter how sound and alive a congregation may be, there are only a few individuals at any one time who are ready to enter into the truths of the Cross. The Spirit would have us prayerfully watch for the hungry heart, feeding the few in preference to offending the many. Furthermore, those about us have a right to observe over a period of time whether or not our witness and our walk are valid. "And let us not be weary in well-doing: for in due season we shall reap, if we faint not" (Gal. 6:9).

53 *Results of Reckoning*

It should be evident by now that the truths we have been studying are interrelated, and interdependent. Together, they form a single unit of truth—centered in the Cross and our risen Lord. Their express purpose is to conform us to the image of God's Son. To consolidate and conclude our study, let us consider a few of the *results of reckoning.*

The Continuity "Consider yourselves to be dead to sin"
of the Cross (Rom. 6:11, NASB). Having reckoned upon a finished work, we must be prepared to experience the results of the position taken. Counting ourselves to have died to sin at Calvary is synonymous with taking up that Cross. It is to be expected that the result of this is *daily crucifixion.* In this connection, the principle of distinctions in Chapter 10 is to be remembered: our dead-to-sin reckoning includes two factors—the old man as crucified, and the new man as having died to sin.

The old man crucified. Our reckoning the old man as crucified results in the Spirit's leading us daily in the path of the Cross. He allows us, chiefly through our own mistakes and willfulness, to become enmeshed in situations and circumstances that hold the self-life on the Cross, that crucify it and break its power. There is nothing easy or pleasant about the Cross, but we learn to *glory* in it because its crucifying power frees us from the "law of sin and death" (Rom. 8:2).

The new man dead to sin. As we exercise the reckoning attitude of having died to sin, and hence take up our Cross daily, the result is that we enjoy increasingly the freedom and the abundance of our new life in the risen Lord. We find that the death that we passed through at Calvary now stands between us and the grip of sin and self. In our *standing,* we count on the crucifixion of the old Adamic source; in our *state,* we find ourselves "alway delivered unto death for Jesus' sake" (2 Cor. 4:11). This dying daily *both* holds the self-life crucified, and manifests the Christ-life in us. *The continuity of the Cross in our lives produces continual freedom from the reign of sin.*

The Continuity of Manifestation   "Consider ye also yourselves to be . . . alive to God in Christ Jesus" (Rom. 6:11, NASB). The foremost reason for reckoning ourselves to be in the glorified Lord is that His risen life may be *manifested.* Although our "life is hid with Christ in God," His life is not meant to be hid in us!

The wonderful fact about this reckoning is that out of our being "always delivered unto death," out of our "being made conformable unto his death," His resurrection life emerges. As long as we are in this unredeemed body, which is vulnerable to temptation and prone to sin, we are going to have to count on the crucifixion of the Cross to deal continually with the Adamic life within. But the very things that crucify provide the daily death from which our new life in Christ is revealed. The more death, the more life! "For we which live are alway delivered unto death for Jesus' sake, that the life also of Jesus might be made manifest in our mortal flesh" (2 Cor. 4:11). *The continuity of manifestation has its source in our continual conformity to His death.*

The Continuity of Life Out of Death   "So then death worketh in us, but life in you" (2 Cor. 4:12). This is the cumulative result of our *life-out-of-death reckoning.* What is the essential characteristic of the Lord Jesus that is to be manifested in us? It is the *sacrificial* quality of being poured out for others. We are not struggling believers who barely exist until we finally fall into heaven; we are recipients of resurrection life for ourselves, and sacrificial life unto all! "I am come that they might have life, and that they might have it more abundantly" (John 10:10).

When we reckon ourselves alive to God in our risen Lord, we are thereby taking our position as seated with Him in the heavenlies. We know that the anchor and source of our life is safely and eternally hid with Christ in God. We are assured that nothing, and no one, can touch us apart from His blessed will (Rom. 8:35-39). Our attitude is that of *looking down* on all that He takes us through—we are not under His circumstances, but above them all in our victorious Lord. Standing in our position, we learn in whatever state we are in, "therewith to be content"; we learn how to be abased, and we learn how to abound (Phil. 4:11, 12).

We enter each day (even Monday), and each situation, from that blessed vantage point of *looking down*. Resting in our risen Lord gives us rest in our pilgrim path. We abide in Him, accepting everything from His nail-pierced hands. "*In* every thing give thanks: for this is the will of God in Christ Jesus concerning you" (1 Thess. 5:18).

Always to be remembered is the fact that the One in whom we live in glory is forever viewed as "a Lamb as it had been slain" (Rev. 5:6). While we abide in and reckon on our life in the Lamb of God, and are taken through the Spirit's processing, His sacrificial lamb-like qualities will be manifested in and through us. Death works in us, but life in others.

Another blessed result of being always delivered to death is *a growing knowledge, by experience, of our crucified, risen Lord.* As the Holy Spirit delivers us day by day to the path of the Cross, we suffer infirmities, reproaches, necessities, persecutions, and distresses "for Jesus' sake." "That I may know him" is closely related to "the fellowship of his sufferings" (Phil. 3:10). Our confidence in the Lord Jesus develops as we realize that His grace is sufficient for all these things, and that His strength is made perfect in our weakness (2 Cor. 12:9, 10). We are compelled to prove His faithfulness at every point of need.

Although we are living in our risen Lord, we are camping in this body of humiliation, and serving in this world of death. Therefore, our Father keeps us in the place of need and helplessness in ourselves. "We have this treasure in earthen vessels, that the excellency of the power may be of God, and not of us" (2 Cor. 4:7). As we are kept dependent, we grow in His submissive, yielded life. "I come to do thy will, O God" (Heb. 10:9). Abiding in the Lord Jesus, it is effortless and natural to yield. The only struggle in the matter of yielding erupts from the self-like; that source never was, never will be, not ever can be, in the subjection to the Father (Rom. 8:7).

Paul's urgent plea for the believer's yielding and consecration is based on reckoning. "I beseech you therefore, brethren, by the mercies of God, that ye present your bodies *a living sacrifice*" (Rom. 12:1). To present our bodies is to yield our faculties, our new life in Christ. "Yield yourselves unto God, as those that are alive from the dead [new creation], and your members as instruments of righteousness unto God" (Rom. 6:13). Life-out-of-death reckoning results in our becoming a "living sacrifice." Such a one is always delivered to death— but, out of that daily death, new life is constantly manifested.

Our reckoning maintains us in *the life-out-of-death principle*. This taking up our Cross renders us a "grain of wheat," and results in our losing our old life. The Holy Spirit "buries" us here in this situation and there in that location, so that we might not abide alone but that there may be a rich harvest of golden grain "for Jesus' sake." It is comforting to realize that the same process of the Cross that holds the old man crucified, causes the new man to be manifest. The burial of the "grain of wheat" makes the old life powerless, and the new life fruitful (John 12:24, 25, NASB).

Some of the "graves" out of which His sacrificial life arises are the ministry, the mission field, the home, the school, the hospital, and the place of employment. Are these not the very places in which His resurrection life must be manifested, where His poured-out life needs to be shared and received? It is as we reckon on our heavenly position that we are able to rest in any "grave." He had prepared for us, rejoicing in His victory that emerges from our daily deliverance to death. We abide in the Lord Jesus, that He may bring us through all the processing required for fruitful life and service, "not somehow, but triumphantly."

Hereby we learn that "all things are for your sakes, that the abundant grace might through the thanksgiving of many redound to the glory of God. For which cause we faint not; but though our outward man perish, yet the inward man [new man] is renewed day by day" (2 Cor. 4:15, 16). "And we know that all things work together for good to them that love God, to them who are the called according to his purpose. For whom he did foreknow, he also did predestinate to be conformed to the image of his Son" (Rom. 8:28, 29).

Take heart, reckoning pilgrim! The *continuity of life out of death leads to the Crown.* "It is a faithful saying: For if we be dead with him, we shall also live with him: If we suffer, we shall also reign with him" (2 Tim. 2:11, 12). "When Christ, who is our life, shall appear, then shall ye also appear with him in *glory*" (Col. 3:4). Maranatha!

54 Foundation of Reckoning

Reckoning on our life-union with the Lord Jesus Christ establishes us in the full *assurance* of salvation. On this foundation we are able to reckon on our *eternal, unconditional security* in Him. Until we are grounded in the truths of substitution and union, we are not prepared for the more demanding reckoning of our *identification* with Him in His death and resurrection—and on to ascension.

The believer who does not realize that he is eternally secure in Christ—a birth truth for babes—is certainly not going to be able to trust Him for emancipation from sin and maturity of growth. Those who begin weakly, and are not instructed concerning their *position* in the Lord Jesus, are apt to remain weaklings. They move mainly up, down, and backward, with rarely any forward spiritual progress and abiding growth. For the most part, they subsist on experiences and so-called blessings; they seem to go from one crisis to another, never really settling down to reckon on Christ risen as the source of their life here and now.

It has been felt necessary to include the following selected material on Eternal Security (author unknown). These truths may be of help to any believers who are attempting to enter on the reckoning of identification before they are settled in that of *justification.*

"If you recognize in the Word of Truth
    that the Lord Jesus Christ is the Savior because He is God
    the Son who became the Son of Man, and as such bore in
    His body the sins of the world;

"And if you rest in Him
in self-surrender for fellowship, relying with confidence on Him alone for deliverance from the guilt and penalty of your sins and from the power of indwelling sin;

"Then there are *twelve proofs* that you can never be lost:

1. Because in the eternal, sure *purpose of God,* you are a 'vessel of mercy' and will finally be 'conformed to the image of His Son.' 'That He might make known the riches of His glory on the vessels of mercy, which He had afore prepared unto glory.' 'For whom He did foreknow, He also did predestinate to be conformed to the image of His Son' (Rom. 9:23; 8:29).

2. Because *God's infinite power* is no longer hindered by your sins, but can wholly keep you safe, for the Blood of Christ still removes your guilt. 'He is the propitiation for our sins' (1 John 2:2).

3. Because *God's love* for you, supremely expressed at Calvary, can now be manifested 'much more' and so accomplish His every desire for you. 'God commendeth His love toward us, in that, while we were yet sinners, Christ died for us. Much more then, being justified by His Blood, we shall be saved from wrath through Him. For if, when we were enemies, we were reconciled to God by the death of His Son, much more, being reconciled, we shall be saved by His life' (Rom. 5:8-10).

4. Because of His delight in the Son, God can never reject the *prayer of the Son* asking Him to keep 'them which Thou hast given Me.' 'I pray for them . . . for they are Thine.' 'Holy Father, keep through Thine own Name those whom Thou hast given Me' (John 17:9, 11).

5. Because the *death of the Son,* having a value equivalent to the punishment demanded for all your sins, has paid also for sins you now commit. 'There is therefore now no condemnation to them which are in Christ Jesus.' 'Who is he that condemneth? It is Christ that died, yea rather,

that is risen again, who is even at the right hand of God, who also maketh inercession for us' (Rom. 8:1, 34).

6. Because by the *resurrection of Christ* God has broken your connection with Adam and joined you to Christ for acceptance and life. 'You, being dead in your sins . . . hath He quickened [enlifed] together with Him, having forgiven you all trespasses.' 'Yield yourselves unto God, as those that are alive from the dead' (Col. 2:13; Rom. 6:13).

7. Because, although your sin could hurl you into hell, Christ as your *Advocate* defends you. 'Christ is . . . entered . . . into heaven itself, now to appear in the presence of God for us.' 'Now once in the end of the world hath He appeared to put away sin by the sacrifice of Himself' (Heb. 9:24, 26).

8. Because Christ 'ever liveth *to make intercession*' for you, Satan has no power to unsave you. 'He is able also to save them to the uttermost that come unto God by Him, seeing He ever liveth to make intercession for them' (Heb. 7:25).

9. Because the Holy Spirit has taken over your body as *His personal, permanent home.* 'I will pray the Father, and He shall give you another Comforter, that He may abide with you forever' (John 14:16).

10. Because the Holy Spirit has planted in you *the very life of God,* making God your real Father. 'Which were born, not of blood, nor of the will of the flesh, nor of the will of man, but of God' (John 1:13).

11. Because the Holy Spirit has now united you with Christ and you are *a very part of Himself.* 'For by one Spirit are we all baptized into one Body' (1 Cor. 12:13).

12. Because the Holy Spirit in you is the *seal* that your salvation is a finished transaction. 'Grieve not the Holy Spirit of God, whereby ye are sealed unto the day of redemption' (Eph. 4:30).

"Though your present sins cannot unsave you, remember there are *other penalties* you bring upon yourself, the least of which is chastisement at your Father's hand." "Do not faint when He corrects you; for those whom the Lord loves He disciplines" (Heb. 12:6, Weymouth).

Further, "to accept and teach that a Blood-bought child of God can fall from grace is to assault the very *nature, character,* and *sovereign purpose* of God, as well as His *justice* and His *love.*

"Such teaching is an assault on the *nature* of God in that believers are declared to be 'partakers of the divine nature' (2 Peter 1:4); 'born, not of blood, nor of the will of the flesh, nor of the will of man, but of God' (John 1:13); and indwelt by the Holy Spirit of God (John 14:16, 17).

"It is an assault on the *character* of God—His faithfulness and truthfulness, in that the life He imparts He gives His pledge to maintain. His promise is, 'I give unto them eternal life; and they shall never perish, neither shall any man pluck them out of My hand' (John 10:28): 'and shall not come into condemnation; but *is* passed from death unto life' (John 5:24).

"Also, the doctrine of 'falling from grace' is an assault on the *sovereign purpose* of God as set forth in Romans 8:28-30, where the believer is seen in the purpose of God in the eternity of the past, in His foreknowledge and predestination, and in the eternity of the future sharing the very glory of Christ (John 17:22-26).

"Then, it is an assault on the *justice* of God, in that God declares concerning the believer, 'Your life is hid with Christ in God' (Col. 3:3), and that there is now 'no condemnation to them which are in Christ Jesus,' and no separation 'from the love of God, which is in Christ Jesus our Lord' (Rom. 8:1, 37-39). Thus, we can thank our Heavenly Father for His justice, for it is this which preserves the child of God from a second charge:

'Payment, God cannot twice demand,
First at my bleeding Surety's hand,
And then again at mine.'

"Lastly, it is an assault on the *love* of God, in that God declares His love 'an everlasting love' from which nothing 'shall be able to separate,' for He is 'able to keep you from falling, and to present you faultless before the presence of His glory with exceeding joy' (Jer. 31:3; Rom. 8:39; Jude 24)."

Part Five

A GUIDE TO SPIRITUAL GROWTH

55 *"The Way Up Is Down"*

The two basic truths to be learned in spiritual progress are: the bankruptcy of self; our riches in Christ.

It is the utter faithfulness of the Father that so deeply impresses the awakened believer, the one who hungers to "grow in grace, and in the knowledge of our Lord and Saviour Jesus Christ" (2 Peter 3:18). "I will sing of the mercies of the LORD for ever: with my mouth will I make known thy faithfulness to all generations" (Ps. 89.1). Through all my failure, my Father is working for my victory.

And at first it seems quite the opposite of faithfulness when the sovereign Father sets the hungry one's faith and feet on the path of His purpose. That is because there is the negative side of death as well as the positive side of life in the working out of His purpose to conform us to the image of His Son (Rom. 8:29). He has decreed that "all things [both negative and positive] work together for good to them that love God, to them who are the called according to his purpose" (Rom. 8:28).

The negative comes first, when the Father begins to transmit that purpose to the life of the Christian in terms of spiritual growth. This is when He may not seem to be very faithful. Nevertheless, "faithful are the wounds of a friend," because "a friend loveth at all times" (Prov. 27:6; 17:17).

Failure Categorized   With some, the downward trend begins early in the Christian life. After a time of faithfulness in Bible study and memorization, church activity, prayer, and witnessing, there comes a decline.

Guilt-fostered attempts are made to regain the ground lost, but without avail. Heartbreaking as it is, the badly shaken Christian is being prepared early to realize the power of the self-life.

For most, the awakening comes much later. A pastor, for instance, after years of training and the hard work of becoming established in the ministry, is confronted with failure in both life and service. All of his praying, preaching, visitation, and counseling, have not brought into being a growing and spiritual congregation.

Another leader has been successful in developing a large Sunday school and congregation, including an impressive missionary budget, only to realize at last that all has been man-centered and not established on the Lord Jesus Christ and wholly for His glory.

A faithful layman has given time, talent, and treasure to his church, serving in various capacities of responsibility for many years. Ultimately he becomes discouraged and even disillusioned due to his own lack of growth in Christ, and the dearth of spiritual development in the lives of those whom he serves.

A Christian wife and mother seeks to establish and maintain a Christ-centered home for her family, as well as faithfully to carry out her church duties and activities. Often husband and children fail to respond to the Savior, resulting in heartache and sometimes tragedy.

Teen-aged believers revel in their church activities and the fellowship of other groups. Then, off to college. All too often the sophistication of the present-day campus and classroom, whether secular or Christian, overwhelm the immature. The result is spiritual failure and conformity to the carnal crowd.

On the other hand, many Christian young people make spiritual progress during their schooling and respond to a missionary challenge, only to turn aside before the goal is realized. Still others go to the foreign field, but drop out after the first term abroad.

Lastly, there is the missionary who has labored faithfully on the field term after term, who finally comes to the place of hunger for a deeper work in his life, as well as in the lives of those being served.

Failure   Need, spiritual need! This is the prerequi-
Recognized   site for growth in Christ. All of these circumstances of failure have been controlled by our ever-faithful Father, the God of circumstances. He knows what needs we need to keep us needy! It is true that the downward path (the negative side) has been the consequence both of the workings of self and the tactics of the enemy. Nevertheless, it is also true that the Father has seen to it that it happened, in order that the hunger caused through failure might be satisfied in the Lord Jesus Christ.

Countless Christians today are in the midst of utter failure—that they know. What they do not as yet know is that at the same time they are in the midst of the Father's purpose for them. During the initial downward process they have been blinded to the work of His faithful hands, in order that they might come to realize something of the extent of their weakness and the overpowering strength of the self-life. Down! and yet—"nor depth . . . shall be able to separate us from the love of God, which is in Christ Jesus our Lord" (Rom. 8:39).

Ever paradoxically, our Father uses our negatives to bring forth His positives. Our sin meant death for His Son, that we might have life (John 3:16). He was made to be our sin on the Cross, that we might be made the righteousness of God in Him (2 Cor. 5:21). "What shall we say then? Shall we continue in sin, that grace may abound? God forbid!" (Rom. 6:1, 2). God's "all things" working together for our good are in His hands, not ours! He is our Sovereign, we are His subjects. We cannot escape from His eternal love—"the Lord corrects and disciplines every one whom He loves" (Heb. 12:6, Amplified).

Many children of God today have all but given up. Self and the world have been steadily taking over in their once bright Christian lives and service. Most have simply quit trying to live the Christian life; many have become sick and tired of church for various reasons, and no longer attend regularly if at all. Others are no longer attempting to maintain a Christian home; while there are those who have dropped out of

Bible school or seminary, the pastorate, the mission field. Many Christian couples once had a hunger and vision for full-time service, but nothing came of it; hence, seeming failure and guilt have hung over their lives as a dark pall.

There are other couples who have entered into their life service and labored diligently for years, but there has not been solid spiritual growth or lasting fruit. They seek to carry on, trying one thing after another, but never seem to quite find *His* answer to the hunger and need of their hearts and lives. It seems to them that the only alternative is to quit as gracefully as possible and get into something that they can handle.

Failure Utilized These are some of the conditions that the Father uses to prepare us to see and enter into that which He has already given in the Lord Jesus. There must be this drastic revelation of self, by the most effective means suited to the individual—all in the realm of personal failure.

The agonizing downward process brings us from simply believing on Him at Calvary, to living in Him in heaven—from substitution, to personal identification. As lost sinners we were prepared by the Spirit to see and accept the Lord Jesus as our Substitute; as defeated believers we have to be prepared by the Spirit to see and abide in the Lord Jesus as our Life. There is no alternative, and He has been faithfully and quietly carrying it out all through the fruitless and failure-ridden years. "Beloved, think it not strange concerning the fiery trial which is to try you, as though some strange thing happened unto you" (1 Peter 4:12).

When the Father has us prepared by means of Romans 7, He opens the liberating truths of Romans 8—but not until! It is first, "O wretched man that I am! who shall deliver me from the body of this death?" and then, "I thank God through Jesus Christ our Lord" (Rom. 7:24, 25). Then, "Come, and let us return unto the LORD; for he hath torn, and he will heal us; he hath smitten, and he will bind us up" (Hosea 6:1). "Faithful is he that calleth you, who also will do it" (1 Thess. 5:24).

56 *Think Position!*

Our position in the Lord Jesus Christ is made up of two parts: death and life. Identification with Him in His death issues in identification with Him in His life. Spiritual growth is the result of the old man abiding in the death of the Cross, and the new man abiding in the risen life of Christ. The way of the Cross doesn't end at the Cross!

The principles on which our Father carries out His purpose in us are eternal and unchanging. He is "the Father of lights, with whom is no variableness, neither shadow of turning" (James 1:17). He begins in the heights, goes down to the depths, and returns to the heights.

Let us consider this principle as illustrated in the work of the Lord Jesus. He came down to earth from His heavenly glory (John 17:4); He was made to be our sin on the Cross, and willingly died as our Redeemer (Rom. 5:8); He took us down into His death to sin as our Deliverer (Rom. 6:4); He then brought us as "new creations" in Himself to His eternal position in heaven (2 Cor. 5:17; Eph. 2:4-6). Life, death, harvest!

Position Above   Our Father begins by placing each believer *above*—in Christ—the very moment he repents and receives Him as his personal Savior. "Ye are risen with him through the faith of the operation of God, who hath raised him from the dead. And you, being dead in your sins . . . hath he quickend [re-created] together with him, having forgiven you all trespasses" (Col. 2:12,13). Yes, "your life is hid with Christ in God" (Col. 3:3). This is exactly where the

Father has positioned every believer, whether or not he is aware of the wondrous fact; whether in service, or out of service; whether victorious, or defeated.

Position   Although the Christian has been positioned
Unknown   above, he is unaware of this fact when he
                      comes to the Savior at the foot of the Cross.
What he sees is that the penalty of his sins has been paid, and that he is thereby assured of his place in glory. Therefore, most new converts begin to live and work *for* Him from the motive of gratitude for their salvation. The usual exhortation they are given is, "Now get busy and serve the Lord." This they seek to do on the basis of the birth truths. From this inadequate ground the majority of young Christians go down in defeat.

Others, more thoroughly taught, move forward in the knowledge of their reconciliation to God, their acceptance in the Lord Jesus, as well as their completeness and eternal security in Him. Even with this firm foundation on which to stand, they have yet to learn that more is needed. The resultant failure in trying to live by these basic truths is the Father's preparation for the Christian to realize his need for deliverance.

The Holy Spirit then begins to reveal the truths that will deliver him from the reign of sin (Rom. 5:21). The Lord has promised that "ye shall know the truth, and the truth shall make you free" (John 8:32). This freedom comes not from general truth in the Word, important as that is, but from specific truths.

In the key Book of Romans nothing is said about growth until the problem of righteousness is completely settled. To the middle of Romans 5 the subject is justification from sins based on the substitutionary work of the Lord Jesus, and on this birth truth many attempt to gain maturity. After Romans 5:11, Scripture begins to speak of "justification of *life*" and "reigning in *life*" (vv. 17, 18)—the life we need for the Lord Jesus to be manifested.

It is important to note that Romans 1:1–5:11 presents God's remedy for the *penalty* of sins, while Romans 6–8 presents God's remedy for the *power* of sin. The Blood secures forgiveness for my sins; the Cross secures deliverance for me, the sinner. These are facts that not only bring new birth and promise heaven, but provide His overcoming resurrection life for the here and now. "I am come that they might have life, and that they might have it more abundantly" (John 10:10).

Position
Appreciated
It is the captive, dominated by the wretched self-life, to whom the identification truths call. This struggling person, long plagued by doubt, defeat, discouragement, and depression, is being prepared to enter into the reality of the provision set forth in Romans 6–8. Through the experience of prolonged personal failure, he has been made aware of self's bankruptcy.

In the light of that realization he is able to appreciate the positional truth that self, the old man, was identified with the Lord Jesus in His crucifixion (Rom. 6:6). This is the gospel for the Christian! Our Saviour dealt not only with the symptoms but with the disease, the root as well as the fruit. We have His substitution for our sins; we have identification with Him in His death for sinful self.

Our Father takes us down until the self-life is uncovered, and then up as the truth of the Christ-life is discovered. This spiritual principle cannot be circumvented. To attempt to "climb up some other way" is futile. God's truth, ministered in God's way by God's Spirit, alone frees. And that freedom is centered in our invulnerable position "in Christ."

The Holy Spirit knows what processing is required for each individual to learn that self deserves nothing but death, and that the Lord Jesus Christ is his life. To learn *all* the truth about the former takes a lifetime, to say the least; *all* the truth about the latter will not be exhausted throughout the eternity. Hence He patiently teaches enough about self through failure to enable us to learn of Christ for triumph.

Position
Accepted
Through the work of the Cross, our Father has not only positionally freed us and made each of us "accepted in the beloved" (Eph. 1:6), but has also made us "complete in him." "For it is in Christ that the fullness of God's nature dwells embodied,

and in him you are made complete" (Col. 2:9, Weymouth). It is in Him we are to abide; He is the very source of our Christian life. To abide is to remain where one has already been enlifed and positioned. It is in Him that we rest, fellowship, and grow—far above all.

Where is the Lord Jesus today? He is risen and set at the Father's right hand (Eph. 1:20, 21). It is when the Christian understands his *death position* that he is enabled to see his *life position* in the risen Lord Jesus. Therefore he counts himself re-created, alive to God in Christ Jesus (Rom. 6:11b).

The believer's enlightened faith follows effortlessly, because he now sees himself exactly where he has been positioned all along: "For ye are dead [unto the old self-life, at Calvary], and your life [new creation, raised in His resurrection and ascension] is hid with Christ in God" (Col. 3:3). Now he can begin walking "in newness of life" (Rom. 6:4).

When the Holy Spirit gives us adequate apprehension of our risen position, we are able spontaneously to reckon ourselves "alive unto God in Jesus Christ." Thus we are drawn to the Source of our life, and there we learn to rest—and *abide above*!

57 Keep Looking Down!

In contrast to the popular exhortation to "keep looking up" (from ourselves to Christ), we are to "keep looking down" (from our position in Him) upon our circumstances here on earth.

Think of the faithfulness of the Holy Spirit, as He works patiently and thoroughly in the life of the growing Christian. He ministers the Cross, and He ministers Christ. It is the finished work of the Cross for the old nature, and the abundant life of the Lord Jesus for the new nature.

Of the Holy Spirit's ministry in the life of the believer the Lord Jesus said, "He will honor and glorify Me, because He will take of (receive, draw upon) what is Mine and will reveal (declare, disclose, transmit) it to you" (John 16:14, Amplified). He not only reveals the scriptural truths concerning Christ and the Cross to our faith, but also transmits their reality to us.

Love Motive   The babe in Christ has started to live for the Savior and to serve Him with all his heart. "He gave His all for me, now the least I can do is give my all for Him." The motive is right, but the motivation is wrong! He is seeking to live and serve on the basis of the birth truths and in the strength and ability of self, not yet understanding that God judicially condemned and crucified the old nature at Calvary. There his position "in Adam" ended; there his position "in Christ" began (2 Cor. 5:17).

The well-meaning believer is seeking to "save his life," not comprehending the spiritual principle, "If any man will come after me, let him deny himself, and take up his cross daily, and follow me. For whosoever will save his life shall lose it" (Luke 9:23, 24). The Holy Spirit is causing him to become aware of the fact that "in me (that is, in my flesh) dwelleth no good thing" (Rom. 7:18). This is the turning point, usually years in the making, where the growing Christian begins to be centered in Christ rather than in self—"not I, but Christ."

Hate Motive   Once the awakened one is brought to see self for the enemy that it is, he finds himself hating the old nature. "He that hateth his life in this world shall keep it unto life eternal" (John 12:25). Now he appreciates the Spirit's application of the Cross for what it brings— freedom from the dominion of the old life. Instead of avoidance of the Cross, he rejoices in its work of holding the Adamic nature in the place of death, inoperative. "God forbid that I should glory, save in the cross of our Lord Jesus Christ, by whom the world is crucified unto me, and I unto the world" (Gal. 6:14).

When the Christian begins to take God's side against himself, he is ready to contemplate the Lord Jesus from God's standpoint, and not self's. Then the Holy Spirit is free to carry out the second part of His ministry in the hungry heart, conforming him to Christ's image. "But we all, with open face beholding as in a glass the glory of the Lord, are changed into the same image from glory to glory, even as by the Spirit of the Lord" (2 Cor. 3:18).

Faith Motive   "Even as by the Spirit of the Lord." It is the Spirit who enables the believer to reject continually the old life ("consider yourselves to be dead to sin"), and who shows him more and more fully his life *in Christ* ("consider yourselves to be . . . alive to God in Christ Jesus" [Rom. 6:11, NASB]). He begins to abide where he has long ago been positioned, in Christ risen. "Set your minds and keep them set on what is above . . . where Christ is, seated at the right hand of God" (Col. 3:2, 1, Amplified).

The Holy Spirit's ministry ever proceeds in balance. On the one hand, He transmits the crucifying death of the Cross to the self-life. The works, doings, practices of the flesh are more and more held inoperative; such things as "immorality, impurity, indencency, idolatry . . . enmity, strife, jealousy, anger [ill temper], selfishness, divisions [dissensions] . . . envy . . . and the like" (Gal. 5:19-21, Amplified).

On the other hand, in conjunction with the death process of the old man, the Spirit develops the life process (growth) of the new man. As we abide above in the Lord Jesus, looking upon His glory in the Word and fellowshiping with Him, the Holy Spirit increasingly produces His fruit: the life of the Lord Jesus in and through us. "The fruit of the (Holy) Spirit [the work which His presence within accomplishes]—is love, joy (gladness), peace, patience (an even temper, forebearance), kindness, goodness . . . self-control (self-restraint, continence)" (Gal. 5:22, 23, Amplified).

Death Motive   Even the new life, the Lamb-life, is taken into death in the growing Christian's daily walk. This "newness of life" is a sacrificial life, in contrast to the old life of self-preservation. Sacrifice is the very nature of his new life. As he grows, that life is manifested to the Father's glory, and for the sake of others. "So then death worketh in us, but life in you" (2 Cor. 4:12).

Here is the principle of the grain of wheat, the paradoxical principle of growth. The Holy Spirit works it out in the daily life and ministry, whatever the calling may be. "Unless a grain of wheat falls into the earth and dies, it remains [just one grain; never becomes more but lives] by itself alone. But if it dies, it produces many others and yields a rich harvest" (John 12:24, Amplified).

Life Motive   The Spirit of Christ carries on this development process throughout our being, in our everyday life here *below*, "that the life also of Jesus might be made manifest in our mortal flesh" (2 Cor. 4:11). But our life source, our home, our position, is the Lord Jesus at the Father's right hand. The Spirit has placed us in Christ, in the light *above*. "Truly our fellowship is with the Father, and with his Son Jesus Christ" (1 John 1:3).

In this invulnerable position above we are developed, matured, and used for His glory in the darkness of this age. We are in the world, but not of it. Our life resources that are from above are more than adequate to meet the needs found in this sphere of death. There are innumerable influences in this sinful world that would draw us to a level below that which is ours, "hid with Christ in God" (Col. 3:3). The Spirit of God has but one standard for the growing believer: God's very best as it is in Christ Jesus. Nothing lower, nothing secondary.

"By the which will we are sanctified through the offering of the body of Jesus Christ once for all. . . . But this man, after he had offered one sacrifice for sins forever, sat down on the right hand of God. . . . Having therefore, brethren, boldness to enter into the holiest by the blood of Jesus, by a new and living way, which he hath consecrated for us, through the veil, that is to say, his flesh; and having an high priest over the house of God; let us draw near with a true heart in full assurance of faith. . . . Let us hold fast the profession of our faith without wavering" (Heb. 10:10, 12, 19-23).

In these pages we are seeking to set forth the glorious position and spiritual resources of the Christian, and to examine some teachings and life levels that are current today. It isn't a matter of whether or not these are wrong—some of them are—but whether or not they are at *His* level. Anything less than that which He has given us in Christ risen is too low. In Him we are to *abide above,* and keep looking down.

58 *Law Versus Life*

Not law, but grace; not I, but Christ. The principle of law applied to the believer dooms him to Romans 7, while the law of the Spirit of life in Christ Jesus delivers him to Romans 8.

Identification with Christ includes the position of *death* for the old nature, and the position of *life* for the new nature. It is the work of the Holy Spirit to block self and its sinful works, and to foster the new life and its fruit.

Spiritual growth does not involve effort on the part of the Christian, for the indwelling Spirit transmits the life of the Lord Jesus from source to servant. Neither is there struggle connected with the daily deliverance from the tyranny of self, for the Spirit transmits the finished work of the Cross to that sinful element.

Where these death-dealing and life-giving identification truths are unknown to the believer, he finds no alternative but to try to keep the law as a "rule of life." This erroneous expedient consists of applying the principle of law for the control of conduct—its prohibitions for self, its commands for life. But the Scriptures teach us that the Holy Spirit, "the Spirit of life in Christ Jesus," ministers Christ to us, not law. "For the law was given by Moses, but grace and truth came by Jesus Christ" (John 1:17).

Most of the depressing law burden placed on believers emanates from Calvinism and its Covenant theology. Many are unaware of the legalistic aspect of this teaching, since its tenets are well known for providing the Christian with the solid scriptural foundation of justification and eternal security. Let us now consider some of the aspects of this theology as it affects those who long to grow in Christ.

Justification   Nothing need be said further regarding the faithful stand the Calvinists have established concerning foundational truths such as the inspiration of the Word, and the complete justification of the believer. (See Chapter 10.) Humanly speaking, the doctrinal basis on which we rest today is due to the scholarship and integrity of such Reformed theologians as Berkhof, Bonar, Hodge, Kuyper, Machen, Pink, Ryle, and Warfield.

Sanctification   The Covenant theologians have ever remained well within the scope of Reformation doctrine. We can be thankful for this with regard to justification by faith, but when it comes to sanctification via Christ our life, it is a different matter. Substitution is clearly proclaimed; identification (our death to the law and our life in Christ) by and large has not been recognized.

The Covenant movement's dependence on law for spiritual growth is caused by a combination of errors. Reformation theology is antidispensational and primarily restricted to two covenants, works and grace. Prophetic Scriptures are spiritualized, resulting in amillennialism. The church is considered to include the saints of all ages, the distinctive Body of Christ not being discerned. In thus merging Israel with born-again believers, the law is brought right on past Calvary and fastened on the Christian. In all the realm of sanctification Covenant Calvinism fails "to distinguish the things that differ."

This theology prevents the Christian from seeing and freely taking his stand as having died to the law and being now alive to God in the Lord Jesus. "You also were made to die to the law through the body of Christ, that you might be joined to another, to Him who was raised from the dead, that we might bear fruit for God" (Rom. 7:4, NASB). We have died to the old life and are now alive in the new, to bring forth "fruit"— the fruit of the Spirit in contrast to the "works" of the law.

Following are representative statements regarding sanctification by well-known Covenant theologians:

Arthur Pink

"Is the disciple to be above his Master, the servant superior to his Lord? Christ was 'made under the law' (Gal. 4:4), and lived in perfect submission thereto, and has left us an example that we should 'follow His steps' (1 Peter 2:21). Only by loving, fearing, and obeying the law, shall we be kept from sinning.

"There is an unceasing warfare between the flesh and the Spirit, each bringing forth 'after its own kind,' so that groans ever mingle with the Christian's songs. The believer finds himself alternating between thanking God for deliverance from temptation and contritely confessing his deplorable yielding to temptation. Often he is made to cry, 'O wretched man that I am!' (Rom. 7:24). Such has been for upwards of twenty-five years the experience of the writer, and it is still so." (*The Doctrine of Sanctification*, pp. 71, 121.)

H. Bonar

"Redemption forms a new obligation to law-keeping as well as puts us in a position for it. Yes, Christ 'hath redeemed us from the curse of the law,' but certainly not from the law itself; for that would be to redeem us from a divine rule and guide; it would be to redeem us from that which is 'holy and just and good.' " (*God's Way of Holiness*, pp. 81, 83.)

J. C. Ryle

"Genuine sanctification will show itself in habitual respect for God's law, and habitual effort to live in obedience to it as a rule of life. There is no greater mistake than to suppose that a Christian has nothing to do with the law and the Ten Commandments, because he cannot be justified by keeping them. The same Holy Spirit who convinces the believer of sin by the law, and leads him to Christ for justification, will always lead him to a spiritual use of the law in the pursuit of sanctification." (*Holiness*, p. 27.)

Charles G. Finney

(Although he was by no means a Reformed theologian, his baneful influence concerning the law has continued to affect the present-day church.) "It is self-evident that the entire obedience to God's law is possible on the ground of natural ability. To deny this, is to deny that man is able to do as well as he can. The very language of the law is such as to level its claims to the capacity of the subject, however great or small that capacity may be. 'Thou shalt love the Lord thy God with all thy heart, with all thy soul, and all thy mind, and with all thy strength.'

"Here then it is plain, that all the law demands, is the exercise of whatever strength we have, in the service of God. Now, as entire sanctification consists in perfect obedience to the law of God, and as the law requires nothing more than the right use of whatever strength we have, it is, of course, forever settled, that a state of entire sanctification is attainable in this life, on the ground of natural ability." (*Finney's Lectures on Systematic Theology*, p. 407.)

We turn now to the words of two men who, in contrast to the above, based their teachings on the identification truths:

William Kelly

"Every believer is regarded by God as alive from the dead, to bring forth fruit [not works] unto God. The law only deals with a man as long as he lives; never after he is dead. 'For ye died, and your life is hid with Christ in God.' And that is not at all what is said of us after a 'second blessing,' . . . or any other step of imaginary perfection. We *begin* with it. . . . I am identified with Christ dead and risen. It is no longer the law dealing with me to try if it can get any good out of me. I have relinquished all by receiving the Lord Jesus, and I take my stand in Him dead and risen again . . . as one alive from the dead, to yield myself to God.

"The Gospel supposes that, good and holy and perfect as the law of God is, it is entirely powerless either to justify or sanctify. It cannot in any way make the old nature better;

neither is it the rule of life for the new nature. The old man is not subject to the law, and the new man does not need it. The new creature has another object before it, and another power acts upon it, in order to produce what is lovely and acceptable to God—Christ the object, realized by the power of the Holy Spirit." (*Galatians*, pp. 125, 137.)

Kelly further states, "Some good men who in grievous error would impose the law as a rule of life for the Christian mean very well by it but the whole principle is false because the law, instead of being a rule of life, is necessarily a rule of death to one who has sin in his nature. Far from a delivering power, it can only condemn such; far from being a means of holiness, it is, in fact, the strength of sin (1 Cor. 15:56)." (*The Holy Spirit*, p. 197.)

C. I. Scofield

"Most of us have been reared and now live under the influence of Galatianism. Protestant theology is for the most part thoroughly Galatianized, in that neither the law nor grace is given its distinct and separate place as in the counsels of God, but they are mingled together in one incoherent system.

"The law is no longer, as in the divine intent, a ministration of death (2 Cor. 3:7), of cursing (Gal. 3:10), or conviction (Rom. 3:19), because we are taught that we must try to keep it, and that by divine help we may. Nor does grace, on the other hand, bring us blessed deliverance from the dominion of sin, for we are kept under the law as a rule of life despite the plain declaration of Romans 6:14—'For sin shall not have dominion over you; for ye are not under the law but under grace.' " (*The Fundamentals for Today*, Vol. 2, p. 367.)

How sad to realize that while Calvinism so effectively refutes Arminianism in the real realm of justification, its Covenant theology fails the believer in the realm of sanctification just as badly as does Arminianism.

59 The Conference Question: Time

The Holy Spirit is well able to provide the hungry heart with abundant truth through the ministry of a Christ-centered conference. However, the believer must be willing to provide the Spirit adequate time to manifest the reality of that truth.

The present-day conference question can probably best be considered by looking at the parent of nearly all "Deeper Life," or "Victorious Life," conferences. We refer, of course, to the great Keswick Convention founded in England a century ago "for the deepening of the spiritual life."

There is no question but that its purpose has been abundantly realized in the lives of many through the years. Its spiritual influence has been multiplied by the establishment of such annual gatherings in other countries, as well as by the spread of its fine literature.

The Keswick method of presenting the message of liberation and growth is quite unique, and has been more or less emulated by most other conferences of this type. The theme for the first day is sin in the life of the believer. The searchlight of God's Word is faithfully focused on indwelling sin.

On the second day the subject is God's provision for deliverance from the domination of sin and self in the life of the defeated Christian. Here the identification truths are set forth, as centered in Romans 6, with the Cross as the key to freedom from sin's power.

On the third day consecration is dealt with. On the fourth day, the fullness of the Spirit. On the final day of the series the subject is Christian service, with emphasis on missionary outreach.

It is probably through English Keswick, more than any other human means, that the Spirit of God has been pleased to make the identification doctrines clear and available to us today. It has been a long, uphill battle to release these truths on the scale that we now have them; and the awakening today among hungry-hearted believers is mainly due to that Convention as an avenue of the Spirit's work.

Coupled with the vast number who have been brought into the deeper truths of the Cross and the Christ-life, there has been an even vaster number who have been frustrated and disillusioned, returning to their problems in home and ministry more disheartened than ever. It is this spectrum of believers that we would seek to encourage.

Individual First of all—and this may not seem very encouraging—the reason for much of the failure lies mainly with the individual rather than the conference. There are those who attend simply to enjoy the messages and fellowship; they do not really mean business concerning growth in the Lord Jesus Christ. Others want to learn how to "live a better Christian life" while at the same time retaining their love for self. In this condition, they are bound to return home with little spiritual progress.

On the other hand, it must be said that the disappointment and failure of many others finds much of its cause in the conference method. Several observations are shared here in the prayerful hope that definite adjustments may be forthcoming in the spiritual life conventions for the good of all concerned.

Method The progression of truth during Keswick's annual series of meetings is very well conceived: first dealing with sin, then deliverance, consecration, infilling, and finally, service. All the doctrine necessary for freedom from the old life and establishment in the new is there, clearly and pointedly presented. However, these truths should bring about more fruit than is usually evidenced in the lives of those who attend.

The method is much like the law: just and good, but weak

through the flesh (Rom. 7:12; 8:3). The believer is not able to keep up with the pace at which the truth is presented. Clear comprehension requires time, and appropriation must be based on comprehension. What the Convention calls for at the end of the week should not be looked for at the end of a year!

Time   The delivering and establishing principles of truth are there, but the governing principle of *time* is not. Consider the second day with its presentation of the all-important identification truths—the Cross in its separation of the believer from the dominion of sin. In actuality, it takes years for the Holy Spirit to prepare the Christian for, and bring him into the reality of, his identification with the Lord Jesus in death and resurrection—to say nothing of his position of ascension.

Yet, the conference rolls onward the next day, and the hungry-hearted one is duly pressed into consecration—in preparation for the vital infilling of the Spirit on the following day. It is on the second day that the light begins to fade for the majority of those who honestly seek victory through Keswick and similar conferences. For some of these the conference ends on the second day as far as their comprehension and participation go.

Others valiantly move on, seeking to reckon on their death and resurrection in Christ, to enter into consecration, and then to receive the fullness of the Spirit—all by faith, but without sufficient understanding. They do not yet have an adequate grasp of the truth of identification to prepare them to advance into the following steps. The problem is compounded when they are all too often pressured at each step to enter into the truth presented. This causes them to attempt to claim and appropriate that for which they are not prepared.

The results are inevitable. There is a return home with high hopes for "victory all the way," only to find it soon slipping from their grasp. Then comes the disillusionment concerning the very truths that the Father has supplied for freedom and spiritual growth.

Those who are able to progress through the week on the

basis of truth apprehended and who go home with victory that lasts, have had adequate teaching and preparation prior to attending the Convention.

For true and abiding progress, the Holy Spirit always establishes the individual in one step before He takes him into the next. We have seen that there must be true conviction of sin and need in the hungry heart before the identification truths can be understood, let alone entered into. Without the reality of the work of the Cross, there can be no true consecration—self will be dedicated to God instead of the new life.

Moreover, the Spirit will not control and fill one who is dominated by self; He must first apply the death of the Cross to the old nature before He can form Christ in the new nature. And it goes without saying that Spirit-motivated and Christ-honoring service must be the outgrowth of all the previous foundational steps. Most service carried out during the development of these steps is primarily for the preparation of the servant.

Awakening   It is certainly true that many needy believers who attend the conferences receive adequate light to be awakened to the possibilities of the Father's answer to their failure and longed-for growth in the Lord Jesus. They are introduced to the realm of liberating and maturing truth that is in the Word of God. This in itself is invaluable, since many faithfully study the Book of Romans all their lives without seeing the message of identification. These awakened ones, with further study of the Scriptures and their newly-discovered deeper-life books, can make healthy progress through the carefully paced teaching of the Spirit of Christ.

60 The Conference Question: Emphasis

The Spirit of Christ cannot manifest the life of the Lord Jesus through the self-life. He has only crucifixion for the old man. Until the Adamic nature is dealt with by the death of the Cross, He is not free to fill the new nature with the life of Christ. Hence the conference without the Cross for the life is essentially a conference without Christ as the life.

Throughout the first fifty years or more of English Keswick's history it was the policy to invite only speakers who were experientially in the good of the truths they taught. They were to be able to share, and not just preach; to teach, and not simply exhort. Upholding this policy did much to preserve the key truths of the Convention, and to guard against deviation and dilution.

Paucity It must be said, however, that this is not wholly the case at the present time, nor has it been for a good many years. Certainly there are many fine and faithful speakers on Keswick conference platforms today, but at the same time it is affirmed that some who speak are not well enough qualified to do so. They are gifted preachers, but not necessarily Keswick speakers.

The needy believers who attend these conventions bear the brunt of this growing weakness of the unique Keswick message. Because it is essential not only to present the identification truths, but to present them effectively, it would be better not to hold a conference where fully qualified speakers are unavailable. In the face of so much slippage and barrenness throughout the Church, there needs to be a return to the original platform standards.

Time We have already considered the fact that the Keswick method of presentation does not give adequate time for the majority of believers attending to enter into that which is expected of them by the end of the week. Through the years it has not only been the unqualified speakers, but the qualified as well who have contributed to this problem.

Most conference speakers seem to forget how long it was before they were able to see and understand the identification truths, to say nothing of sharing them with others. To some extent, they are expecting the average believer in just four days to enter into that which took them years simply to understand! At the next convention, ask a speaker just how long a period it was for him.

Emphasis Mainly due to the inadequacy of many speakers at deeper-life conferences, there has been a shift of emphasis away from *the centrality of the Cross* in the overall message presented. The key to spiritual growth is the Cross. It was there that the ground of death was established from which the Christian partakes of the resurrection life of the Lord Jesus Christ. No Cross for death results in no Christ for life.

The Holy Spirit does not reveal this key to the unprepared heart, neither does He share these truths through speakers who are in a similar condition. The reproach to be borne, and the extreme difficulty of properly sharing the message of the Cross, are understandable. Nevertheless, it is imperative to present the truth of identification if there is to be any liberation for those in need.

It must be the Cross, or nothing, for any life-giving ministry to believers. For speaker as well as listener, as it was for Paul, "God forbid that I should glory, save in the cross of our Lord Jesus Christ, by whom the world is crucified unto me, and I unto the world" (Gal. 6:14).

If the believer fails to gain access to the truths of the Cross during a conference, he will have little or nothing. No matter what decisions or commitments he is brought to, all will inevitably come down and great will be the fall thereof. There will be nothing to prevent the reassertion of the sinful self-life and the consequent sinking back into defeat and despair.

In all deeper-life ministry, wherever and whenever the identification truth of the Cross is not central, the emphasis shifts to the filling of the Spirit. Important as is His fullness and control, He does not fill the new life until the old is firmly established in the death of the Cross. This principle of life out of death is inviolate! "*Except* a corn of wheat fall into the ground and die, it abideth alone; but if it die, it bringeth forth much fruit" (John 12:24).

Personnel   It must be remembered that we are not dealing here with the typical Bible or prophetic conference. These comments have to do with conferences whose specific purpose is to minister identification truth.

There are certain pitfalls involved in the establishing of such a conference. For one thing, there is the possibility of conference directors choosing speakers on the basis of their popularity rather than for the explicit truths that need to be shared. On the other hand, some are simply ill-advised, and are not able to discern the proper leadership required for such gatherings. Convention councils are too often, like some church boards, composed of unqualified members.

Literature   The responsibility of sponsoring deeper-life conferences is tremendous. It includes not only the selection of speakers but the choice of literature. Keswick-type conferences usually have a well-stocked book table, but the fact that it is well-stocked too often proves to be a dubious blessing. There just aren't that many top-level books available in the area of spiritual growth, even after one hundred years of faithful Keswick ministry and writing.

One of the results of a poor choice of speakers is that their secondary books will also blunt the effectiveness of the literature outreach. Therefore, books have to be chosen with equal discernment. Since the identification and related truths are new to many of the believers attending the conferences, they need careful guidance as to what they read in the growth realm. If the selections are of the highest caliber they will be studied for years, whereas the speakers may be heard only briefly. In meeting this responsibility it is advisable to offer only the best of deeper-life literature, all in harmony with the truths shared from the platform. Then, no matter what books the eager heart chooses, he will consequently go home with gold for growth.

The Individual   What about the needy one who attends the conference? Dear friend, trust the Father for His very best as it is in Christ Jesus. Settle for nothing less; the Holy Spirit never will. Watch for the Cross. He is not there, He is risen! But you must be taken *there* in order to see and know Him where He is.

If the conference ministry is lacking in the "word of the cross," there will be a crippling lack in the presentation of the Lord Jesus Christ, no matter how clearly He is set forth. The Spirit of Christ ministers resurrection life out of death; with Him it is ever "dead indeed unto sin, but alive unto God"—and so it must ever be with us.

Even where spiritual truth is shared in proper balance, do not allow yourself to be coerced to enter into realms for which you are not ready, truth that you do not yet clearly understand. No matter who might be ministering, or what conference you are privileged to attend, until the Holy Spirit makes a truth clear to you He will not take you into its experiential reality.

Then, my soul, wait and be still;
  Thy God shall work for thee His perfect will.
If thou wilt take no less, *His best* shall be
  Thy portion now and through eternity.

                                        —*Freda Hanbury*

61 Conditions—Cause or Effect?

The Christian is not called upon to meet conditions in order for the Holy Spirit to fill him. The Spirit ministers to the believer so that Christ may be the fulfillment of all conditions pertaining to abundant life.

The established trend in the conference ministry has already been mentioned, that of strong emphasis on the filling of the Spirit at the expense of adequate emphasis on the work of the Cross. The messages naturally focus on the finished work, but if solid groundwork has not been laid the sought-for result will not be achieved.

In any ministry to Christians where the positional facts of identification are not presented as the basis of spiritual development, there will be no true preparation for experiencing the Lord Jesus as one's life. Attempts will be made to build on other areas of truth that we are not meant to produce spiritual growth.

Confession Error
Most deeper-life ministries are being erroneously founded on the fullness of the Spirit. There are some that rely on confession and cleansing for this fullness (1 John 1:9). It is taught that if one will faithfully confess and forsake his sins as they occur, he will then be able to maintain a spiritual walk. Important and blessed as this provision is for restoration of fellowship, it was not intended to be a means of growth. This expedient deals only with symptoms, and never was meant to reach the cause: indwelling sin and the self-life. The Cross alone does

that, Crucifixion for the source of sin, confession and cleansing for its symptoms.

Holiness Error Another ministry to believers built on a misplaced emphasis is that of "holiness by faith," or what might be termed instant spirituality. The believer is urged to forsake all known sin, to yield unreservedly to the Spirit, and by faith appropriate His fullness. Then he is filled, since he has asked in faith for something that is God's will for him, and has believed that he has received (1 John 5:14,15). On the basis of this by-faith filling he is henceforth to live a yielded, holy life.

This method has brought about a great deal of struggle in the attempt to maintain such a step, often resulting in disillusionment, especially among eager young people. The reason is that co-crucifixion with Christ is by-passed. Self is still rampant. The Spirit of God does not give immediate holiness of life by faith or any other means. True, His method of producing holiness is by faith, but it is through *the process of growth*. The Spirit matures the new life in Christ as He holds the old life in the position of death via the Cross. There are no shortcuts to maturity.

Authors Errors such as these should be obvious enough for the hungry believer to avoid. But we must be careful in our study of spiritual growth books that are available, since they tend to reflect the conference trend of undue emphasis on the filling of the Spirit. Or, it may be possible that the conference problem has been influenced by the literature—a somewhat vicious circle.

The deeper-life books include the identification truths, or else they would not be classed as such. But there is a factor in all but a few that tends to annul the work of the Cross, and to transfer most of the work to the defeated believer. He is exhorted to be filled with the Spirit before he has been felled by the Cross!

The titles were referred to are some of the finest obtainable in the growth realm, written by authors who clearly delineate the identification truths. These include such venerable leaders as Andrew Murray, Watchman Nee, L. S. Chafer, Evan H. Hopkins, James H. McConkey, N. B. Harrison, Ruth Paxson, most of the Keswick writers, and many others. However, when it comes to the believer being filled with the Holy Spirit, without exception all place far too much of the onus on the hapless Christian. The very results of the Spirit's fullness, they require him to produce for that fullness!

Conditions   Some of the typical requirements laid on the failing one before he can hope for the Spirit's fullness are: "put away all sin in the life"; "there must be full obedience in all things"; "complete abandonment to the Spirit"; "self must be dethroned"; "unqualified surrender"; "absolute separation from the world"; "complete separation from all defilement of the flesh and spirit"; "total obedience and complete consecration, with Jesus enthroned in the heart"; "the old life must be cast out." Over and above all these conditions is the constant call for the believer to "yield" himself to God in order to be filled. It might be asked, "Which self?"

Reversal   The cart must not be placed before the horse. It is not for the believer to put sin out of his life—that is the work of the Spirit. The yielded life is not a prerequisite for His fullness, but its result. We came to the Lord Jesus just as we were, with all our sin; we are to come to the Spirit just as we are, with our spiritual need.

Responsibility   As a matter of fact, if the immature believer could meet any one of the above-mentioned conditions he wouldn't need to be filled with the Spirit. However, in order for anyone to meet them, he must first be filled (controlled) by the Spirit. This is an extremely important point, and one of the chief causes for many Christians giving up all hope of ever being filled.

To compound the problem, many of these leaders further insist that if and when one is filled, that blessed infilling can be maintained only by continual obedience, yieldedness, surrender, separation, etc. If there is sin, the filling is lost. They admit that the individual does need the Spirit's help in meeting these conditions, but they still place too much of the burden on him.

In saying this, we make reference to most deeper-life authors and speakers, past and present. It is not that their valuable ministries are to be rejected in any way, but it is necessary to note this trend in order that the emphasis may be turned back to the Cross. That is where the Holy Spirit keeps it. For the most part, the growth conferences and literature faithfully present the identification truths—the work of the Cross is there. But it has become a matter of too little Cross, and too much "condition." In relation to all other aspects of the Christ-life, the believer's position of death with Christ suffers from a nullifying imbalance.

As a result, the child of God is drawn out of his position of rightful need, to that of wrongful responsibility: "The responsibility for this fullness of the Spirit is, in a tremendous sense, in your own hands." "It is not now a question of His fullness; it is a question of your receptiveness." "You may have all the fullness that you make room for. In a profound sense it rests on you."

Romans 6:13 There is a statement in the midst of the identification truths that explains the reason for this inversion of responsibility. The scriptural key that reveals how this problem developed, and how it can be rectified, as in Romans 6:13: "Yield yourselves unto God, as those that are alive from the dead." In almost every instance where this verse is touched on, the first half receives all the emphasis; indeed, the second half is usually neglected altogether. For every page that has to do with the believer's union with Christ in His death, there is usually a chapter or more dealing with his responsibility to yield to God for the fullness of the Spirit.

The emphasis must always be on the all-important statement, *"as those that are alive from the dead."* The whole of Romans 6 is contained in this clause. There the Cross is central, where it ever should be. There the Holy Spirit's ministry is seen, as He "transmits" life out of death to the risen believer.

Yielded Nature Dear friends in Christ Jesus, it must be proclaimed! When the Christian thoroughly comprehends his participation in the finished work of the Cross, he will be able to yield himself (as a new creature in Christ, not the self-life) to God as one who is alive from the dead. Yes, "alive unto God in Jesus Christ our Lord." There will be no conditions required for the filling with the Spirit. Emphasis on the meeting of conditions arises from failure to establish the believer in truth that renders conditions needless. Where others posit surrender, the Spirit places the *Cross*.

Christ-centered Further, we must not make the filling with the Spirit an end in itself. The life must be Christ-centered if He is to make it fruitful and full of joy. The Holy Spirit's ministry is to glorify the Son, and to this end the Father and the Spirit work together, "that in all things he [the Son] might have the preeminence" (Col. 1:18).

Sir Robert Anderson has said well, "In proportion therefore as mind and heart are fixed on Christ, we may count on the Spirit's presence and power, but if we make the Holy Spirit Himself the object of our aspirations and worship, some false spirit may counterfeit the true and take us for a prey."[1]

Our prayer, with Paul, is, "that He would grant you, according to the riches of His glory, to be strengthened with might by His Spirit in the inner man, that *Christ* might feel completely at home in your hearts" (Eph. 3:16, 17, lit.).

[1]*Your Problem Solved*, p. 7 (tract by K. Wuest, Chicago: Moody Press).

62 *The Spirit's Ministry*

Normally, the Holy Spirit fills the Christian as a result of the balanced application of death and life. By death (the Cross), that no flesh should glory in God's presence; by life (growth), that Christ may be all (1 Cor. 1:29; Col. 3:11). No experience could ever bring that about.

This is a call to return to the Cross and to abide above in Christ. The Christian life is not developed through an experience, or even a series of experiences, no matter how enthralling they may be. Rather, spiritual maturity and fruitfulness develop as one grows in grace and in the knowledge of the Lord Jesus Christ. There will be valid experiences resulting from growth, but they will glorify Him and never self.

Spirit-filled   It is true that the waiting disciples were instantly filled with the Holy Spirit on the Day of Pentecost. Not long afterward, the Spirit filled them again (Acts 4:31). It was also for a specific purpose that Paul was immediately filled with the Spirit shortly after his conversion. Nothing powerful or spectacular occurred at the time of his filling, and there were no signs involved. Rather the Lord said to Ananias concerning Paul, "He is a chosen vessel unto me, to bear my name before the Gentiles, and kings, and the children of Israel: for I will shew him how great things he must suffer for my name's sake" (Acts 9:15, 16).

Anti-spirit   There is no denying that many believers are suddenly filled with the Spirit for reasons that are related primarily to service. Such instances, however, are not meant to be the norm, nor are they to be the means of growth into the image of the Lord Jesus. The misguided insistence on seeking an experience has wrecked, and is wrecking, untold numbers of lives, whether that experience be "by faith" or "by conditions." It does not matter whether it be a "baptism of the Spirit," a "second blessing," "higher life," "entire sanctification," or "tongues." No such experience is able to establish a Christian in the life that is Christ. Rather, all tend to turn him from Christ and establish him but deeper in the life that is self.

Experience-centered attainment fosters spiritual pride, which in turn causes divisions among children of God. The Holy Spirit unites, in Christ; self divides, in selfish experiences. At best, there is a concentration on self and the Spirit, rather than on Christ and the Cross.

We have noted that the emphasis in conference ministry has shifted from crucifixion to surrender. The Holy Spirit, however, does not fill the Christian on the basis of yieldedness. The old life is enmity against God and will never surrender, hence the Spirit must minister the death of the Cross to that nature. The new life has only love for God, and will always yield, hence the Holy Spirit freely ministers the life of Christ to that nature.

Spirit-control   Apart from occasional and special instances, the Spirit controls and fills the believer as a result of the growth that He gives. It is not a matter of surrender so as to get and to have, but of growth in Christ so as to be and to give. It is not to be powerful or gifted, but to be weak and dependent. He will see to that. "My grace is sufficient for thee: for my strength is made perfect in weakness" (2 Cor. 12:9). "Unto them which are called . . . Christ the power of God, and the wisdom of God" (1 Cor. 1:24).

To be filled with the Holy Spirit is to be filled with the life of the Lord Jesus Christ. It is to have His life manifested in our mortal flesh (2 Cor. 4:11). That growth is transmitted by the Spirit of the Lord, from glory to glory is transforming us into the image of the Son (2 Cor. 3:18). And growth of the new is always balanced by the Spirit's application of the death of the Cross to the self-life. Surrender of self is no substitute for the death of self. The one is to glory in self, the other is to glory in the Cross (Gal. 6:14).

The trend in deeper-life teaching has not only been moving away from the Cross to center on Spirit-filling, but has gone beyond this to focus on the responsibility of the Christian. It is, "yield, surrender, abandon, obey, separate, consecrate, cease from sin, cast out self," or the Holy Spirit will neither be able to function nor fill. What this amounts to is a mighty believer, but a weak and helpless Spirit of the living God. This emphasis on human responsibility may have seemed quite harmless once, but it is far from that now.

The Lord Jesus was explicit in explaining to the disciples just what the Spirit's ministry was to be on behalf of His own. He said, "I will send him unto you" (John 16:7), and that He did, at Pentecost (Acts 2:4). He also informed them that "He shall not speak of himself . . . he shall glorify me: for he shall receive of mine, and shall shew [transmit] it unto you" (John 16:13, 14). He laid down no conditions; all was to be through the faith by which they lived. True faith is centered in the Word, including faith for growth. "Sanctify them through thy truth: thy word is truth" (John 17:17).

Spirit-motivated   The Holy Spirit took charge while we were yet "dead in sins" and brought us to the Lord Jesus by faith. He will conform us to Christ's image by faith. He is God, dwelling within each believer, and He will abide with us forever (John 14:16). The union is absolute, since we are "in the Spirit, if so be that the Spirit of God dwell in you" (Rom. 8:9). His indwelling is a relationship of life. "For the law of the Spirit of *life* in Christ Jesus hath made me free from the law of sin and death" (Rom. 8:2).

The Spirit of Christ within is at work, and has been from the moment we were saved. He is not cringing in some corner of our being, in some dark garret, hopefully waiting for a series of conditions to be met so that He may have the privilege of filling us. Far from it! We have been bought with the price of Calvary and re-created in Christ Jesus; therefore the Spirit is able to carry out God's eternal purpose in us by means of that finished work and flowing life.

How vast the number of believers today who are utterly defeated! Many of these are being tempted by the tinseled offer of instant holiness, or by self-centered, neurotically induced, socalled "gifts of the Spirit." They do not realize the blessed fact that, ever since their new birth, the Spirit has been faithfully ministering within by taking them down into defeat that self might be revealed and repudiated.

At the very time they are crying out, "O wretched man that I am!" the Spirit has them at the turning point where He can begin to transmit the life that is "not I, but Christ," thereby enabling them to begin to "thank God through Jesus Christ" (Rom. 7:24, 25). But they know it not. May many see it now!

Both in the natural realm and in the spiritual, healthy growth takes time—the Spirit's time. "He shall be like a tree planted by the rivers of water, that bringeth forth his fruit *in his season*" (Ps. 1:3). "And therefore will the LORD *wait*, that he may be gracious unto you, and therefore will he be exalted, that he may have mercy upon you . . . blessed are all they that *wait* for him" (Isa. 30:18). "Now the God of hope fill you with all joy and peace in *believing*, that ye may abound in hope, through the power of the Holy [Spirit]" (Rom. 15:13).

63 The Spirit's Goal

The pride of self has come from another; our humility of life must also come from Another. The Lamb of God said of Himself, "I am meek and lowly in heart" (Matt. 11:29). It is the Lamb-life that the Holy Spirit ministers within.

We are exhorted in the Word neither to "grieve" (by sinning) nor "quench" (by resisting) the indwelling, sensitive *Holy* Spirit (Eph. 4:30; 1 Thess. 5:19). But this we do daily in the course of our spiritual development. Nevertheless, in the midst of the grief we cause Him by our sin, He carries on the work to which He was commissioned by our risen and glorified Lord. He does not sulk and quit His ministrations.

The Holy Spirit took into consideration beforehand all that He would have to endure. He simply turns from fruit-bearing to conviction, and to chastening (child-training). Painful as it is, His conviction brings us to confession of sin and restoration to fellowship with Himself, with our risen Lord, and the Father (1 John 1:9). The chastening may well be "grievous: nevertheless afterward it yieldeth the peaceable *fruit* of righteousness unto them which are exercised thereby" (Heb. 12:11).

The Spirit of Christ   Spirit-fostered growth can never be attained through meeting conditions or having experiences. Nor does the Spirit depend on such means. He is carrying out the commission of the Lord Jesus Christ. He is in charge. "No man can [even] say that Jesus is the Lord, but by the Holy [Spirit]" (1 Cor. 12:3).

The Word further calls us to be "filled with the Spirit" (Eph.

5:18). The purpose of His infilling is to manifest the life of the Lord Jesus in us. Galatians 5:22 and 23 enumerate the facets of the fruit of the Spirit—"love, joy, peace, longsuffering, gentleness, goodness, faith, meekness, [self-control]." These are the characteristics of Christ Himself. To be filled with the Spirit is to be filled with the Lord Jesus.

The Spirit of Truth   It was "through the [same] eternal Spirit" that the Lord Jesus "offered himself . . . to God" at Calvary (Heb. 9:14). "Ye are manifestly declared to be the epistle of Christ . . . written not with ink, but with the Spirit of the living God" (2 Cor. 3:3). We obtain our growth by "obeying the truth through the Spirit" (1 Peter 1:22). We are to "walk in [dependence on] the Spirit, and ye shall not fulfill the lust of the flesh" (Gal. 5:16).

Especially bitter is the disappointment of the one who has truly sought to depend on the Spirit and yet has sunk down into failure and darkness. Often his heartbreak is brought about by overemphasis on the fullness of the Spirit in deeper-life books and conferences. Even so, the Spirit uses this disillusionment to bring defeat and thereby prepare the heart for victory and growth in the Lord Jesus.

The failing one finds that, just where he depended on the Spirit most, and just when he needed Him most, He did not seem to respond. Rather, He seemed to make him all the more miserable and needy. The Spirit of God will never give power through faith in Himself, but will ever increase the believer's realization of his need of Christ. In this He is faithfully carrying out His mission of glorifying the Lord Jesus, all the while speaking not of Himself but remaining hidden. He has not even revealed His name.

Throughout this discovery of weakness the hungry heart is slowly being turned to the truth of the Word, from which the Spirit of truth never deviates. When his faith is finally shifted to the dual growth center—the Cross and the ascended Lord Jesus—then the Spirit begins to respond accordingly.

The Spirit of the Cross   The Cross is to be gloried in, and the Son glorified. As the Cross is applied to the old life, the awakened one finds himself more free to concentrate on the Lord Jesus above. This focused faith brings the very heart of the Spirit's ministry into action. The joyful and dependent believer is resting in the positional truth that "the law of the Spirit of life in Christ Jesus hath made me free from the law of sin and death" (Rom. 8:2). Now he is beginning to receive the reality of that freedom in his daily life.

How is this Spirit-wrought "not I, but Christ" life experienced? When one is reckoning within the scope of identification with Christ, the Holy Spirit inevitably transmits the finished work of both death and life to the Christian. The self-life is going to feel the cut of the Cross, while the growing life of the crucified and risen Lord Jesus within will be manifested in sacrifice for others.

The hunger that the Spirit gives to the heart of the growing one is expressed in Paul's determined cry, "That I may know him, and the power of his resurrection, and the fellowship of his sufferings, sharing the likeness of his death" (Phil. 3:10, Conybeare). To know Him is the very core and *raison d'etre* of one's life in Christ. "This is life eternal, that they might know thee the only true God, and Jesus Christ, whom thou hast sent" (John 17:3). The Spirit's transmission of these truths into reality of life results in death working in us, but life in others (2 Cor. 4:12).

The Spirit of the Lamb There is no list of conditions to be met, no yielding called for in order to be Spirit-filled. The Lamb-like life that the Spirit ministers and manifests is by nature yielded. It fills and overflows the one who believes and grows. Putting one's "all on the altar" is simply *self*-sacrifice, hence unacceptable. God's altar is the Cross. It is here He crucified self. Reckoning on that finished work brings forth the sacrificial life of the Lamb, obedient and pliant in the Father's hand. "Lo, I come to do thy will, O God" (Heb. 10:9). "Let this mind be in you, which was also in Christ Jesus: who . . . made himself of no reputation, and took upon him the form of a servant . . . he humbled himself, and became obedient unto death, even the death of the cross' (Phil. 2:5, 7, 8).

Christ-centered servants, filled with the Spirit, are not conscious of power, but of weakness. God's Spirit-led servants are base and despised, "that no flesh should glory in his presence" (1 Cor. 1:29). Paul's bodily presence was weak, and he testified, "My speech and my preaching was not with enticing words of man's wisdom, but in demonstration of the Spirit and of power; that your faith should not stand in the wisdom of men, but in the power of God" (1 Cor. 2:4, 5).

The Spirit's Goal   Paul, filled with the Spirit, was God's frontline warrior, church planter, writer, and sufferer. John, likewise filled with the Spirit, was Jesus' heart-companion; quiet, deep, devotional. Paul was taken to glory, but was not allowed to share what he saw there. John was also taken to glory, and he wrote what he saw in "The Revelation of Jesus Christ" (Rev. 1:1). It matters not whether the Spirit makes of us a flaming Paul, or a faithful John; He *is* going to make us like the Lord Jesus Christ, "from glory to glory."

What is the true manifestation of the power of the Spirit? Many Christians think they should become dynamic, powerful, and even flashy personalities in order to radiate "victory" and "spirituality." But the Word defines the result of His filling thus: "For this cause we also, since the day we heard it, do not cease to pray for you, and to desire that ye might be filled with the knowledge of his will in all wisdom and spiritual understanding; that ye might walk worthy of the Lord unto all pleasing, being fruitful in every good work, and increasing in the knowledge of God; strengthened with all might, according to his glorious power, unto all *patience* and *longsuffering* with joyfulness" (Col. 1:9-11).

64 *Life Via Literature*

The good has always been the enemy of His best. No books can replace the Book, and only those of highest caliber can assist in opening its treasures. Therefore, seek the best and shun the secondary.

In conjunction with the Word of God, the greatest aid to spiritual growth comes through deeper-life literature. As to feeding, it must be primarily the Word. But desired growth can be substantially aided by concentration on the best writings. Secondary books, good at they may be, just will not do.

It must be pointed out that there are not many of the better titles available today. The enemy has thus far succeeded in keeping some of the older ones out of print, while any number of his are being produced for unsuspecting hearts, even by evangelical publishers. However, our Lord has seen to it that adequate material for healthy growth can be obtained by any hungry Christian.

It is important to select only superior growth literature, whether it be for the purpose of study, sharing, or selling. Much could be said about the mass of questionable and even harmful material that is available in most of our Christian bookstores. Once the best books are discovered, the reader's discernment and requirements keep him from dropping to the level of the secondary. It makes all the difference when the awakened believer is early introduced to the tried and true writings on the Christ-life. Even so, caution must be exercised in studying most of the better books.

In the early stages, the eager Christian never dreams of questioning an author who presents the identification truths.

Such teaching seems so far in advance of other spiritual literature that in his estimation these authors can do no wrong. This attitude is not as harmful as it may seem at first, since the Spirit in time gives adequate discernment whereby the believer is able to glean the gold without accepting or rejecting the whole.

We find this admixture in many of the best growth books. The main problem centers in their teaching on the filling of the Spirit. Despite this and other lesser difficulties, the priceless truths are there for all who hunger for His best. Brief comments concerning some of these books and their authors may be of help here, especially to those whom the Lord has only recently begun to stimulate. Some of these titles may be out of print, but the rest should be carried by most Christian bookstores, and be available at conference booktables and in church libraries. (See bibliography at end of book for further information on these books.)

Romans, Verse by Verse—William R. Newell. The anchor book of them all in the growth realm. A doctrinal and devotional study of the identification truths, as well as of the entire epistle. This is a lifetime treasure that all should have.

The Wealth, Walk and Warfare of the Christian—Ruth Paxson. Highly commendable textbook on Ephesians.

His Side Versus Our Side—N. B. Harrison. Textbook on Galatians. Recommended for early-stage growth. Study manual available.

Galatians—William Kelly. Advanced study of deep exposition.

The Normal Christian Life—Watchman Nee. In recent years the Lord has used this book to awaken and instruct many concerning the identification truths.

The above is Nee's best book, and is within the realm of growth. Most of his other titles cannot be recommended as they are more or less centered in his extreme teaching regarding the local church, similar to that of the exclusive branches of the Plymouth Brethren.

Several of the Nee books promulgate his "release of the spirit" teaching, which involves one in unsound and dangerous spirit-warfare such as emerged from the Welsh Revival. Actually, Nee took a great deal of this material directly from the controversial book, *War on the Saints*, which was written as a result of the Revival's excesses.

The Person and Work of the Holy Spirit—S. Ridout. A safe and sound treatment. Seven fine lectures regarding the Holy Spirit.

The Law of Liberty in the Spiritual Life—Evan Hopkins. This is considered to be the standard textbook of the original Keswick teaching, Hopkins being one of the founding fathers of the movement. It is the prototype of all Keswick writings, and naturally very clear on the truths of identification.

Born Crucified—L. E. Maxwell. Contains outstanding teaching and illustrations concerning identification.

Bone of His Bone—F. J. Huegel. A fine treatment of the subject of our union with Christ.

Abide in Christ, and its sequel *Like Christ*—Andrew Murray. These two are Murray's finest, and are based on identification. Of his sixty devotional books, there are probably fifteen or twenty now in print. Such titles as *The True Vine, Waiting on God, The Prayer Life, God's Best Secrets,* and *The Holiest of All,* contain growth teaching that is unsurpassed.

Murray's books dealing with the Holy Spirit are not recommended as he tended to confuse the baptism of the Spirit with His fullness, similar to the teaching of R. A. Torrey and others.

Joshua—H. L. Rossier. Old Testament study geared for growth. Exceptional.

What Is Man?—T. Austin-Sparks. A sound treatment of the subject of soul and spirit. Identification centered.

Every-Member Evangelism—J. E. Conant. An old book that the Lord has kept in print. Not only valuable concerning church outreach, but contains some outstanding chapters on the subject of identification.

Hudson Taylor's Spiritual Secret—Dr. and Mrs. Howard Taylor. Biographical account of this great missionary leader's discovery of the life that is Christ.

Rightly Dividing the Word of Truth—C. I. Scofield. A small booklet well suited to establish the new believer on a solid footing for growth.

The Cross of Calvary—Jessie Penn-Lewis. Few have made the identification truths clearer than this author. However, outside of this realm her writings cannot be recommended. Concerning "the baptism" and "warfare," her teachings are too extreme to be followed. She was mainly influenced in this direction by the Welsh Revival and its leader, Evan Roberts.

The New Life—Reginald Wallis. Once again in print, this little book is one of the best on the subjects of the self-life, the Cross, and the Christ-life.

There is other literature for growth that could be mentioned, but the above titles will serve to set a high standard for the hungry heart. It is unfortunate that all of the books by all of these authors cannot be recommended; nevertheless the discerning believer is encouraged to dig for the golden truth while allowing the slag to lie.

Most of these writings yield richer treasure with the years of study. As the Christian grows, the Holy Spirit takes him deeper into the truth presented; it seems as though He renews the material every five or ten years. "We have received, not the spirit of the world, but the Spirit which is of God; that we might know the things that are freely given to us of God." "God hath revealed them unto us by his Spirit: for the Spirit searcheth all things, yea, the deep things of God" (1 Cor. 2:12, 10).

There are two reasons for the careful and prayerful study of the highest in growth material. The most important consideration is one's own spiritual development—so that the Lord Jesus may be glorified, and others drawn to Him.

It is also important to know the literature well enough to be able to share it intelligently with others. Books can work day and night, year in and year out, and never tire. Furthermore, they can present the truth far better than most of us.

When one is burdened to point out these truths to others, it is extremely vital to share the right book with the right person at the right time. Begin with something simple, preferably a deeper-life tract. If the response is favorable, then present something a little more definite. If the reaction is otherwise, pray and wait—for years, if necessary.

Often such literature is received by one who is as yet unprepared, and it may collect dust on the shelf indefinitely, patiently awaiting the Spirit's time. When that time comes, the newly inspired heart wonders why it didn't "discover" such glorious truth long before!

65 *Identification Leadership*

In the ministration of the growth truths, the one who shares must have a spiritual parent-heart of love and understanding. Such leadership has the Spirit-fostered yearning of Paul, "My little children, of whom I travail in birth again until Christ be formed in you" (Gal. 4:19).

Pastors are like all others when it comes to spiritual development, since our Father is no respecter of persons. There has to be preparation of heart by the Holy Spirit prior to any realistic apprehension of the Christ-life. The fact of the pastor's theological training makes little or no difference in this growth realm, for even if our sound seminaries clearly taught the identification truths the Spirit rarely reveals these by formal academic means. Moreover, the student-stage is usually somewhat premature for the necessary needs and realizations to be generated in the life.

It is a lamentable fact that the majority of our sound pastors never become really interested in these positional doctrines, nor aware of their indispensable nature. They faithfully preach the gospel and general teachings for the Christian life. They present more or less "the whole counsel of God"—with the exception of the very truths that make all the difference in the life and service of the Christian.

Awakening   On the other hand, it is heartening to note that in the midst of this needy situation the Holy Spirit is quietly awakening the minds and hearts of an increasing number of shepherds. To this end He is using deeper-life conferences and literature, as well as some true-to-the-Word tape ministries.

Nevertheless, there has been much misunderstanding among pastors concerning conferences for spiritual growth. This is mainly because they present "deeper truth," as well as the fact that they are "outside the church." Concerning these barriers, there are one or two factors that should be considered.

Such conventions came into being because growing believers must have not only milk, but the meat of the Word. The Holy Spirit will never allow the heart that He has stimulated to starve. If the scriptural nourishment for maturity in Christ is not available in the local church, He will provide it elsewhere and by other means. Actually, these "other means" are often utilized by the Spirit to bring the food back into the churches, where He would have it.

The Keswick movement was never meant to be, and never has been, in competition with sound churches. In 1875, the original Keswick settled down in the capable hands of devout churchmen and subsequently made its mark throughout the world. Those gifted men of God, without peer today, being dead yet speak by means of their books. The present-day church would be yet more spiritually impoverished were it not for the ministry of such faithful leaders of past days.

There are other factors to be considered in connection with the deeper truths and the church ministry, some of which the pastor soon discovers when he is awakened to the realm of identification. No matter what means the Spirit uses to reveal these truths to him, the revelation always comes as a wonderful surprise. "Why didn't I see long ago what is now so obvious?"

The pastor has been highly trained in the Word, which he loves and memorizes; he also depends on the Spirit of truth in his study and use of it. Yet the entire subject of the Cross in the life of the believer is closed to him until the Spirit has prepared his heart.

Before long he realizes that identification is church doctrine in the very strictest sense; it has to do exclusively with the members of the body of Christ. It is marvelous positional truth, centered in the Cross that means death and the Lord Jesus who means life—not just new birth, but His ascended life. As he begins to realize in experience something of the release from the old and growth in the new, the shepherd's attention refocuses on his flock. "Feed my sheep."

"This is just what my people need. Order twenty-five copies of *The Complete Green Letters*, and let's get started!" Now there comes another, but sad, surprise. The need is not necessarily the call in any realm of service, whether it be church or mission field. The tendency here is to forget the processing needed to prepare one for these truths, no matter how clearly (or vehemently) presented. When the newly awakened pastor attempts to teach or preach identification, he is bound to suffer frustration and disillusionment.

When it comes to sharing the deeper truths, there are two important factors that must be taken into account. First, it is imperative to know the doctrines scripturally and to some extent experientially. Second, it is every bit as necessary to know *how* to share them. It takes time for the Spirit to impart a clear understanding of identification, and it takes time for Him to teach the intricacies of sharing effectively.

Pastor   When the pastor's presentation is premature, there is the tendency to preach instead of to share. He may resort to exhortation and pressure to compensate for his failure to prepare hearts. This is also a chronic conference problem: the content is Calvinistic (sound), but the application is Arminian (pressure).

What if the Holy Spirit were to enlighten even a dozen of the congregation? It is one thing to see believers awakened, and quite another to be able to establish them on the path to maturity. The Lord gives just a few at a time, so that each may be given the required care to enable him or her to begin to grow.

Congregation   Rarely is there more than a handful at any time who are ready to hear the message of crucifixion with Christ. Were the eager pastor to stand up on the Lord's Day and unburden his heart concerning the need for the Cross in the life of the believer, he would perceive but a flickering spark here and there amidst a glassy sea of eyes. There has been faithful preaching and the church is composed of believers who love the Lord, yet they are in no way prepared for death to self, to say nothing of the Christ-life.

As for the enthusiastic pastor's initial attempts at apprising his fellow ministers of his newly found treasure, we will refrain from mentioning the results here. The average awakened leader has been trained and has pastored for some fifteen or twenty years, therefore he should understand the necessity of quietly waiting on the Lord for a further period in preparation for this deeper ministry. Although there will be some unlearning involved, none of the former experience need be looked on as wasted; all fits into the underlying foundation.

"O my God, I trust in thee: let me not be ashamed. . . . Yea, let none that wait on thee be ashamed. . . . Shew me thy ways, O LORD; teach me thy paths. Lead me in thy truth, and teach me" (Ps. 25:2-5).

66 *The Silent Minority*

The Holy Spirit has ever carried out the eternal purposes of the Father through His little flock. The nature of that flock is Lamb-like; dependent, humble, silent. Only when they are sufficiently prepared will the Spirit give them freedom to speak; only those whom He has conditioned can receive what they have to share.

Much as the Lord has used spiritual conferences, they are by no means His be-all or end-all for deeper-life teaching. Especially in recent years, the Holy Spirit has been awakening and preparing leadership for small study groups throughout the body of Christ. These are known as Bible studies, deeper-life studies, growth groups, etc. Some are held in sound churches, many in Christian homes. Some are led by awakened pastors, but most by lay people. In these days, however, there are other types of groups that should be avoided. Let us briefly examine some of them.

Dangerous The hungry-hearted believer should at all costs avoid any type of secular or "Christian" sensitivity training group, including those called prayer therapy. This destructive and subversive "sensitivity" technique is being implemented, mainly by government grants, throughout many school systems, government projects, business corporations, and is now even filtering into sound churches.

The U.S. Congressional Record of March 11, 1969, states: "Group criticism compels the participant to bare his soul before ten or fifteen other persons who are required to do likewise under the direction of a group leader. The individual is pressed to seek out real or fancied shortcoming in his personality and thinking, to humble himself and give up his independence of mind and judgment, to make himself dependent upon the good opinion of the leader and others in the group. The individual's 'problems' become group property."

This is being reflected in the "Christian" groups by uninhibited "honesty" and confession, with the molding of one's beliefs to the prevailing low level. If there were a high spiritual level, the group would not exist. They are of necessity self-centered and emotionally motivated—never Spirit-controlled and Christ-centered.

Care must be taken to avoid study groups that are affiliated with or mainly composed of those from modernist, holiness, or cultist churches. Such groups engage in sharing, confession, testimonies, non-doctrinal discussion, cult study, or tongues and healing. These gatherings put self first, not Christ.

Secondary Some Bible study meetings are comparatively large. They often utilize quite sound literature, but may be led and attended by those who are more or less ecumenical and worldly. The level is far too low for those who would *abide above.*

There are also many true-to-the-Word Bible studies that are capably led and attended by hungry hearts. For the most part, general Bible teaching is given, having little or nothing to do with the deeper truths. Such studies are valuable as far as they go, even to the laying of a good foundation for spiritual growth.

Compromising On a large scale there are numerous Christian organizations and churches seeking to minister according to the theory of accommodation. Their method is to descend to the level of those whom they attempt to reach in order to gain rapport and thus a response.

This is a costly procedure. In utilizing the world's methods, music, dress, speech, and attitudes, the Christian is inevitably pulled down to the world's level instead of drawing the worldling to a spiritual level. The price paid is infinitely too high for what little is gained.

Identification   In direct contrast to the foregoing, there is the small Bible study group designed for the purpose of presenting the identification truths as the basis for growth in the Lord Jesus Christ. The following thoughts are shared to help guide those who would lead and those who would be led in this type of gathering.

The purpose of the identification study group is to enable hearts to progress in the opposite direction—not down, but up. Not down to the world's sinful level, but up to Christ's glorious level, and that via the Cross. This is not a way of escape, but a full preparation for the world's dire needs. Our ministry to others must ever be from the standpoint of our being hid with Christ in God, and never from the standpoint of the world itself. "We do not stand in the world bearing witness to Christ; we stand *in Christ* bearing witness to the world."

The group is comparatively silent because it is composed of those who are aware of their personal need for growth and maturity in the Lord Jesus. They do not attempt to share to any great extent until He has them prepared for the outreach of His choice. As always, the little flock is a silent minority; not superior to any, just humble and needy.

Leadership   When it comes to forming a group of this nature, whether the leadership be pastor or layman, it is best to gather a few hungry hearts in a church, parsonage, or Christian home affiliated with a sound church. Although the Bible is to be central, a textbook will help guide, such as Hopkins' *Law of Liberty*, or the growth chapters in Conant's *Every-Member Evangelism*. We might even suggest *The Complete Green Letters*.

It has been found best to meet only once or twice a month. This gives the individual sufficient time to study thoroughly the assigned reading. And what is even more important, it gives the Holy Spirit time to work some of the truth studied down from the head to the heart and life by means of everyday experience.

The meetings should be continued just long enough to clarify the identification truths, and give an introduction to the best growth literature. In this way the individual will not become dependent either on the leader or the group, and yet will be able to study further and go on with the Lord. The hungry heart will never give up, and those who learn the hard way are better prepared to properly teach others.

Solid
Foundation
Sometimes it is necessary to divide a group, if it becomes obvious that all are not doctrinally prepared for identification. It is the responsibility of the leader to make certain that each one is established in the foundational doctrines, i.e., assurance, acceptance, and eternal security in the Lord Jesus Christ. Until this groundwork is sure, there can be no advance into the deeper growth truths. Harrison's *New Testament Living* is suitable for use with preparatory groups. The fatal temptation of both leaders and students is to want to hurry through the all-important basic teaching so that they can "get to the good part."

This is the Achilles heel of the conference movement, as well as of many deeper-life groups: hungry hearts are being taught the growth truths without *first* being established in the birth truths. Unless this is rectified, the work is bound to come undone—the Holy Spirit will never build on sand.

God's Terms
In true identification study the Spirit will turn the heart and life away from the world and its ways, back to the finished work of the Cross. From there He turns the heart and life still further from the world and its self-centered methods, up to the risen Lord Jesus Christ.

It is not a matter of the believer conforming to the world to reach the worldling. The Lord Jesus came into this world, but He was never of it; it is the same with the Holy Spirit. As we abide in the Lord Jesus and walk in the Spirit, the same will be true of us. The Father offers His Son to the world as Savior, and to the believer as Life, *on His terms!* He has met all needs at the Cross, and this is the only place where all find their needs met.

Holy Spirit Conviction   It is mainly through Christ-centered and Cross-centered Christians that the Spirit convicts of "sin . . . righteousness . . . judgment" (John 16:9-11). Under true conviction of sin the stricken one will come to the Lord Jesus on His terms; all of his selfish demands and pet arguments will be instantly discarded. Now, nothing matters but that which God says in His Word. The convicted heart will settle for nothing less than God's will, under God's conditions!

This is the disposition of the healthy convert and of the awakened believer who will make spiritual progress. As He did with Paul, the risen Lord has stopped them in their tracks, and their submissive response is, "Lord, what wilt thou have me to do?" (Acts 9:6). It takes far more than an accommodating approach to produce this heart attitude.

Resting in Him   Our life in this world is to be the expression of our growth in Christ and fellowship with Him in Glory. "If [since] you have been raised up with Christ, keep seeking the things above, where Christ is, seated at the right hand of God. . . . For you have died, and your life is hidden with Christ in God" (Col. 3:1-3, NASB). Abide above, for the burden below!

67 *Psychic Healing*

The Holy Spirit's ministry to the Christian (whether in sickness or in health) is to conform him to the image of the Lord Jesus Christ, and that upon the foundation of his eternal security. No "healers" ever manipulate from that solid ground!

The modern "gifts" of tongues and healing have a common source. They are not of the Spirit, but of the flesh, and function primarily in the realm of the nervous system.

Whether carried on at a somber cathedral altar, on a spectacular TV program, or in a wild tent meeting, there is no basic difference. None but the psychosomatic condition is affected by healers. Now and then some sufferers may be relieved of their neuro-induced symptoms, but actual healing of organic sickness never occurs by such means.

Doctrine   The basic claim of the healing movement is that healing is included in the Atonement, that it is not God's will for Christians to be sick, but that all should be in perfect health. This premise has been based on Isaiah 53:4-6: "Surely he hath borne our griefs, and carried our sorrows: yet we did esteem him stricken, smitten of God, and afflicted. But he was wounded for our transgressions, he was bruised for our iniquities: the chastisement of our peace was upon him; and with his stripes we are healed . . . the LORD hath laid on him the iniquity of us all."

The word "borne" refers to our Lord's life-identification with our earthly griefs and sorrows. The words "with his stripes we are healed" set forth the result of our Lord's death-identification with our iniquities. He shared with us the former in His life on earth, but He was made to be the latter in His death on the cross.

"In the book, *If You Need Healing Do These Things,* the author says, 'Healing is in the Atonement, therefore it includes all.' This error would be avoided if people had a fair knowledge of dispensational truth, and would remember that the removal of the entire curse placed upon the human family is in the Atonement. But we have not received all that was wrought out for us in the Atonement. We are still 'waiting for the adoption, to wit, the redemption of our body' (Rom. 8 :23)."—*B. F. Cate.*[1]

"God can, and does, heal today, but not always. He is not committed to a covenant promise today, but is perfectly free to exercise a proper discrimination regarding the spiritual advisability of doing so where His people are concerned. No believer who has a history with the Lord will deny that He has used physical weakness and sickness as a means to develop the graces of the Holy Spirit and a spiritual dependence upon the power of God.

"At the same time there are many who have prayed earnestly for deliverance and have received it. In both cases the Lord works on the principle of the highest benefit to the believer, which is his or her spiritual life and growth."—*C. H. Maskery.*[2]

Concerning God's principle of the highest benefit to the believer: "Hudson Taylor once told me that his greatest spiritual blessings had come to him in connection with his various sicknesses; and later he made the remarkable statement to me that all of the most important advance movements which had taken place in connection with the China Inland Mission, including its inception, had come as a direct result of some physical breakdown through which he had been called to pass."—*Henry Frost.*[3]

Diagnosis   Just how correctly diagnosed are the cases of cancer, TB, blindness, deafness, etc., that

---

[1]*The Nine Gifts of the Spirit Are Not in the Church Today,* p. 31.
[2]*The Pentecostal Error,* p. 30.
[3]*Miraculous Healing,* p. 45.

healers claim to have cured? "It is extremely easy for a layman to be misled regarding the exact nature of a disease. No layman is qualified either to diagnose his own sickness, or to determine whether he is completely healed. Public testimonies of healing at moments of great excitement and emotional stress are worthless. For that matter, even doctors are occasionally deceived. We have all known cases where doctors disagree."—W. H. Boggs, Jr.[4]

"Few physicians of even life-long practice are really good diagnosticians; perhaps there is none of whatever eminence who has not been more than once wholly deceived in the nature of the disease he has been called upon to treat—as the autopsy has proved."—B. B. Warfield.[5]

Psychosomatic Illness It has been admitted from the platform of a large healing campaign that seventy percent of all who apply for healing cards are suffering from psychosomatically induced symptoms. Mayo's claims it to be an even higher percentage in their medical work. Of those who are screened and thus admitted to the healing line, a certain number actually do experience some relief.

One often hears healing claims concerning goiters, tumors, and cancers, such as, "They disappear right before your very eyes!" But—"There was a woman in St. Luke's Hospital, New York City, who had a tumor, to all, even the most skilled, diagnosis. But the tumor simply disappeared on the administration of ether and the consequent withdrawal of nervous action."—B. B. Warfield.[6]

"First of all, the majority of the patients cured under such conditions (Lourdes) are neuropaths. That is to say, they are persons whose illness is to a preponderant extent due to mental causations.

"Before a group of European physicians in Paris in 1932, a French neurologist gave an incredible demonstration of the

[4]*Faith Healing and the Christian Faith*, p. 22.
[5]*Miracles: Yesterday and Today*, p. 188.
[6]Ibid., p. 188.

potential power of suggestion. After the man who was the subject had been blindfolded and informed that his right arm had just been burned above the elbow, there soon developed, on the specified place on his arm, a large red spot surmounted by a water blister. Yet the man had not been touched by any object.

"After three years of investigations, a special committee of the British Medical Association had this to say in their report, 'Divine Healing and Cooperation Between Doctors and Clergy: As far as our observation and investigation have gone, we have seen no evidence that there is any special type of illness cured solely by spiritual healing which cannot be cured by medical methods which do not involve such claims.

"The cases claimed as cures of a miraculous nature present no features of unique and unexpected character outside the knowledge of any experienced physician or psychiatrist. We can find no evidence that organic diseases are cured solely by such means as spiritual healing. The evidence suggests that many such cases claimed to be cured are likely to be either instances of wrong diagnosis, wrong prognosis, remission, or possibly of spontaneous cure.' "—*V. Edmunds and G. Scorer.*[7]

God's Will   Finally, we must consider God's will in the subject of healing. "God's primary purpose for His children is the forming of the image of Christ in them (Rom. 8:28, 29). Whether He heals or not will depend upon which will contribute to the accomplishment of that purpose."—*A. Hay.*[8]

"It takes a lifetime to learn and really believe in our hearts that there is sometimes something better than release from pain and sorrow, and that is a deep likeness to the Lord Jesus Christ which means fruitfulness.

"I would witness to the fact that the deepest, the most abiding spiritual lessons which God has been pleased to teach me were learned in consequence of and during my various experiences of sickness. This last is particularly true in respect to

[7]*Some Thoughts on Faith Healing,* pp. 88, 89.
[8]*New Testament Order for Church and Missionary,* p. 195.

the prayer-life, the praise-life, the life of dependence upon God, and the life which chooses to live, not for the seen but for the unseen, not for the temporal but for the eternal."—*Henry Frost.*[9]

"As in the apostolic days so now the desire exists for the manifestation of the Spirit in marvelous ways; but a life sober, righteous, holy, lived in the hope of the glory to come, is the more excellent way of the Spirit's manifestation and undeniable proof of His indwelling. The prayer should not be so much for this or that gift, or this or that result, as for Christ Himself to be made manifest to us and through us. The Apostle who was most filled with the Spirit sums all up in the one great word, 'For me to live is Christ."—*W. F. Erdman.*

"It is a serious mistake to presume that the Christian can maintain a neutral or passive attitude toward error. Contrariwise, he must oppose error as definitely as he embraces truth. Error is never static or stagnant, but is always aggressive. For that reason it has never died a natural death, nor can we ignore it to death.

"Error ceaselessly seeks to corrupt, efface, and neutralize the truth, and to destroy all whom it enmeshes in its tentacles. The grand reason then for opposing error is to retrieve precious souls from its blight, and to deliver them from bondage to freedom, from darkness to marvelous light."—*W. D. Miller.*[10]

"Is it not significant that in groups today in which the Corinthian errors regarding the gifts of the Spirit are taken as normal and sought, there appear finally along with them the same manifestations of carnality and disorder that were evidenced in the Corinthian church?"—*A. Hay.*[11]

[9]*Miraculous Healing,* p. 45.
[10]*Modern Divine Healing,* p. 9.
[11]*New Testament Order for Church and Missionary,* p. 195.

68 Tongues Trauma

True spiritual growth is free, but not cheap; it is gradual, deep and thorough, never sudden or shallow; always Christ-centered, never self-centered. The Holy Spirit upholds and transmits God's highest. Stoop not!

In all of our failure the Spirit has but one purpose, God's purpose. He faithfully unmasks the self-life in order to reveal the scriptural remedy for it—our identification with Christ in His death to sin (Rom. 6:6). Then heart becomes energized for the life that is Christ, the abiding as a branch in the Heavenly Vine. The believer begins to see that he needs to settle down and, in dependence on the Holy Spirit, "grow up into him in all things . . . even Christ" (Eph. 4:15).

Self-betrayal But often because of extended defeat, darkness, depression, and despair, some are unwilling to go upward for God's best at the Spirit's measured pace within the bounds of the Word of God. They want victory at once; they demand power *now*! And, as always, there are those pressing in who are ready to promise self what it wants, when it wants it.

These aggressive ones insist that what the hungry-hearted believer has missed is "the baptism of the Holy Ghost"; that he must seek the Holy Ghost and receive Him for power; that he must tarry for his Pentecost and speak in tongues as in the apostolic days. In some there is a response to this temptation to take a possible shortcut as a quick and easy way to "get the blessing." Now it has become the blessing, rather than the Blesser—tragic evidence of the continued reign of self.

Self-centeredness   The Holy Spirit raises us to the level of Christ in glory, but self ever lowers us to its natural level of error. Because of self-centeredness, there is a response, an anticipation generated in the heart by means of the endless testimonies presented by these people—tall and tantalizing tales of "signs and wonders," "baptisms of power," "dramatic healings," "multitudes saved and sanctified," "abundant financial blessings." On and on it goes.

As the eagerness intensifies, the desperate desire for the blessing increases. Before long the unsuspecting one is taken to a church service, which is followed by a stay at the altar. Or he may be invited to a motel or hotel dining room for a dinner meeting to hear some "great and powerful" leader in the movement tell startling stories. Included are impressive success testimonies by businessmen, along with the singing of many choruses. After the meeting the individual or couple will be invited to gather with a few others in another room.

Or he may find himself in a small home gathering where there are Bible discussion (mainly from certain sections of the Book of Acts), testimonies, singing, and possibly speaking in tongues. Regardless of the setting, these meetings follow a common pattern in order to gain a common end—the bitter end.

The believer becomes ever more vulnerable. He is determined to get the blessing, he wants it now, and he is afraid to resist the claims and promises extolled because he doesn't want to "resist the Spirit," or miss anything that God might have for him. What little scriptural support he is given for the so-called "baptism of the Holy Ghost" is always out of context and in complete disregard for the clear dispensational distinctions of the Word.

By now, anticipation has overcome reason. It is no longer (if it ever was) a matter of "rightly dividing the word of truth" (2 Tim. 2:15). "For the time will come when they will not endure sound doctrine . . . and they shall turn away their ears from the truth, and shall be turned unto fables" (2 Tim.

4:3, 4). The deflected Christian is pressing, praying, and pleading for the Holy Spirit to do something that He has already done; to do something extra that *He* cannot and will not do.

The seeker is confused, but "God is not the author of confusion" (1 Cor. 14:33). He is now pursuing an emotional experience. He may receive such, but it will not be of the Holy Spirit! The ministry of the Spirit is within the scope of the "rightly divided" Word, and centered in the risen Lord Jesus Christ. It is never otherwise, and never less.

In the after-meeting the emotion-charged seeker is awaiting the blessing that is purported to make everything right, that will bring in "the Holy Ghost and tongues" to set him apart as one of the spiritual elite, entirely sanctified.

Self-expression Finally, the moment of moments arrives. On his knees with others closely gathered around, all cry out to "Jesus" (rarely is He given His title of "Lord") and plead with the "Holy Ghost" to come, enter, and bestow the blessing. Hands are laid on him, with rubbing and pressure applied to head and limbs. He is admonished to relax, to let his mind go blank, to loosen his tongue and let the Spirit take over. It is under these conditions that the mental and physical climax is reached. This may take one of several forms, depending on the emotional preparation involved and the make-up of the individual.

(1) There is a sudden burst of uncontrolled paroxysms accompanied by the sensation of electrical pulsations surging up through the body. The limbs take on the characteristic jerking and the "tongues" pour forth in a rushing babble of unrelated gibberish. (Reminiscent of the phone call a mother received one night: "My dear, your daughter is lying on the Mission floor, chattering like a monkey!")

(2) With others the emotional release results in tears and/or laughter, with an interplay of babbling in the supposed "language." This may go on for an hour or two, until the agitation of the nervous system subsides and the cerebral brain can regain control. In whatever manner the experience may appear,

the nerve pattern has been formed; now, with a little practice, the recipient is able to induce at will his "gift of tongues."

(3) There are also those who experience nothing in the after-meeting, but later—sometimes weeks later, in another meeting or even alone—they suddenly find themselves in possession of their long-awaited "baptism."

(4) In some cases there is a disappointing anticlimax, and the individual never does attain the blessing. As a consequence, his faith is crushed—the Spirit has evidently refused to give the blessing although the conditions have been met. Or there may come a cloud of guilt, with the feeling that he is not worthy of the "gift."

Whether in a church, tent meeting, motel room, or living room, whether within the erratic Pentecostal movement or the sedate and seemingly intellectual neo-tongues movement, the process of conditioning and its results are the same: unscriptural, out-of-Spirit control, emotional and spiritual catastrophe. Are these fleshly manifestations the glorious fruit of the Holy Spirit? Hardly!

69 Tongues Trauma (continued)

Spiritual growth is not a result of emotional experiences, or "signs and wonders." Rather, it comes through realization of our spiritual position. "Believers do not depend upon signs, because they are believers." As we abide in the Lord Jesus the Holy Spirit faithfully manifests His fruit in the life, quietly, normally, and for the Father's glory.

What really happens to people in this climactic "baptism and tongues" experience? Are these the actual tongues of the carnal Corinthian church that Paul had to circumscribe so firmly? Something happens to these seekers—physically, morally, spiritually—and we shall see whether it is of the Holy Spirit.

Physical   Concerning the source of the tongues experience, Dr. Ernst Lohmann explains the process: "What physical occurrences accompany this phenomenon? The lower nerve-centers (the ganglionic system, or the 'vegetative' nerves, as they are called), which have their chief seat in the region round the pit of the stomach, i.e., solar plexus, are excited to increased activity. At the same time the central region of the higher nervous system (cerebral), which in a normal state of affairs is the medium of conscious perception and action, becomes paralyzed. There is a reversal of the order of nature. The lower nerves take over the duty of the higher ones.

"This state of things comes to pass negatively, by the higher system losing its natural supremacy under the pressure of illness, or artificially by hypnosis, auto-suggestion, etc.; and positively, by the lower nerves being in some way excited artificially to increased activity, whereby they get the upper hand. Those in this condition feel as it were an electric stream pass through the body, which is an exciting of the lower nerves by which a feeling of bliss is produced, and the jaws are moved in speaking in tongues. . . ."[1]

This initial breakthrough is brought about purely by psychological means, and never by the Holy Spirit. The individual is open and willing, and desperate to receive. He responds without question to all commands such as, "Raise your hands and praise God," "Say Amen," "Shout hallelujah!" The repetitive singing of well-known choruses, and the rhythmic clapping of the hands coupled with the overpowering influence of the music's beat, contribute both to the lulling of the cerebral system and the stimulating of the auto nerves.

When the initial short circuit of the nervous system has occurred, the nerve pattern is thereby established and tongues speaking may be triggered at will. At first some stimulus may be required, but soon it is simply a matter of choice. Actually, some find themselves unable to control the babbling when stirred by the excitement of a meeting.

There are other penalties involved in this unnatural stimulation. The nervous system becomes affected; the highs are too high, and the inevitable lows are too low. Extended periods of deep depression occur, often resulting in nervous breakdowns. A far cry from the miraculously-given languages of the transitional early church days, and further still from the Christ-centered ministry of the Holy Spirit!

Moral   There are not only nervous breakdowns, but moral breakdowns as well. All of the movements based upon "the baptism of the Holy Ghost" have a long history of moral laxity. For one thing, immorality is bound to show up in a realm where there is this type of physical stimulus of the lower nervous system.

Then too, there is a type of psychotic lying that takes hold of those who propagate these experiences. In regard to testimonies, all rationality and integrity seem to disappear. It never

[1]*The Overcomer* (1910), p. 114.

occurs to these people to question what they are told concerning miracles, signs and wonders, healings, raising of the dead, and the like. In the retelling, usually to one who "doesn't have the Spirit," there is much embellishment. Most of these stories start out as a lie, and never do recover.

At times it is not a matter of outright lying, but simply a lack of rationality when it comes to these assertions. Every range of mentality, from the lowest to the highest, is infected. In a recent Pentecostal book the following testimony was given by a young man who graduated magna cum laude from a leading American university, with a degree in theology. In seeking "the baptism of the Holy Ghost," he said that the leader of the meeting stood before him for a moment, and then in Christ's name "cast Satan out" of him. Instantly he knew that a demon had left; he felt himself physically shaken and distinctly smelled burning sulphur. And he claimed to know that smell well from chemistry lab!

Spiritual　　In this movement the tragic toll is greatest in the spiritual realm. This type of error produces nothing but unscriptural unreality centered in bondage to a nerve-fostered experience. Without reality and growth in the risen Lord Jesus Christ, its followers rely on a constant round of meetings and renewed experiences to keep going—to say nothing of renewed "salvation." This endless circle and other related woes are the result of the initial error of holding far too low an estimate of the new birth. Instead of resting on the finished work of the Cross, they insist on another reception of the Holy Spirit, and the necessity of maintaining one's own salvation. (See Chapter 7).

Contrast　　As Dr. L. S. Chafer has commented, "Where do the leaders of these great errors ever declare that God, impelled by infinite love and acting in sovereign grace, and on the ground of the absoluteness of the finished work of Christ, does save the chief of sinners on no other condition than that he *believe*?

"Do they preach that, since the sin question is settled—past, present and future (Col. 2:13)—unforfeitable, unchangeable, eternal life is God's absolute gift to all who *believe?* Do they preach that being found in Christ every human merit and demerit, in the divine reckoning, passed; and the one who believes is so transferred to the perfect merit of Christ that he will never perish, but will endure as Christ endures? The preaching of the Gospel of Grace consists in the proclamation of these eternal glories, and apart from these announcements, *there is no Gospel.* "[2]

With no secure foundation on which to build, there can be little or no true spiritual development. Small wonder those in the movement are trapped at its so-called Pentecost, since they have yet to become. established at Calvary. "Ye have need that one teach you again . . . the first principles of the oracles of God . . . let us go on unto perfection [full growth]; not laying again the foundation of repentance from dead works, and of faith toward God, or the doctrine of baptisms, and of laying on of hands . . ." (Heb. 5:12; 6:1, 2).

Until the Holy Spirit establishes the believer on the solid Rock, Christ Jesus, He makes no attempt to take that one forward in God's eternal purpose. These experience-centered people rely on the Holy Spirit for what He will not do, and fail to rely on the Lord Jesus Christ for what He has done. "If ye will not believe, surely ye shall not be established" (Isa. 7:9).

In the new birth, the Spirit's baptizing work eternally unites the believer to the Lord Jesus as Head and to all members of the Body—the Church (Eph. 1:22, 23; 1 Cor. 12:12-27). Taken out of the old creation in Adam, he is positioned forever as a new creation in Christ risen (2 Cor. 5:17). The false baptism separates from this knowledge; it also separates believers from each other.

"Thank God, we may and should be filled with the Spirit, with a fullness which means nothing less than the dethronement of self, and the enthronement of Christ, or, in the terminology of Paul, the reckoning of self to have died in Christ's death, and of ourselves newly alive in His resurrection. The craving today, on the part of many believers, for sensuous signs, is most unhealthy; it is destructive of sober

²*True Evangelism.*

312

Bible study, and invariably leads to pitiful extremes of belief and conduct.

"I feel compelled, therefore, to warn all seekers after fuller blessing against this unscriptural teaching about the Baptism of the Spirit and Tongues."—*William G. Scroggie.*[3]

Think of all the Father has done to position us at His own right hand in His Beloved Son (Eph. 1:6). He has blessed us with all spiritual blessings in heavenly places in Christ, therefore we are complete in Him (Eph. 1:3; Col. 2:10). There is nothing for us to do but *abide above!*

[3]*The Baptism of the Holy Spirit: Speaking in Tongues,* p. 29.

70 *The Five Points of Calvinism*

1. Total Inability or Total Depravity   Because of the Fall, man is unable of himself to savingly believe the gospel. The sinner is dead, blind, and deaf to the things of God; his heart is deceitful and desperately corrupt. His will is not free, it is in bondage to his evil nature. Therefore, he will not—indeed he cannot—choose good over evil in the spiritual realm. Consequently, it takes much more than the Spirit's assistance to bring a sinner to Christ—it takes regeneration by which the Spirit makes the sinner alive and gives him a new nature. Faith is not something man contributes to salvation—it is God's gift to the sinner, not the sinner's gift to God.

2. Unconditional Election   God's choice of certain individuals to salvation before the foundation of the world rested solely on His own sovereign will. His choice of particular sinners was not based on any foreseen response or obedience on their part, such as faith, repentance, etc. On the contrary, God gives faith and repentance to each individual whom He selected. These acts are the result, not the cause of God's choice. Election therefore was not determined by or conditioned on any virtuous quality or act foreseen in man. Those whom God sovereignly elected He brings through the power of the Spirit to a willing acceptance of Christ. Thus God's choice of the sinner, not the sinner's choice of Christ, is the ultimate cause of salvation.

3. Particular Redemption or Limited Atonement   Christ's redeeming work was intended to save the elect only and actually secured salvation for them. His death was a substitutionary endurance of the penalty of sin in the place of certain specified sinners.

In addition to putting away the sins of His people, Christ's redemption secured everything necessary for their salvation, including faith that unites them to Him. The gift of faith is infallibly applied by the Spirit to all for whom Christ died, therefore guaranteeing their salvation.

4. The Effica-cious Call of the Spirit or Irresistible Grace In addition to the outward general call to salvation which is made to everyone who hears the gospel, the Holy Spirit extends to the elect a special inward call that inevitably brings them to salvation. The external call (which is made to all without distinction) can be, and often is, rejected; whereas the internal call (which is made only to the elect) cannot be rejected; it always results in conversion. By means of this special call the Spirit irresistibly draws sinners to Christ. He is not limited in His work of applying salvation by man's will, nor is He dependent on man's cooperation for success. The Spirit graciously causes the elect sinner to cooperate, to believe, to repent, to come freely and willingly to Christ. God's grace, therefore, is invincible; it never fails to result in the salvation of those to whom it is extended.

5. Persever-ance of the Saints All who are chosen of God, redeemed by Christ, and given faith by the Spirit are eternally saved. They are kept in faith by the power of Almighty God and thus preserved to the end.

Summary Salvation is accomplished by the almighty power of the triune God. The Father chose a people, the Son died for them, the Holy Spirit makes Christ's death effective by bringing the elect to faith and repentance, thereby causing them to willingly obey the gospel. The entire process (election, redemption, regeneration) is the work of God and is by grace alone. Thus God, not man, determines who will be the recipients of the gift of salvation.

71 *The Five Points of Arminianism*

1. Free Will or Human Ability Although human nature was seriously affected by the Fall, man has not been left in a state of total spiritual helplessness. God graciously enables every sinner to repent and believe, but He does not interfere with man's freedom. Each sinner possesses a free will, and his eternal destiny depends on how he uses it. Man's freedom consists of his ability to choose good over evil in spiritual matters; his will is not enslaved to his sinful nature. The sinner has the power to either cooperate with God's Spirit and be regenerated or resist God's grace and perish. The lost sinner needs the Spirit's assistance, but he does not have to be regenerated by the Spirit before he can believe, for faith is man's act and precedes the new birth. Faith is the sinner's gift to God; it is man's contribution to salvation.

2. Conditional Election God's choice of certain individuals to salvation before the foundation of the world was based on His foreseeing that they would respond to His call. He selected only those whom He knew would of themselves freely believe the gospel. Election therefore was determined by or conditioned on what man would do. The faith that God foresaw and on which He based His choice was not given to the sinner by God (it was not created by the regenerating power of the Holy Spirit) but resulted solely from man's will. Who would believe (and therefore who would be elected to salvation) was left entirely up to man. God chose those whom He knew would, of their own free will, choose Christ. Thus the sinner's choice of Christ, not God's choice of the sinner, is the ultimate cause of salvation.

3. Universal Redemption or General Atonement   Christ's redeeming work made it possible for everyone to be saved but did not actually secure the salvation of anyone. Although Christ died for all men and for every man, only those who believe on Him are saved. His death enabled God to pardon sinners on the condition that they believe, but it did not actually put away everyone's sins. Christ's redemption becomes effective only if man chooses to accept it.

4. The Holy Spirit Can Be Effectually Resisted   The Spirit calls inwardly all those who are called outwardly by the gospel invitation; He does all that He can to bring every sinner to salvation. But inasmuch as man is free, he can successfully resist the Spirit's call. The Spirit cannot regenerate the sinner until he believes; faith (which is man's contribution) precedes and makes possible the new birth. Thus, man's free will limits the Spirit in the application of Christ's saving work. The Holy Spirit can only draw to Christ those who allow Him to have His way with them. Until the sinner responds, the Spirit cannot give life. God's grace, therefore, is not invincible; it can be, and often is, resisted and thwarted by man.

5. Falling From Grace   Those who believe and are truly saved can lose their salvation by failing to keep up their faith, etc. (All Arminians have not agreed on this point; some have held that believers are eternally secure in Christ.)

Summary   Salvation is accomplished through the combined efforts of God (who takes the initiative) and man (who must respond)—man's response being the determining factor. God has provided salvation for everyone, but His provision becomes effective only for those who, of their own free will, "choose" to cooperate with Him and accept His offer of grace. At the crucial point, man's will plays a decisive role; thus man, not God, determines who will be the recipients of the gift of salvation.

LIVE POSITIONALLY
"CRUCIFIED, RISEN, SEATED"
(Gal. 2:20; Eph. 2:6)

LIVE POSITIVELY
"FULLY PERSUADED"
(Rom. 14:5)

LIVE POSSESSIVELY
"ALL THINGS ARE YOURS"
(1 Cor. 3:21)

LIVE TRIUMPHANTLY
"MORE THAN CONQUERORS"
(Rom. 8:37)

Bibliography

Austin-Sparks, T. *What Is Man?* London: Witness and Testimony Publishers, 1963.

Boggs, Wm., Jr. *Faith Healing and the Christian Faith.*

Bonar, Horatius. *God's Way of Holiness.* Chicago: Moody Press, n.d.

Cate, B. F. *The Nine Gifts of the Spirit Are Not in the Church Today.* Des Plaines, IL: Regular Baptist Press, 1956.

Chafer, Lewis Sperry. *True Evangelism.* Grand Rapids: Zondervan Publishing House, 1919.

Conant, J. E. *Every-Member Evangelism.* New York: Harper and Row, 1922.

Edmunds, Vincent & Scorer, G. Gordon. *Some Thoughts on Faith Healing.* London: The Tyndale Press, 1956.

Finney, Charles G. *Finney's Lectures on Systematic Theology.* Grand Rapids: Wm. B. Eerdmans Publishing Co., 1957.

Frost, Henry. *Miraculous Healing.* Grand Rapids: Zondervan Publishing House, 1979.

Harrison, Norman B. *His Side Versus Our Side.* Minneapolis, MN: His International Service, 1940.

_____. *New Testament Living.* Minneapolis, MN: His International Service, 1953.

Hay, Alexander R. *New Testament Order for Church and Missionary.* Welland, Canada: New Testament Missionary Union, 1947.

_____. *What Is Wrong in the Church?* Vol. 2. Welland, Canada: New Testament Missionary Union, n.d.

Hopkins, Evan H. *The Law of Liberty in the Spiritual Life.* Fort Washington, PA: Christian Literature Crusade, 1953.

Huegel, F. J. *Bone of His Bone.* Grand Rapids: Zondervan Publishing House, 1972.

Kelly, Wm. *Lectures on The Epistle of Paul the Apostle to the Galatians.* Oak Park, IL: Bible Truth Publishers, n.d.

_____. *Lectures on the New Testament Doctrine of the Holy Spirit.* Los Angeles: Berean Bookshelf, n.d.

Lohman, Ernst. *The Overcomer.* Bournemouth, England: The Overcomer Bookroom, 1910.

Maskery, C. H. *The Pentecostal Error.*

Maxwell, L. E. *Born Crucified.* Chicago: Moody Press, 1945.

Miller, W. D. *Modern Divine Healing.* Fort Worth, TX: Miller Publishing Co., 1946.

Murray, Andrew. *Abide in Christ.* Three Hills, Canada: Prairie Book Room, n.d.

_____. *God's Best Secrets.* Grand Rapids: Zondervan Publishing House, 1950.

_____. *Like Christ.* Three Hills, Canada: Prairie Book Room, n.d.

_____. *The Holiest of All.* Old Tappan, NJ: Fleming H. Revell Co., n.d.

_____. *The True Vine; Waiting on God; The Prayer Life.* Chicago: Moody Press, n.d.

Nee, Watchman. *The Normal Christian Life.* Fort Washington, PA: Christian Literature Crusade, 1961.

Newell, Wm. R. *Romans, Verse by Verse.* Chicago: Moody Press, 1938.

Penn-Lewis, Jessie. *The Cross of Calvary.* Fort Washington, PA: Christian Literature Crusade, n.d.

Penn-Lewis, Jessie and Roberts, Evan. *War on the Saints.* Bournemouth, England: The Overcomer Book Room, 1939.

Paxson, Ruth. *The Wealth, Walk and Warfare of the Christian.* Old Tappan, NJ: Fleming H. Revell Co., 1939.

Pink, Arthur W. *The Doctrine of Sanctification.* Grand Rapids: Baker Book House, 1955.

Ridout, Samuel. *The Person and Work of the Holy Spirit.* Neptune, NJ: Loizeaux Brothers, Inc., Publishers, 1899.

Rossier, H. L. *Joshua.* Sunbury, PA: Believers Bookshelf, n.d.

Ryle, J. C. *Holiness.* London: J. Clarke & Co., Ltd., n.d.

Scofield, C. I. *Rightly Dividing the Word of Truth.* Grand Rapids: Zondervan Publishing House, 1964.

_____. *The Fundamentals for Today.* (Feinberg, Chas. L., ed.) Grand Rapids: Kregel Publications, 1958.

Scroggie, Wm. Graham. *The Baptism of the Spirit: Speaking With Tongues.* London: Marshall, Morgan & Scott, Ltd. n.d.

Taylor, Howard. *Hudson Taylor's Spiritual Secret.* Chicago: Moody Press, 1932.

Wallis, Reginald. *The New Life.* Neptune, NJ: Loizeaux Brothers, Inc., Publishers, 1947.

Warfield, Benjamin B. *Miracles: Yesterday and Today.* Grand Rapids: Wm. B. Eerdmans Publishing Co., 1953.